D0710464

Europea: Ethnomusicologies and Modernities

Series Editors: Philip V. Bohlman and Martin Stokes

1. *Celtic Modern: Music at the Global Fringe*, edited by Martin Stokes and Philip V. Bohlman, 2003.
2. *Albanian Urban Lyric Song in the 1930s*, by Eno Koço, 2004.
3. *The Mediterranean in Music: Critical Perspectives, Common Concerns, Cultural Differences*, edited by David Cooper and Kevin Dawe, 2005.

Europea: Ethnomusicologies and Modernities

Series Editors: Philip V. Bohlman and Martin Stokes

The new millennium challenges ethnomusicologists, dedicated to studying the music of the world, to examine anew the Western musics they have treated as "traditional," and to forge new approaches to world musics that are often overlooked because of their deceptive familiarity. As the modern discipline of ethnomusicology expanded during the second half of the twentieth century, influenced significantly by ethnographic methods in the social sciences, ethnomusicology's "field" increasingly shifted to the exoticized Other. The comparative methodologies previously generated by Europeanist scholars to study and privilege Western musics were deliberately discarded. Europe as a cultural area was banished to historical musicology, and European vernacular musics became the spoils left to folk-music and, later, popular-music studies.

Europea challenges ethnomusicology to return to Europe and to encounter its disciplinary past afresh, and the present is a timely moment to do so. European unity nervously but insistently asserts itself through the political and cultural agendas of the European Union, causing Europeans to reflect on a bitterly and violently fragmented past and its ongoing repercussions in the present, and to confront new challenges and opportunities for integration. There is also an intellectual moment to be seized as Europeans reformulate the history of the present, an opportunity to move beyond the fragmentation and atomism the later twentieth century has bequeathed and to enter into broader social, cultural, and political relationships.

Europea is not simply a reflection of and on the current state of research. Rather, the volumes in this series move in new directions and experiment with diverse approaches. The series establishes a forum that can engage scholars, musicians, and other interlocutors in debates and discussions crucial to understanding the present historical juncture. This dialogue, grounded in ethnomusicology's interdisciplinarity, will be animated by reflexive attention to the specific social configurations of knowledge of and scholarship on the musics of Europe. Such knowledge and its circulation as ethnomusicological scholarship are by no means dependent on professional academics, but rather are conditioned, as elsewhere, by complex interactions between universities, museums, amateur organizations, state agencies, and markets. Both the broader view to which ethnomusicology aspires and the critical edge necessary to understanding the present moment are served by broadening the base on which "academic" discussion proceeds.

"Europe" will emerge from the volumes as a space for critical dialogue, embracing competing and often-antagonistic voices from across the continent, across the Atlantic, across the Mediterranean and the Black Sea, and across a world altered ineluctably by European colonialism and globalization. The diverse subjects and interdisciplinary approaches in individual volumes capture something of—and, in a small way, become part of—the jangling polyphony through which the "New Europe" has explosively taken musical shape in public discourse, in expressive culture, and, increasingly, in political form. Europea: Ethnomusicologies and Modernities aims to provide a critical framework necessary to capture something of the turbulent dynamics of music performance, engaging the forces that inform and deform, contest and mediate the senses of identity, selfhood, belonging, and progress that shape "European" musical experience in Europe and across the world.

The Mediterranean in Music

Critical Perspectives, Common Concerns, Cultural Differences

Edited by
David Cooper
Kevin Dawe

Europea: Ethnomusicologies and Modernities, No. 3

The Scarecrow Press, Inc.
Lanham, Maryland • Toronto • Oxford
2005

SCARECROW PRESS, INC.

Published in the United States of America
by Scarecrow Press, Inc.
A wholly owned subsidary of
The Rowman & Littlefield Publishing Group, Inc.
4501 Forbes Boulevard, Suite 200, Lanham, Maryland 20706
www.scarecrowpress.com

PO Box 317
Oxford
OX2 9RU, UK

British Library Cataloguing in Publication Information Available

Library of Congress Cataloging-in-Publication Data

The Mediterranean in music : critical perspectives, common concerns, cultural
differences / edited by David Cooper and Kevin Dawe.
    p. cm. — (Europea ; no. 3)
  Includes bibliographical references (p.   ) and index.
  ISBN 0-8108-5407-4 (hardcover : alk. paper)
  1. Ethnomusicology—Mediterranean Region. 2. Music—Mediterranean
Region—History and criticism. I. Cooper, David, 1956– II. Dawe, Kevin. III.
Series.

ML3799.M43 2005
780'.9182'2—dc22

                                    2004024704

⊖™ The paper used in this publication meets the minimum requirements of
American National Standard for Information Sciences—Permanence of
Paper for Printed Library Materials, ANSI/NISO Z39.48-1992.
Manufactured in the United States of America.

Contents

Series Foreword

Takis Theodoropolous could have been referring to this volume when he said:

> All this confirms, without a doubt, what all Mediterranean people know, that the Mediterranean doesn't exist.... This is why I have the clear sensation that the Mediterranean, rather than existing for itself, is a necessary condition for the existence of its inhabitants. (cited by Plastino, p. 187)

One might add that it is also, and has for a long time been, a "necessary condition" for European scholarship in the modern period. The movements of people, ideas and technologies across the ancient Mediterranean, drawing together (in order to transcend) the heritage of Asian and African civilizations, inspired modern European imaginings of its classical roots. The fragmentation of the Roman Empire inspired the European efforts to forge a new destiny, casting the new arrivals (then as now) as barbarians and outsiders, pitted against civilization, modernity and democracy in an unending struggle. The ideological battlefield of the twentieth and twenty-first century in the Mediterranean area, between social democracy, fascism and communism, and increasingly (in the view of some) between Christianity, Judaism and Islam, have inspired contemporary efforts to imagine new conceptions of civility and peace, reaching across national and ideological barriers, and what we persist in imagining as cultural and civilizational divides. The concentration of wealth and poverty in the Mediterranean area today, of economic stability and desolation, challenge Europeans and those living elsewhere in the Mediterranean area with some of the toughest questions about what globalization has produced, and what it still might be.

The music scholarship on and of the Mediterranean has been intensely bound up with this intellectual and political history. In the north, it has been the site of some of the most fraught and violent efforts to excise polluting difference, efforts that have, predictably enough for those versed in Freudian and deconstructive theory, produced some of the most deeply rooted and persistent musical pleasures in the region (the love of "Arab" music in Spain and Turkey, of "Turkish" music in Greece and the Balkans, of Jewish and Rom music in Central Europe). These efforts have their complex and confusing echoes, refractions and reflections in the South, and in the borderlands between. But music scholarship in the area has also touched on intriguing possibilities, as the contributors to this volume show. It accesses domains of gendered and sexual performativity where unexpected cultural resources can be glimpsed. It alerts us to the complex play of cultural power and subversion in households, cafes and bars. It exposes unexpected aspects of nation-state development, unexpected in the determination of some to consider nations in dialogue, rather than violent opposition to other. With mass media and travel (of one kind or another), music, we find, offers opportunities to piece together fragments of highly mobile lives and suggest how they might be made intelligible and pleasurable, rather than—as is often the case for so many—confusing, alienating and oppressive.

An imagined Mediterranean musical space also allows us to gather as scholars and performers, and have conversations that would not otherwise be possible, bringing together truly diverse styles of thinking, talking and writing about music. Music scholarship in Europe and North America has gained a significant critical edge in recent decades, but at the (perhaps necessary) expense of a certain uniformity of style and method. These create new blind spots: places, times, experiences, practices that escape the critical eye, or things that we think we know but have actually ceased to think about critically. Cooper and Dawe's volume offers scholarship on Mediterranean musical genres and practices with a sharp critical edge, but also a conversation of diverse methods and styles. Beyond challenging a certain hegemony, one that continues to marginalize popular and vernacular practice, this conversation also challenges music scholarship to consider the complex whole of music making—imagined in such different ways by ethnomusicologists, folklorists, historical musicologists, popular music scholars—in new ways.

As this volume reminds us, we cannot think about male performativity without thinking about its effects on women, and vice-versa. We cannot think about domestic sites of reception and consumption without also thinking about intellectual production and the structures of media dissemination. We cannot think about the musical imaginings of those who move freely around the Mediterranean without thinking, also, about those who are stuck, trapped or exploited.

The Mediterranean poses significant challenges in the study of "Europe", every step forward an undermining of certainties, and a posing of new questions with significant implications, as Michael Herzfeld pointed out long ago, for all those invested in European categories of thought and political practice. Cooper and Dawe's book moves the study of European music in new directions, and towards fresh perspectives on music making and music scholarship in general.

Martin Stokes

Acknowledgments

David Cooper and Kevin Dawe would like to thank all of the contributors to this volume. It should be noted that authors' original spelling and orthography generally have been retained.

Drs. Cooper and Dawe are grateful to Ian Sapiro for his expert assistance with the editing and typesetting of this book. His involvement in and dedication to the project is very much appreciated.

In addition, the editors would like to thank the series editors of *Ethnomusicologies and Modernities*, Professors Martin Stokes and Philip Bohlman of the University of Chicago, for their interest in, and helpful comments and advice on, the collection.

The help and support of Bruce Phillips, Sam Grammar and their colleagues at Scarecrow Press in the production of the book is gratefully acknowledged.

At the University of Leeds, the editors wish to express their appreciation to Professor Dionisius Agius and the Centre for Mediterranean Studies for co-hosting the original conference from which this book took its inspiration.

Finally, David Cooper and Kevin Dawe are grateful for all the love and support of their families.

Introduction

Kevin Dawe and David Cooper

Social geographer Doreen Massey notes in *Space, Place and Gender* that "as a result of the fact that it is conceptualized as created out of social relations, space is by its very nature full of power and symbolism, a complex web of relations of domination and subordination, of solidarity and co-operation" ([1994] 2001: 265). Geology and climate, flora and fauna, patterns of human settlement, history and culture have combined to give us the legacy of the place that we now call "the Mediterranean," a site which certainly exhibits the characteristics of space as defined by Massey. Clearly evidenced in the Mediterranean are socially and culturally based responses to a common and unique set of circumstances. People have worked the sea and its littoral, fished its waters and farmed its lands, for millennia. When we talk of "the Mediterranean" we are, of course, at all times describing a place and its people, that is, a diverse range of societies and cultures that share common concerns and traits. The Mediterranean then is a place of the mind as much as a physical location, often idealized as a unified area (see Bradford 1971 and Braudel 1972) yet, clearly diverse in many respects. The Mediterranean remains a space for critical dialogue for competing and often antagonistic voices and functions as a meeting place for diverse and interdisciplinary approaches. Although a unified approach to Mediterranean Studies has been posited in historical and geographical studies, as John Morgan O'Connell remarks in this book, this approach is informed by a generally Eurocentric perspective which views the Mediterranean as "a cultural hearth for the development of European civilization and implicitly ignores the complex cultural processes that underlie the demographic constitution of the area."

Mediterranean Studies is a context for the thorough and rigorous re-examination of "the Mediterranean" by scholars, themselves engaging with the concept, but also with what it means to peoples of the region and the wider world. This volume has its roots in a conference, *Traditional Music of the Mediterranean*, organized by Dionisius Agius and David Cooper and jointly hosted by the Centre for Mediterranean Studies and the School of Music at the University of Leeds in February 2001. The book therefore contains a broad range of approaches to the study of Mediterranean cultures and societies, reflecting the interests of the editors and the contributors, whose backgrounds vary. The influence of Mediterranean studies as a broad field of enquiry involving critical perspectives, common concerns and cultural differences is clearly mirrored in the ethnomusicological writing here. Although the conference provided the matrix and stimulus for the book, with a key-note address by John Morgan O'Connell and papers by Ruth Davis and Eno Koço, it has now developed into a broader consideration of issues beyond just notions of "traditional" music and how these are con-structed in a Mediterranean context. We are immediately challenged to see how these local traditions are reconfigured as they come within the reach of global cultural flows, mediated by cultural industries which are now firmly rooted in a Mediterranean context, as elsewhere. Only re-cently have scholars of music begun to challenge their preconceptions of the Mediterranean as a musical area. Clearly, the boundaries of the Mediterranean in music have always been contested and negotiated as part of the history and cultural politics of the region, whether in the policies of the Ottoman Turks or the recordings of modern Corsican polyphony, whether in Lachmann's Palestinian recordings of the 1930s or in the lyrics of Algerian singers in Paris, whether in Theodorakis's experiments with rebetiko or Irish musicians' adoption of the bouzouki.

Anthropologists have always attended to a critical examination of the Mediterranean, their work providing a very useful model for eth-nomusicologists. Michael Herzfeld's highly influential *Anthropology through the Looking-Glass: Critical Ethnography in the Margins of Europe* (1989) reveals as much about the problems of research and scholarship in the Mediterranean area as the area concept itself. Herzfeld (1982) discusses the ways in which "the Mediterranean" is constantly negotiated and contested within and without academia, in politics and prose, on the inside and the outside and within the media and folklore studies as much as within domestic space. Although Herzfeld focuses on nation building in Greece, his ideas can be applied to a number of different cultural contexts; indeed, he draws on a "tradi-tion" of anthropological research in the region in his own work in Crete where he relates the micropolitics of everyday life to national political events (1991). Herzfeld's Cretans are caught up in an ongoing negotia-tion of space, place and gender. As much as their "manly" perform-ances provide a site of contest and competition, so too does Herzfeld's writing on the subject within and without the academy (1985).

Put very simply, in an examination of the cultures of the Mediter-ranean we learn as much about ourselves as the people whose lives we write about. In "the Mediterranean" we find different ways of being in the world, whether we regard ourselves as European, west Asian or North African. From the outset we concur that a study of "the Mediter-ranean" in music is inherently and necessarily a reflexive enterprise.

Identity and difference are negotiated in the very words we use and the pages we write. The ways in which cultural difference is negotiated, identities are constructed and history is (re-)written in notions of "the Mediterranean" in music are common concerns in this book.

The present study investigates a number of musical cultures that have been traditionally seen to demonstrate common threads, trends and interactions. We consider the music of Greece, Crete, Turkey, Albania, Corsica, Italy, Spain, Morocco, Algeria and Palestine. We also explore music popular amongst the Algerian diaspora in Paris and the ways in which Irish musicians continue to take inspiration from the Mediterranean soundscape.

The five sections of the book reflect ongoing trends in an ethnomusicology of the Mediterranean region. In the first, "Nation and History," John Morgan O'Connell not only provides reference to the history of writings on "the Mediterranean" as an area concept but also traces the development of nationalist agendas in modern Turkey, wrapped around the musical Mediterranean as a place inhabited by the East. Dafne Tragaki notes the "interpretive moves" (Feld 1995) that various commentators and ideologues have made in approaching and appropriating the bouzouki-based urban musical tradition of rebetiko as a form of cultural politics. And in a very personal study of Albanian urban lyric song, Eno Koço relates the development of the genre to the history and politics of the region. These three chapters demonstrate how various influential figures, whether ethnomusicologists, composers or politicians, have had the power to affect or at least challenge policy at the time (Gazimihâl in Turkey, Xenos and Theodorakis in Greece and Xhurri in Albania).

In "Broadcasting and New Media," Ruth Davis considers Robert Lachmann's radio broadcasts not only as a valuable document of the rich and diverse music cultures he found in 1930s Palestine, but as a means of promoting understanding between peoples of European and Near Eastern descent. Lachmann's research was conducted at a time of intense political and cultural turmoil in Palestine and demonstrates how ethnomusicological research is ideologically based. Tony Langlois offers a contemporary examination of the impact of media consumption practices on regional identity formation in North Africa, global musical media apprehended by the local concept of houma—a notional community or neighborhood that imposes certain obligations upon its constituents.

"Men and Women" revisits the literature on Mediterranean gender studies represented with force in the work of, for example, Stanley Brandes (1981), Michael Herzfeld (1985) and David Gilmore (1987).

These writers note and debate the fundamental role of the concepts of honor and shame and how these shape the lives of men and women across Mediterranean society. Kevin Dawe and Loren Chuse discuss these and other ideas in two case studies, the former on the lyra music of Crete, the latter on women singers in flamenco. Both these forms now come within the remit of "world music"—a theme which is further explored in the next section.

In "Mediterranean Music," Caroline Bithell traces the growth of Corsican polyphony from a local men's music to one in which the influence of the wider Mediterranean plays an increasing role. Bithell notes that Corsica has always been a place of musical contacts, its "anchors and sails" providing the means for the navigation of new musical opportunities. As it has been taken up by the media, film and television, modern pajella self-consciously explores its Mediterranean roots in the context of "'world music." Goffredo Plastino's analysis of the music and lyrics of the band Dounia and of Cecilia Pitino draws on the notion posited by Miriam Cooke that "placing oneself in the perspective of Mediterranean thinking . . . opens the possibility of reconceptualizing the Mediterranean as both a physical and virtual place" (2004: 185–86) which, he suggests, undermines concepts of center and margin, which are now being reconfigured in the minds of a new generation of Italian musicians, exploring both their musical roots and their musical futures.

In the concluding section, "The Traveling Mediterranean," Gabriele Marranci draws on his fieldwork in Algeria and Paris to examine raï's development as a potent marker of Algerian immigrant identity. This music continues to travel in various forms through the heartland of the Algerian diaspora, as much as it has become, in the hands of Khaled and others, an important force on the "world music" scene. The final chapter, by David Cooper, explores notions of real and imagined kinship between the musical practices of Ireland and the Mediterranean. This extends our frame of reference, for at the "global fringe," we find a meeting of imagined musical worlds—those of Celtdom and the Mediterranean. At its margins the Mediterranean remains a place "full of power and symbolism." Musical cultures are entangled in "a complex web of relations of domination and subordination, of solidarity and co-operation" (Massey [1994] 2001: 265). These ideas clearly inform our critical perspectives on the music of the Mediterranean, inscribed as they are with both common concerns and cultural differences.

Bibliography

Bradford, Ernle. *The Mediterranean: Portrait of a Sea.* London: Hodder and Stoughton, 1971.

Brandes, Stanley. *Metaphors of Masculinity: Sex and Status in Andalusian Folklore.* Philadelphia: University of Pennsylvania Press, 1980.

Braudel, Fernand. *The Mediterranean and the Mediterranean World in the Age of Philip II.* 2 vols. Translated by Siân Reynolds. New York: Harper and Row, 1972.

Feld, Steven. "Notes on a 'World Beat.'" 238–46 in *Music Grooves*, edited by Charles Keil and Steven Feld. Chicago: University of Chicago Press, 1995.

Gilmore, David. *Honor and Shame and the Unity of the Mediterranean.* Washington: American Anthropological Association, 1987.

Herzfeld, Michael. Ours Once More: Folklore, Ideology and the Making of Modern Greece. Austin: University of Texas Press, 1982.

———. The Poetics of Manhood: Contest and Identity in a Cretan Mountain Village. Princeton: Princeton University Press, 1985.

———. Anthropology through the Looking-Glass: Critical Ethnography in the Margins of Europe. Cambridge: Cambridge University Press, 1989.

———. A Place in History: Monumental and Social Time in a Cretan Town. Princeton: Princeton University Press, 1991.

Massey, Doreen. *Space, Place and Gender.* 3rd edition. Minneapolis: University of Minnesota Press, [1994] 2001.

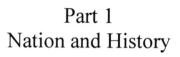

Part 1
Nation and History

Chapter 1

Sound Sense: Mediterranean Music from a Turkish Perspective

John Morgan O'Connell

Sound Sense

This chapter considers the ways in which humans make sense of sound. In particular, it shows how individual scholars attempted to provide distinctive interpretations of Turkish history, interpretations that disclose divergent ideological positions constructed within the realm of musical discourse. From this perspective, the music of the Mediterranean provided a neutral space for articulating political dissent during a major period of social change that attended the collapse of the Ottoman Empire and the foundation of the Turkish Republic in 1923. Under the autocratic leadership of Mustafa Kemal Atatürk (1881–1938), native scholars were encouraged to write a new history of the Turkish state by providing a central Asian definition of Turkish identity and by ascertaining a Turkic epicenter for cultural evolution within that frame. As part of this process, Turkish musicologists scrutinized expressive culture in the Mediterranean to validate larger claims of Turkish cultural hegemony stemming from an Asian hearth and to interrogate the Eurocentric prejudices of orientalist historiography where Turkish music was traditionally viewed as an underdeveloped moment within a European trajectory. By emphasizing an Asian rather than a European provenance for music in the Mediterranean, scholars were able to challenge the classical focus of musical studies and to propose instead an original source for all world musics. Significantly this original source was Turkish and not Greek. While such a reading of Turkish history did not go unchallenged, the Mediterranean provided an ideal focus for excavating relevant sound materials, for formulating new cultural theories and for testing heterodox constructions of Turkishness not conforming to the purist ideals of a newly established national elite. In this way, Turkish scholars developed a unique perspective on Mediterranean music, a perspective that made sense of sound, a sound sense of history.[1]

A Sense of Mediterranean Sounds

Mediterranean music as a singular concept has received surprisingly little scholarly attention. This may, in part, represent a hesitancy among academics (for institutional and professional reasons) to study musical practices which are not deemed consistent with national and/or ethnic interests. In part, it may also represent a failure on the part of specialists to deal effectively with musical traditions that do not conform to clearly defined Western and non-Western categories indicative of musicological and ethnomusicological modes of inquiry respectively. While a unified approach to Mediterranean Studies can be found in the realm of historical and geographical studies, the approach is—generally speaking—informed by a Eurocentric perspective, a perspective which views the Mediterranean as a cultural hearth for the development of European civilization and which implicitly ignores the complex cultural processes which underlie the demographic constitution of the area. To some extent, anthropologists have tried to make sense of this diversity by examining social themes underpinning cultural practices in the region. In this respect, they have studied honor and shame (Gilmore 1987), engendered performance (Herzfeld 1985), narrative violence (Gilsenan 1996) and political sentiment (Abu-Lughod 1986) to provide a unifying paradigm applicable to all Mediterranean peoples.[2] In a similar vein, some ethnomusicologists have been inspired by this anthropological precedent. Operating under the auspices of the recently founded International Council for Traditional Music study group, "Anthropology of Mediterranean Music,"[3] they too have sought to develop a synthetic approach to Mediterranean Studies. By co-opting the methodological tools of their parent discipline, they have applied these with some effect to the various musical traditions in the region. In short, these scholars have tried to present a unified approach to Mediterranean music by examining the diverse musical traditions of distinctive peoples resident upon the Mediterranean littoral.

Perhaps an integrated approach to the music of the Mediterranean is to be found in—and not around—the Mediterranean Sea. Following Bradford's (1971) classic account of Mediterranean history, I have attempted to develop a unified theory of Mediterranean music by examining the intersection of Asia and Europe evident in the region's history. According to Bradford, the Mediterranean Sea—especially its division into significant eastern and western sectors—shaped the migrations, the conflicts and the politics of Mediterranean peoples. Apart from one period of unification (under the Romans), the history of the region is portrayed as a constant flux between opposing forces resident in the East and the West, be they Carthaginians and Romans, Arabs and Vikings, Muslims and Christians or Ottomans and Spaniards. For him, the control of the Mediterranean Sea—rather than the conquest of the Mediterranean littoral—represented the crucial determinant of regional power: that is, determining colonization, trade and strategy. While the multicultural fabric of the Mediterranean Basin was enriched by successive waves of settlement (generally issuing from the East), the dominant powers in control of the sea facilitated the emergence of unique expressive cultures. These cultures crystallized about the courts of the ruling elite and benefited from the artistic contributions of diverse and subservient peoples. In this respect, Bradford's account of the Ottoman Sea is especially pertinent. Viewing Ottoman hegemony in the Mediterranean during the fifteenth century as a triumph of Asia over Europe, he attributes the expansion of Turkish power in the western Mediterranean to the maritime prowess of Barbarossa (d. 1546) and to the regional disinterest of Western powers. Tracing the rapid conquest by the Turks of the eastern Mediterranean after the fall of Byzantium in 1453, he notes the ways in which the multicultural character of the new empire was translated into the mutual exchange of artistic practices from East to West (through conquest) and from West to East (through trade). While Bradford's narrative is open to criticism,[4] his focus upon the mediating properties of the Mediterranean Sea and his exposition of East–West exchange within that framework is extremely significant for the following discussion.

The Sounds of an Ottoman Sea

Bradford's account provides a useful framework for studying the musical legacy of Ottoman rule. On the one hand, the Mediterranean not only enabled the Turkish conquest of the Aegean (1451), the Adriatic (1451–81), the Levantine (1512–20) and the Barbary (1520–66) shores, but it also facilitated the diffusion of Turkish cultural practices into these conquered areas, cultural practices which were promoted in the provincial courts of Ottoman rule and which confirmed the supremacy of Ottoman political domination in the region. On the other hand, Turkish expressive culture underwent a profound transformation as non-Muslim artisans from the Mediterranean littoral sought the patronage of new Turkish overlords to create a new syncretic urban style, Ottoman art. In the musical realm, this transformation was most apparent. Turkish art music (türk sanat müziği) abandoned the musical legacy of its Persian past and opted instead (broadly speaking) for the acculturating influences of Byzantium.[5] While this exchange of artistic preferences from East to West was gradual, the influence of a Mediterranean musical culture was profound. As some authorities demonstrate,[6] the emergence of a unique Ottoman aesthetic after the sixteenth century can—in part—be related to the preservation of Byzantine music in an Ottoman soundscape where new musical modes, new musical forms, new musical instruments and new performance practices bear testimony to the endurance of a regional aesthetic. In particular, Ottoman musical treatises demonstrate a new theoretical vigor during the period. Sometimes written by non-Turks, these treatises show the evolution of Ottoman modal conceptions from a closed system (the Persian model) to an open system (the Arabo/Turkish model) perhaps informed by a Byzantine theoretical precedent.[7] Although the development of Turkish art music is complex, the diffusion of a distinctive Ottoman musical style throughout the eastern Mediterranean was aided by the multicultural attributes of the Ottoman soundworld (where resident populations were predisposed to a regionally specific aesthetic) and by Christian music theorists (who reconceptualized musical practices following a Greek Orthodox prototype).[8] In short, Turkish art music was a sonic articulation of an Ottoman Sea, a sea of sounds with a decidedly Mediterranean flavor.

Turkish folk music (türk halk müziği), however, remained resolutely independent of this Mediterranean cultural influence. Intimately associated with the westward migration of Turkic peoples from central Asia, this ancient musical tradition was conservative (rather than innovative), rural (rather than urban), monocultural (rather than multicultural) and steadfastly land-based in contrast to the maritime adaptability of its urban counterpart. In this respect, the Turkish conquest of Anatolia (by 1451), the Balkans (by 1481) and Mesopotamia (by 1566) witnessed a very different form of expressive culture preserved largely (intact) by migrant colonizers scattered in peripheral Ottoman provinces. In contrast to Turkish art music, this land-based musical tradition heralded the diffusion of Asian poetic forms, compositional genres, musical instruments and ritual practices to new areas of Turkish settlement. At the vanguard of this Turkic invasion, wandering minstrels (aşıklar) proselytized to frontier settlers (gaziler) heterodox religious practices which were loosely allied to a mystical branch of Islam but which were more firmly grounded in the shamanistic belief systems of central Asia. As religious and political leaders, aşıklar promoted the Turkification of this inland empire by disseminating in song a singular reading of ethnic awareness and by demarcating in sound Turkish cultural hegemony in the occupied territories. Yet at the juncture between the land and the sea, Ottoman cities witnessed the flowering of a heterogeneous sound aesthetic characterized by the intricate conjunction of Turkish art and Turkish folk musical traditions and complicated by the penetration of non-Turkish musical cultures disseminated from the three continents bordering the Mediterranean.[9] In this respect, social hierarchy and ethnic identity were articulated sonically in a broad spectrum of musical tastes ranging from the Western to the Eastern and encompassing the urban and the rural. It was precisely this bricolage of urban musical styles which led to the critical appraisal of expressive culture by nationalist commentators who identified music-making explicitly with the multicultural fabric and implicitly with the societal degeneracy of Ottoman culture. That is, they scrutinized Ottoman sounds to make sense of Ottoman history.

Eastern Sounds in a Western Sea

Turkish musicologists were profoundly informed by this critical perspective. Responding to a larger nationalist concern for rewriting Turkish history, they tried to make sense of this complex Ottoman sound world by reframing Turkish music studies within a wider global framework for comparative purposes and by providing conflicting readings of Turkish history consistent with individual ideological preferences. In particular, the ethnomusicologist Mahmud Ragip Gazimihâl (1888–1961) attempted to present an evolutionist interpretation of Turkish music while studying the traditional musics of the Mediterranean. By examining the penetration of Eastern musical instruments, Eastern musical forms, Eastern theoretical principles and Eastern performance practices into Europe, the author offered a singular interpretation of a well-trodden musical discourse, a discourse which sought to include Eastern musical practices within the development of Western music and which, in turn, sought to impose upon these same musical practices an Ancient Greek pedigree.[10] That is, Mahmud Ragip Gazimihâl wished to include all traditional musics within this canonic version of musical evolution and, in doing so, hoped to establish an enduring connection between the traditional musics of Europe and Asia. Viewing Mediterranean expressive culture as the most Westerly expression of Eastern influence in the European musical context, he attempted to provide a new interpretation of European traditional musics, an interpretation in which the prejudices of orientalist scholarship were tailored to suit the nationalist aspirations of Turkish musicology where the traditional musics of Turkey found an equal—if not a privileged—position. By concluding that he could find "little or no difference between the traditional musics of Asia and Europe" (Gazimihâl 1927b), the author at once reconfigured the musical hierarchies implicit in Western musicology and provided instead an alternative explanation of a quintessential orientalist concern.

Gazimihâl's discussion of Spanish music is of particular interest. Viewing this Mediterranean tradition as the most westerly expression of Eastern influence in the European musical context and publishing his findings in an article entitled "The Equal Status of Eastern Music" (Tr. Şark Musikisinde Seviye) (Gazimihâl 1924b), he outlined the musical characteristics of and the musical practices associated with this influence. In this respect, his examination of the troubadour is extremely illuminating. Outlining the performance practices, the poetic genres, the didactic methods and the cultural values associated with this tradition, he attempted to place the troubadour within a larger global framework, a framework which not only recognized the significance of the troubadour for the development of traditional and art musics in Europe but which also established an enduring link between this bardic tradition and an older shamanistic legacy. According to him, this legacy originated among Turkic peoples in central Asia and persisted at the most ancient strata of Mediterranean musical cultures. Further, Gazimihâl's discussion of Eastern musical styles (especially oriental melismas and modalities), Eastern musical genres (especially poetic forms and texts), Eastern musical instruments (especially aerophones and chordophones) and Eastern musical theories (especially the transmission of ancient Greek music theory via Arab sources) seemed to confirm the importance of Eastern music for the development of Mediterranean—and ultimately—European traditional musics. According to Gazimihâl, it was precisely this legacy which proved the musical connection between Asia and Europe and which necessitated the scholarly analysis of Turkic musical sources. Since traditional musical practices in Turkey could be traced to a central Asian hearth and since a native bardic tradition (in the form of itinerant aşık) was still evident in Anatolia, the author concluded that the study of traditional music in Turkey provided a necessary introduction to the interpretation of historic performance practices in Spain and, by extension, in Europe. Simply put, Gazimihâl argued that he had found the origin of Eastern sounds in a Western sea.

A Sound Sense of History

The article "The Equal Status of Eastern Music" was not written in isolation. It was rather part of a larger series of papers concerning world music written by Mahmud Ragip Gazimihâl between 1923 and 1928 and published in *Millî Mecmua* (Eng. National Periodical)—a journal with an explicitly nationalist agenda catering to the republican ethos and the cultural interests of the newly established Turkish state. While a number of earlier publications concerning non-Western and non-Turkish musical practices existed prior to this series, Gazimihâl's treatment of the issue was comprehensive and systematic. That is, he covered the musical traditions of the Middle East, south Asia, east Asia, southeast Asia and the Americas before turning his attention to the classical and the traditional musics of southern Europe. He organized the series around a number of topics, topics which concerned the cultural history of different musical traditions and which betrayed the ideological biases of his scholarship. In particular, he attempted (Gazimihâl 1927a) to undertake a worldwide investigation of quartertones (*çeyrek sesler*), an investigation which informed his cross-cultural theory of scale structure and which was tested within the limited confines of European traditional musics. By showing the existence of microtonal inflections within the European arena and by developing a theory of quartertone tonality to suit,[11] Gazimihâl was able to satisfy a contemporary concern for pitch measurement in musicology and he was able to employ the interpretative tools of comparative musicology to develop a theory of universal music (evrensel müzik), a theory which undermined the distinction between the musical systems of Asia and Europe, a theory which sought to prove the central Asian origin of all music and a theory which elevated accordingly the study of Turkish traditional music (with its central Asian pedigree) to the central stage of theoretical discourse.

Gazimihâl's excursion into the world of music was not without precedent. Since the late nineteenth century, a number of Turkish musicologists were actively involved in examining non-Ottoman musical sources for methodological and comparative purposes.[12] In the former or methodological category, music theorists hoped to standardize musical practice by notating Turkish art music from oral sources and by developing a systematic theory of Ottoman music to suit. Inspired by the Westernizing ethos promoted by the Tanzimat Reforms (after 1839), Turkish musicologists (especially in Mevlevi circles) began to employ the practical (such as sonometric measurements) and the analytic (such as Helmholtz's theory of acoustics) tools of Western musicology to this end. In particular, the famous musicologist Rauf Yekta Bey (1871–1934) not only standardized Turkish musical theory to suit the modernist aspirations of contemporary commentators, but he also began to examine non-Turkish musical practices for comparative purposes (the second category described above). By analyzing the musics of neighboring peoples in the Mediterranean (especially the Greeks and the Arabs) and by employing the tools of Western musicology,[13] he was able to propose a theory of Turkish music, a theory that systematized the measurement of Turkish intervals (using intervallic proportions expressed as logarithms) and that confirmed the Mediterranean provenance of Turkish art music with scientific rigor. As part of the same process, he wrote Şark Musiki Tarihi, the first comprehensive history of Eastern music (Yekta Bey 1926). Employing the stringent historiographic techniques of Western musicology, this history necessitated a detour into the musical practices of neighboring musical traditions and, in doing so, confirmed the Mediterranean origin of Turkish art music. While Yekta Bey's interpretation of Turkish music history appealed to a scholarly audience in Europe (especially in France), his method of analysis and mode of interpretation had limited influence in Turkey. From a republican perspective, his sense of history was not considered sound.

It was precisely this conception of Turkish history which Gazimihâl wished to challenge. Attempting to bypass the Mediterranean focus of contemporary historiography (for religious and political reasons) and hoping to propose instead a central Asian provenance for Turkish music culture, the author began to compile an archive of musical sources from around the world, sources which were generally collected by European researchers (especially by French and German scholars) providing a critical edge to his ideological agenda.[14] Studying in Berlin during the 1920s at the *Fachrichtung für vergleichende Musikwissenschaft* and fully conversant with the techniques of comparative musicology, Gazimihâl focused upon folk musical rather than art musical sources, a focus that was in keeping with his academic training as an ethnomusicologist enabling him to satisfy his historiographic interests and ideological position. Embarking upon a number of field expeditions to record music in Anatolia (in association with the İstanbul Belediye Konservatuvarı [Eng. Istanbul Municipal Conservatory]), he classified the musical (especially the pentatonic structure) and poetic (especially the syllabic structure) characteristics of Turkish folk songs. Publishing his findings in a seminal publication entitled *The Türküs of Analolia* (1928) (Tr. Anadolu Türküleri), he compared his results with similar musical studies among Turkish-speaking peoples of central Asia. Following a methodological precedent initiated by Kodály (1882–1967) and perfected by Bartók (1881–1935), Gazimihâl was able to propose an alternative evolutionary model for Turkish music, a model which looked to central Asia rather than the Mediterranean as a cultural hearth and which satisfied the Asiatic (rather than the European) predilections of contemporary republican scholarship. In this way, Gazimihâl was able to proffer an Asian reading of Turkish history with ethical impunity, that is, a sound sense of history developed from an historical sense of sound.

A Historical Sense of Sound

The two interpretations of Turkish music history outlined above bear the indelible mark of a larger discourse, a discourse which concerned the appropriate constitution of Turkish culture during a turbulent period of historical change. While this discourse can properly be traced in part to the pan-Turkic and essentially Asiatic aspirations of previous constitutional movements and in part to the modernist tenor of contemporary European thought, it was only precisely articulated in 1923 by the sociologist Ziya Gökalp (1876–1924) who, in his influential critique of Turkish culture entitled *The Principles of Turkism* (Tr. Türkçülüğün Esasları), suggested that Turkish art music belonged to the Ottoman or imperial stage of Turkish civilization. Further, he argued that it had not progressed to the Republican or national category exemplified by the folk arts, such as carpet weaving, calligraphy and (in particular) folk music. In the musical realm, Gökalp tended to stereotype artistic sensibility according to its appropriate historical epoch so that Turkish art music and Turkish folk music were confined to their respective Ottoman and Republican categories. It was for this reason that music was the subject of intense public debate during the 1920s. On the one hand, Turkish art music was considered the anachronistic legacy of an imperial past with its multicultural character, divisive religious overtones and conservative disposition. Its history was intimately associated with the demise of a recently discredited political system, a system that was continuously subverted from within (by nationalism) and from outside (by interventionism). The powerful position held by non-Turkish groups (especially Greeks) in this system was unacceptable in Republican eyes.[15] On the other hand, Turkish folk music was equated with the most developed stage of Gökalp's cycle, that is, it was the true artistic expression of modern Turkey. Its history bypassed the Mediterranean preoccupation of orientalist historiography and offered instead the possibility of a new past, a past that was truly Turkic (rather than Greek) in character and that was central Asian (rather than Mediterranean) in origin.

The Principles of Turkism had a profound impact upon Turkish musicology. Gökalp provided the necessary framework for distilling Turkish music history into Ottoman and Republican epochs and for bifurcating Turkish musical style into Eastern (alaturka) and Western (alafranga) categories respectively. In keeping with the climate of major social reforms that attended the foundation of the Turkish Republic, Gökalp helped to articulate a contemporary concern for revolutionary musical change, a concern which sought to define a new national style (millî musiki) and which attempted to reform deviant musical practices according to Western scientific principles, the intended result being the harmonization of Turkish folk melodies to suit the modernist predilections of Republican taste. Gökalp's interest in Turkish folk music had a wider linguistic significance. Following the reform of the Turkish language (1928), scholars examined folk-song texts to develop a new and purified Turkish lexicon and to compare their findings with central Asian prototypes. The result was a new theory of Turkish—the sun language theory (güneş dil teorisi)—a theory which sought to link Turkish with a linguistic precedent (originating in central Asia) and which attempted to explain the evolution of all languages within that frame. Turkish musicologists, too, were profoundly influenced by this theory. For instance, Arel (1940) argued that the nationalist depiction of Turkish art music (as an outmoded survival of Byzantine culture) disguised the logical progression of ancient history from a Turkish hearth. Since Sumerian, Egyptian, Greek and other ancient Asiatic and European civilizations lay within this natural historical succession, he proposed that all Turkish music was the expression of a Turkic rather than a Mediterranean artistic culture. By reframing the history of Turkish music around a central Asian hearth, Arel was able to circumvent the Mediterranean focus of traditional scholarship and to develop, instead, a new history for a new nation. For him, Turkish music (like other Mediterranean musics) was a tangible expression of the East in the West.

Western Sounds in an Eastern Land

Gökalp's thesis had a major influence upon Turkish historiography. On the one hand, Mahmut Ragip Gazimihâl (1924a) refined Gökalp's argument for a musically informed Turkish audience. While Gazimihâl was critical of Gökalp's representation of Turkish music history (especially the Byzantine provenance of "Eastern music") and while he questioned the accuracy of Gökalp's knowledge of Western music history (especially his analysis of harmony and opera), he had a profound respect for Gökalp's sociological principles. Interpolating Gökalp's original premise, Gazimihâl justified the need for change in Turkish music by analyzing the revolutionary transformation of social and artistic systems in Europe during the nineteenth century, by comparing these with contemporaneous Turkish developments (especially in the literary realm) and by emphasizing the obsolete status of "Eastern music" within his evolutionary analysis. Inspired by a Russian precedent and drawing upon an impressive range of musical sources, Gazimihâl proposed a national school of Turkish music, a school where folk musical motifs and themes were collected (during field research) and adapted to the compositional language of a new national style. In his view, this style belonged (like other national musics) to a single universal musical system. To this end, he organized (in association with the newly-established Conservatory of Music) a number of expeditions during the 1920s to document, record and transcribe different regional musical styles throughout Turkey. From these sources, he developed a theory of pentatonicism (later developed by Adnan Saygun, 1960) which not only served to validate contemporary European models concerning the origins of Finno-Ugric cultures but which also served to legitimate a new and different conceptualization of Turkish history, a history which looked to the Turkic regions of central Asia for its roots and which circumvented the Mediterranean focus of an Ottoman past.

On the other hand, Rauf Yekta Bey (1927) was outspoken in his rejection of Gökalp's view of music history. Reacting against Gökalp's characterization of Turkish art music as Byzantine in origin, dismissing Gazimihâl's contention that Ottoman music was merely an underdeveloped stylistic variant of a universal (but implicitly Western) prototype and defending Turkish music in the context of unfavorable educational (1925) and institutional (1926) reforms,[16] he continued to advocate a rigorous musicological approach to the study and preservation of his tradition, an approach which implicitly acknowledged the Ancient Greek theoretical underpinnings of the art tradition. An article entitled,

"How Can Turkish Music Be Improved?" (Tr. Türk Musikisi Nasıl
Islah Olunabilir?) and published in the popular radio magazine, *Telsiz*
(Eng. Wireless), is typical of his reactionary stance (1927). In contrast
to Gazimihâl, he was deeply suspicious of a universal theory of music.
First, he emphasized the fundamental difference between Eastern and
Eestern music by outlining the distinctive tonal composition (twenty-
four note vs. twelve note), the different tonal arrangement (equidistant
vs. non-equidistant) and the disparate textural attributes (monophonic
vs. polyphonic) of both systems. Second, he rejected Gazimihâl's (and
Gökalp's) call for a harmonized national style precisely because Eastern and Western musics are two mutually exclusive and independent
systems, systems which could not be galvanized into a modern synthesis for ideological purposes. Third, he proposed the reconstitution of
Turkish music theory according to western musicological principles—a
position which he validated with reference to a number of foreign journals where Turkish music theory was considered worthy of serious
scholarly attention.[18] Fourth, he advocated the reformation of Turkish
performance practices—employing Western didactic methods—to suit
the modernist sensibilities of Republican taste. That is, he reconfirmed
the Mediterranean characteristics of Turkish art music but recognized
the need for modernization and Westernization. Put another way, he
acknowledged (in public at least) the need for Western sounds in an
Eastern land.

Conclusions

In this chapter, I have shown how Turkish scholars studied sound to
make sense of history. In particular, I have examined the ways in which
the Mediterranean acted as a catalyst for uncovering two conceptions of
Turkish history: one (a maritime conception) which looked to a Mediterranean hearth and the other (a terrestrial conception) which looked to
a central Asian hearth. I have demonstrated that both perspectives represent two distinctive cultural worldviews that are defined historically
(indicative of opposing Ottoman and Republican positions) and articulated sonically (conforming to different European and Asian musical
interests). While I have explained the interpretative position of the Ottoman camp (with its focus upon Turkish art music) in terms of orientalist critique, I have suggested that the musicological raison d'être of
the Republican musical camp (with its focus upon Turkish folk music)
requires a very different explanation. This explanation acknowledges

the nationalist biases of contemporary scholarship and recognizes the Turkic focus of musical theory within this frame. Accordingly, I am drawn to the musical writings of the Turkish musicologist, Mahmut Ragip Gazimihâl, a scholar who was not only a passionate collector of Turkish folk music during the 1920s but who also sought to explain the place of this music in a larger global context. Employing the tools of comparative musicology and interpreting his results by recourse to the principles of Gökalp, he published a world survey of music that at once satisfied the diffusionist stance of his field and the nationalist aspirations of his readership. That is, he argued that all music originated in a central Asian hearth. This hearth, which was Turkish in essence, prescribed the development of all musical traditions in Europe and Asia. From this perspective, he was not only able to interpret the traditional music of Spain within an Eastern musical framework but he was also able to propose a Turkic origin for all Mediterranean musics, a proposition which reconfigured the cultural hierarchies implicit in Western scholarship which placed an Asian (rather than a European) musical tradition at the cornerstone of musical evolution. In Bradford's language, his thesis seemed to confirm the triumph of Asia in Europe.

Notes

This chapter was presented as a keynote address at the Traditional Music of the Mediterranean Symposium in Leeds, Great Britain (February 2001). Research in Istanbul was supported by grants from the Turkish Government, the German Government (DAAD), by UCLA (Chancellor's Dissertation Fellowship), Otago University (Otago University Research Grant) and the Fulbright Commission. I would like to thank Dionisius Agius, David Cooper, Alâeddin Yavaşça, Murad Bardakçı, Cem Behar, Ali Jihad Racy, Dwight Reynolds, Susan McClary, Timothy Rice, Robert Walser and my teachers and colleagues in Istanbul for their knowledge, comments and support.

1. The Turkish language has undergone a profound transformation since 1923, a transformation that has seen the language adopt a Latin (rather than an Arabic) alphabet and has posed some problems of consistency in academic sources. For the purposes of transliteration, I have followed Shaw's example (1977 II: ix) by using the modern standard Turkish spelling system for all technical terms and place names. Where relevant, these spellings can be found in the *Redhouse Turkish/Ottoman–English Dictionary* (1999). I have used Öztuna (1990) as

a source reference for the names of Turkish artists and Turkish institutions where appropriate. Since there is a significant problem concerning the representation of Turkish names and dates during the twentieth century, I have adopted the current convention of supplying Turkish second names where relevant and of rendering Ottoman dates into their European equivalent for all events and citations.

2. Anthropologists have attempted to formulate a unified approach to Mediterranean Studies (see Gilmore 1982). Following a long tradition of relevant scholarship in the Humanities and the Social Sciences (where the Mediterranean as a cultural hearth occupies a significant place in the European historical imagination), they have sought to make sense of diversity in the region by identifying cultural traits characteristic of the Mediterranean Basin. In this respect, they have examined a wide variety of subjects including demography (see Peristiany 1976), kinship (see Campbell 1964), labor (see Gilsenan 1977), peasantry (see Sweet 1969), patronage (see Gellner and Waterbury 1977), settlement (see Kenny and Kertzer 1983), food (see ICAF 1998) and navigation (see Davis 2001) to validate a singular conception of Mediterranean identity. Further, they have studied shared value systems throughout the area to explain similar human behaviors within a complex geographical context and to analyze regional distinctiveness within a larger global framework. In particular, the trope "honor and shame" has provided an important focus for study. Emerging in the 1960s as an important marker of Mediterranean identity (see Pitt-Rivers 1963; Peristiany 1966), this structural dualism has generated a significant literature, a literature that transcends long-established geographical and historical boundaries in the region and that bypasses (for the most part) the Eurocentric preoccupation of traditional scholarship.

3. Ethnomusicologists have been profoundly influenced by anthropological studies of Mediterranean culture. Under the auspices of the International Council for Traditional Music (ICTM), the Music and Anthropology Study Group has sought to provide an integrated approach to Mediterranean Studies through music. Not only does the study group publish an online journal (www.muspe.unibo.it/M&A/), but it also organizes regular meetings in Europe that (to date) have dealt with the following themes: Anthropology of Music (1992), Past and Present (1995), Anthropology and History (1996), Music and Gender (1998) and Trends and Processes (2001). Other pan-regional (in contrast to intra-regional) studies of Mediterranean music can be found in relevant academic publications (see Falvy 1986; Camilleri 1988; Magrini 1993, 2003; De Incontrera 1996; Catalano 1999; Cavallini 2000), musical journals (see *MEMUS*; *Mediterranean Music*) and con-

ference proceedings (see Arcangeli 1988; IMS 1992; Tuksar 1998). A pan-Mediterranean focus is also to be found in the areas of musical composition and sound recording. The prominence of Italian scholars in this area of study is noteworthy.

4. Bradford's thesis is open to criticism. Employing an evolutionist methodology bearing the indelible imprint of Cultural Darwinism, he views the history of the Mediterranean from a distinctly Eurocentric perspective, a perspective which implicitly validates the cultural dominance of European civilization and which denigrates accordingly the legacy of Ottoman influence in the region. While Bradford's anti-Turkish stance is clear, his focus upon the mediating properties of the Mediterranean Sea is also open to scrutiny. As Gilmore notes (1982: 177), a maritime reading of Mediterranean culture excludes many countries with limited geographical relation to and with restricted historical connection to the Mediterranean Sea (such as Portugal). However, I maintain that Bradford's argument (despite its obvious drawbacks) is a useful framework for explaining Turkish historiography. See Braudel (1972) and Davis (1977) for maritime interpretations of Mediterranean historical unity. See also Colicci (1996) for an innovative approach to understanding the mediating properties of the sea in ritual practice.

5. Turkish classical music is known by a number of different names in Turkish. Generally speaking, this ancient tradition is called osmanlı mûsikî and fenn-i mûsikî in Ottoman sources and türk sanat müziği and türk klasik musıkisi in Republican publications. Other expressions are also found, including: divan musıkisi, enderun-i mûsikî, şark musıkisi, türk müsıkisi, alaturka and (more colloquially) ahenk. The choice, spelling and even pronunciation of specific terms in many sources reveal aesthetic preferences and ideological attitudes reminiscent of the alaturka-alafranga debate (see O'Connell 2000).

6. The relationship between Byzantine and Ottoman musical culture is complex. While many authorities recognize the significance of Greek musical influences upon an emergent Ottoman aesthetic in the sixteenth century (see Wright 2000: 3–4; Feldman 1996: 48–49, 62, 495; Popescu-Judetz 1981: 99–100), they are unable to find a firm connection due to inadequate source materials on both sides. While a number of scholars (especially Brandl 1989; Bardakçı 1993; Zannos 1990, 1994; Plemmenos 1997, 2001; and Popescu-Judetz 2000) have explored this relationship during the eighteenth and nineteenth centuries, their results show a gradual Turkification of the Greek orthodox liturgy in Istanbul and they do not (for the most part) indicate an emergent Hellenistic hegemony in the aesthetic realm. The matter is further com-

plicated by the exchange of musical modes, musical meters, musical genres, musical instruments, musical notations and musical practices between both communities during the nineteenth century. However, it must be stressed that I am principally interested here in an early-twentieth century understanding of Byzantine music (Bizans Musikisi) from a Turkish perspective, a perspective which, for nationalist reasons, sought to extricate Greek elements from the canonic realm and label them as non-Turkish (that is, as Byzantine). In this respect, Gazimihâl is echoing the revisionist attitudes of his contemporaries especially Arel (1940) and Ezgi (1933–53).

7. The reforms to the Greek Orthodox liturgy during the nineteenth century had an indirect influence upon the transmission of Ottoman music. Following the lead of Chrysanthos of Madhytos (c. 1810), the Armenian, Hamparsum Limonciyan (1768–1839), developed a widely used alphabetical system of notation that promoted the fixing and the preservation of different musical repertoires. As in Arab music (see Marcus 1989), the new system of notation had important implications for the re-conceptualization of Turkish music theory during the mid-nineteenth century. See O'Connell (1996) for an analysis of solmization in published song anthologies (güfte mecmuaları).

8. After the late seventeenth century, a number of important musical treatises concerning Ottoman music were written. As part of a wider renaissance in the arts (especially in architecture and literature), these treatises not only reflect the gradual demise of Persian influence in, but they also demonstrate the growing significance of non-Turkish commentators for the tradition. In this respect, the treatises/commentaries of Bobowski (c. 1650), Cantermir (c. 1700), Chalathzoglu (1724–28), Arutin (c. 1730), Fonton (1751), Marmarinos (1749) and Toderini (1789) are important non-Turkish sources for our understanding of the emergence of an independent Ottoman aesthetic.

9. Mediterranean music is well documented in Istanbul throughout the Ottoman period. While different styles and genres from Italy, the Balkans, the Levant and North Africa are too numerous to list here, Aksoy (1994) provides a good coverage of relevant traveler sources in Turkish. English translations of many references cited can be found in *The Turkish Music Quarterly*. As Öztuna notes (1990, II: 434–37), the sound-world of the Ottoman capital was characterized by a bricolage of different ethnic musics (including: Arab, Armenian, Greek, Sephardic and Roma musics) and regional styles (that is, from Anatolia, the Balkans, the Levant and North Africa). It was with reference to this multicultural sound-world that nationalist commentators wished to purify Turkish music of its perceived non-Turkish elements.

10. European scholars were particularly interested in the theory of Middle Eastern music. From an Orientalist perspective, they wished to study Ottoman musical practice explicitly to locate a shared theoretical tradition (emanating from an Ancient Greek source) and implicitly to demonstrate the highly developed status of Western music in comparison to its non-Western counterpart. Turkish musicologists were also informed by this Orientalist mind-set as they sought to modernize Turkish musicology according to the scientific principles of the West. In this matter, Rauf Yekta Bey played an important role. Educated initially by Ataullah Efendi (1842–1910) in the Galata Mevlevîhanesi and subsequently by Hüseyin Fahreddin Dede (1854–1911) and Calâeddin Effendi (1849–1907) (within the Westernizing worlds of the Bahariye and the Yenikapı Mevlevîhaneleri respectively), he was sponsored by the Byzantine scholar Abbé Thibaut who encouraged him to publish his findings in French academic sources (see Yekta Bey, 1907a, 1907b, 1922). See Farmer (1925) and Ribera (1929) for contemporary European interpretations of Eastern influence upon Western music. See Gazimihâl (1939) for a Turkish interpretation of this process.

11. The theory of quartertones was not new. Appearing in Lebanon during the eighteenth century (following musical reforms in the orthodox liturgy) and penetrating the Arabo-Turkish musical system during the nineteenth century (through the theoretical writings of Mīkhā'l Mushāqa, 1800–80), the theory provided an alternative to the traditional Pythagorean model. The theory simplified modal analysis into discrete quartertone units demonstrating (in contrast to Pythagorean theory) the equal-tempered influence of Western music. While a number of authors have noted the relationship between the development of a quartertone conceptualization and the emergence of Western cultural practices in the Near East (see Marcus 1989), Gazimihâl's interpretation of this theoretical model is slightly different. Quoting Fox Strangways (1914), he elicited a quasi equal-tempered system from Indian sources. He related his findings to the musical system of Ancient Greece (justified on the basis of a shared Indo-European cultural heritage). Finally, he interpreted not only the musical traditions of Europe but also the intervallic structure of all Turkish musics from this perspective. In short, he provided a universal theory of music that informed the ideological prejudices of his scholarly output.

12. Turkish musicologists explored non-Turkish sources during the early twentieth century to understand the history of Turkish music and to validate individual interpretations of Turkish identity. Following the early attempts by Mithat (1885) and Cağatay (1895) to write general music histories, Yekta Bey (1915, 1926) and Gazimihâl (1924b,

1927a, 1927b) wrote distinctive surveys of Turkish music from a comparative perspective. Arel's (1940) diffusionist interpretation of Turkey's musical past is probably the most controversial of these histories.

13. The influence of Abbé Thibaut (1901, 1902, 1906) upon Rauf Yekta Bey is evident in his earliest writings. See Yekta Bey (1899a, 1899b, 1907a, 1907b). In particular, Thibaut's research into Byzantine chant probably had a considerable influence upon Yekta Bey's theoretical analysis of Ottoman music. This is a subject worthy of further study. I would like to thank Sayın Dr. Murat Bardakçı for pointing out this interesting connection to me (personal communication, March 1994).

14. The French and German sources (which are sometimes translations of the original) referenced by Gazimihâl here include the following journals: *Allgemeine musikalische Zeitung*; *Vierteljahresschaf für Musikwissenschaft*; *Sammelbände der internationalen Musik-Gesellschaft*; *Le monde musicale*; and *La revue musicale*. They also include the following academic publications: Lichtenthal (1839); Vincent (1854); Helmholtz (1877); Gastoué (1907); Emmanuel (1911); Combarieu (1913–19); Busoni (1916); Closson (1916); Wisghnegradsky (1924) and Delacroix (1927).

15. See Shaw (1976–77) for a historical survey of the Phenariot Greeks. See also Brandl 1989; Bardakçı 1993; Zannos 1990, 1994; Plemmenos 1997, 2001 and Popescu-Judetz 2000 for an explanation of the significance of the Phenariot Greeks for Ottoman music.

16. See O'Connell (2000) for an overview of relevant institutional reforms.

17. See Bardakçi (1986) for a representative bibliography of Rauf Yekta Bey's publications in Turkish and non-Turkish sources.

Bibliography

Abu-Lughod, Lila. *Veiled Sentiments: Honor and Poetry in a Bedouin Society*. Berkeley: University of California Press, 1986.

Aksoy, Bülent. *Avrupalı Gezginlerin Gözüyle Osmanlılarda Musıki*. İstanbul: Pan Yayıncılık, 1994.

Arcangeli, Piero. *Musica e liturgia nella cultura mediterranea*. Conference Proceedings. Florence: L. S. Olschiki, 1988.

Arel, Hüseyin S. *Türk Musikisi Kimindir?* İstanbul: 1940.

Bardakçı, Murat. *Türk Musikisi: Rauf Yekta Bey*. İstanbul: Pan Yayıncılık, 1986.

————. *Fener Beyleri'ne Türk Şarkıları*. İstanbul: Pan Yayıncılık, 1993.

Bradford, Ernle. *The Mediterranean: Portrait of a Sea*. London: Hodder and Stoughton, 1971.

Brandl, Rudolf M. "Konstantinopolitanische Makamen des 19. Jahrhunderts in Neumen. Die Musik der Fanarioten." 159–69 in *Maqam, Raga, Zielenmelodik: Konzeptionen und Prinzipen der Musikproduktion*, edited by Jürgen Elsner. Conference Proceedings. Berlin: International Council for Traditional Music. Study Group "Maqam": 1989.

Braudel, Fernand. *The Mediterranean and the Mediterranean World in the Age of Philip II*. 2 vols. Translated by Siân Reynolds. New York: Harper and Row, 1972.

Busoni, Ferruccio. *Entwurf einer neuen Äesthetik der Tonkunst*. Triest: C. Schmidl and Co, 1916.

Cağatay, Ali R. "Fenn-i Musiki Nazariyatı." *Malumat* (1895): 1–7, 9–11, 13–14, 16, 20, 23, 28.

Camilleri, Charles, and Peter Inglott. *Mediterranean Music*. Malta: Foundation for International Studies at the University of Malta, 1988.

Campbell, John K. *Honor, Family and Patronage*. Oxford: Oxford University Press, 1964.

Catalano, Roberto. "Mediterranean World-Music: Experiencing Sicilian-Arab Sound." Ph.D. dissertation, University of California, 1999.

Cavallini, Stefano. *Un'altra musica: Da Marsiglia a Tunisi, da Tangeri a Limassol: la musica nella cultura del Mediterraneo*. Tirrenia (Pisa): Edizioni del Cerro, 2000.

Closson, Ernest. *Eléments d'esthétique musicale*. Bruxelles: P. Lombaerts, 1916.

Colicci, Guiseppina. "Invocation in a Fisherman's Festival for the *Madonna del Lume*: San Diego, California and Porticello, Italy." Ph.D. dissertation, University of California, 1996.

Combarieu, Jules. *Histoire de la musique: Des origines au début XXe siècle*. vols. 1, 2 and 3. Paris: A. Colin, 1913–19.

Chrysanthos of Madhytos. *Theoritikon megha tis mousikis*. Trieste: 1832.

Davis, John. *People of the Mediterranean: An Essay in Comparative Social Anthropology*. London: Routledge and Kegan Paul, 1977.

Davis, Lee. "Navigation in the Ancient Eastern Mediterranean." Ph.D. dissertation, Texas A&M University, 2001.

De Incontrera, Carlo. *Nell'aria della sera: Il Mediterraneo e la musica*.

Monfalcone: Teatro comunale di Monfalcone, 1996.

Delacroix, Henri. *Psychologie de l'art, essai sur l'activité artistique.* Paris: F. Alcon, 1927.

Emmanuel, Maurice. *Historie de la langue musicale.* 2 vols. Paris: H. Laurens, 1911.

Ezgi, Subhi. *Nazarî ve Ameli Türk Musikisi.* 5 vols. İstanbul: Millî Eğitim Basımevi, 1933–53.

Falvy, Zoltán. *Mediterranean Culture and Troubadour Music.* Budapest: Akadémiai Kiadó, 1986.

Farmer, Henry George. *The Arabian Influence on Musical Theory.* London: H. Reeves, 1925.

Feldman, Walter. "Music of the Ottoman Court: Makam, Composition and the Early Ottoman Instrumental Repertoire." *Intercultural Music Studies* 10. Berlin: Verlag für Wissenschaft und Bildung, 1996.

Fox Strangways, Arthur H. *The Music of Hindostan.* Oxford: The Clarendon Press, 1914.

Gastoué, Amédée. *Les origines du chant romain: l'Antiphonaire grégorien.* Paris: A. Picard, 1907.

Gazimihâl, Mahmut. "Musiki ve Ziya Gökalp." *Millî Mecmua* 24 (1924a): 383–85.

———. "Şark Musikisinde Seviye." *Millî Mecmua* 26 (1924b): 414–16.

———. "Musiki: Çeyrek Sesler." *Millî Mecmua* 85 (1927a): 1375–77; 86: 1390–93; 87: 1407–9; 88: 1423–26.

———. "Musiki: Avrupada Çeyrek Sesler." *Millî Mecmua* 91 (1927b): 1473–74; 94: 1519–21; 95: 1536–38; 96: 1545–47.

———. *Anadolu Türküleri ve Musiki İstikbalimiz.* İstanbul: Marifet Matbaası, 1928.

———. *Türkiye-Avrupa Musiki Münasebetleri.* İstanbul: Nümune Matbaası, 1939.

Gellner, Ernest, and John Waterbury, eds. *Patrons and Clients in Mediterranean Societies.* London: Duckworth, 1977.

Gilmore, David. "Anthropology of the Mediterranean Area." *Annual Review of Anthropology* 11 (1982): 175–205.

———, ed. *Honor and Shame and the Unity of the Mediterranean.* Washington: American Anthropological Association, Special Publication 22, 1987.

Gilsenan, Michael. "Against Patron-Client Relations." 167–83 in *Patrons and Clients in Mediterranean Societies*, edited by Ernest Gellner. London: Duckworth, 1977.

———. *Lords of the Lebanese Marches: Violence and Narrative in an Arab Society.* Berkeley: University of California Press, 1996.

Gökalp, Ziya. *Türkçülüğün Esasları*. Ankara: Matbuat ve Irtibarat Matbaası, 1923.

Helmholtz, Hermann L. *Die Lehre von de Tonempfindungen als physiologische Grundlage für die Theorie der Musik.* Braunschweig: F. Vieweg, 1877.

Herzfeld, Michael. *The Poetics of Manhood: Contest and Identity in a Cretan Mountain Village.* Princeton: Princeton University Press, 1985.

ICAF (International Commission of the Anthropology of Food). *The Road of Food Habits in the Mediterranean Area.* Proceedings of the International Congress: Seventh Meeting of the International Commission of the Anthropology of Food. Rome: Istituto Italiano di Anthropologia, 1998.

IMS (International Musicological Society). *Actas del XV Congresso de la Sociedad Internacional de Musicología: culturas musicales del Mediterraneo y sus ramificaciónes.* Madrid: International Musicological Society, 1992.

Kenny, Michael, and David Kertzer. *Urban Life in Mediterranean Europe: Anthropological Perspectives.* Urbana: University of Illinois Press, 1983.

Lichtenthal, Pierre. *Dictionnaire de musique.* Translated by Dominique Mondo. Paris: Troupenas et ce, 1839.

Magrini, Tullia. *Antropologia della musica e culture mediterranee.* Bologna: Il Mulino, 1993.

———. *Music and Gender: Perspectives from the Mediterranean.* Chicago: Chicago University Press, 2003.

Marcus, Scott. *Arab Music Theory in the Modern Period.* Ph.D. dissertation, University of California, 1989.

Mithat Efendi, Ahmet. "Tarih-ı Musiki." *Müntehabat-ı Tercüman-ı Hakikat* (1885): 675–92.

O'Connell, John M. "Alaturka Revisited: Style as History in Turkish Vocal Performance." Ph.D. dissertation, University of California, 1996.

———. "Fine Art, Fine Music: Controlling Turkish Taste at the Fine Arts Academy." *Yearbook for Traditional Music* 33 (2000): 117–42.

Öztuna, Yılmaz. *Büyük Türk Mûsikisi Ansiklopedesi* vols. 1 and 2. Ankara: Kültür Bakanlığı, 1990.

Peristiany, Jean, ed. *Honor and Shame: The Values of Mediterranean Society.* Chicago: University of Chicago Press, 1966.

———. *Mediterranean Family Structures.* Cambridge: Cambridge University Press, 1976.

Pitt-Rivers, Julian. *Mediterranean Countrymen: Essays in the Social Anthropology of the Mediterranean.* Paris: Mouton, 1963.

Plemmenos, John. "The Active Listener: Greek Attitudes towards Music Listening in the Age of Enlightenment." *British Journal of Ethnomusicology* 6 (1997): 51–63.

————. "'Micro-music' of the Ottoman Empire: The Case of the Phenariot Greeks of Istanbul." Ph.D. dissertation, University of Cambridge (UK), 2001.

Popescu-Judetz, Eugenia, and Adriana Ababı Sırlı. *Studies in Oriental Arts.* Pittsburgh: Duquesne University, Tamburitzan Institute of Folk Arts, 1981.

————. *Sources of 18th Century Music: Panayiotes Chalathzoglou and Kyrillos Marmarinos' Comparative Treatises on Secular Music.* İstanbul: Pan Yayıncılık, 2000.

Redhouse, Sir James. *Redhouse Türkçe/Osmanıca–İngilizce Sözlük: Redhouse Turkish/Ottoman–English Dictionary.* İstanbul: Redhouse Yayınevi, 1999.

Ribera, Julián. *Music in Ancient Arabia and Spain: La músiquas de las cantigas.* Translated by Eleanor Hague and Marrion Leffingwell. Oxford: Oxford University Press, 1929.

Salvatore, Gianfranco. *Isole sonanti: scenari archetipici della musica del Mediterraneo.* Rome: ISMEZ, 1989.

Saygun, Adnan. "La musique turque." 573–617 in *Histoire de la musique*, edited by Roalnd-Manuel. Paris: Pleyel, 1960.

Shaw, Stanford. *History of the Ottoman Empire and Modern Turkey* vols. 1 and 2. Cambridge: Cambridge University Press, 1976–77.

Sweet, Louise. *Circum-Mediterranean Peasantry: Introductory Bibliographies.* New Haven: Human Resources Area Files Press, 1969.

Thibaut, P. J. "Assimilation des echoi byzantins et des modes latins avec les anciens tropes grecs." *Revue d'histoire et de critique musicales* 1 (1901): 306–14.

————. "La musique des mevlévis." *La revue musicale* 2 (1902): 346–56, 384–92.

————. "Notes sur la musique orientale: La musique arabe, persane, et turque." *La revue musicale* 6 (1906): 63–66.

Tuksar, Stanislav. *Zagreb 1094–1994: Zagreb and Croatian Lands as a Bridge between Central-European and Mediterranean Musical Cultures.* Zagreb: Croatian Musicological Society, 1998.

Vincent, Alexandre. *Emploi des quarts de ton dans le chant grégorien constaté sur l'antiphonaire de Montpellier.* Paris: A Leleux, 1854.

Wisghnegradsky, Ivan. "La musique à quarts de ton." *Revue musicale* 5, no. 11 (1924): 231–34.

Wright, Owen. *Demetrius Cantemir: The Collection of Notations* 2, Commentary. Aldershot: Ashgate, 2000.

Yekta Bey, Rauf. "Rum Kiliselerinde Musiki." *İkdam* no. 1960 (17 December 1899a): 3.

————. "Osmanlı Musiksinden Çeyrek, Salis, ve Nesif Sedalar." *İkdam* no. 1972 (29 December 1899b): 3.

————. "Musique orientale: Le compositeur du péchrev dans le mode nihavend." *La revue musicale* 7 (1907a): 117–21, 156.

————. "Musique orientale: les modes orientaux." *La revue musicale* 7 (1907b): 176–81.

————. "Eski Türk Musikisinde Dair Tarihi Tetebbular, 1–3." *Millî Tetebbular Mecmuası* (1915): 3–5.

————. "La musique turque." 2945–3064 in *Encyclopédie de la musique* 5, edited by Albert Lavignac. Paris: Delagarve, 1922.

————. *Şark Musikisi Tarihi*. İstanbul: Mahmud Bey Matbaası, 1926.

————. "Türk Musikisi Nasıl Islah Olunabilir?" *Telsiz* 8 (18 August 1927): 1–2.

Zannos, Iannis. "Intonation in Theory and Practice of Greek and Turkish Music." *Yearbook for Traditional Music* 23 (1990): 42–59.

————. *Ichos und Makam: vergleichende Untersuchungen zum Tonsystem der griechisch-orthodoxen Kirchenmusik und der türkischen Kunstmusik*. Bonn: Orpheus-Verlag, 1994.

Chapter Two

A Family of Song: Reflections of Albanian Urban Lyric Song in the Mediterranean

Eno Koço

Introduction

Albania presents a fascinating example of a country whose culture has been brushed by successive waves of influence and yet which, like a beach at high-water mark, has absorbed and developed these influences in its own way, protected from complete domination by its position at the extreme edge of the waves. This chapter discusses the origins and development of a unique branch of music, the Albanian urban lyric song (AULS), which began to appear in the early years of the nineteenth century, had its "golden age" in the 1930s and is still a part of Albanian musical culture today.

Music has always played an important role in Albanian everyday life, in both the country and the towns. The songs which grew up and flourished in the different regions were passed down orally through the generations and this tradition, to some extent, persists today. The Albanian urban lyric songs represented a great step forward in music making, because they were the first Albanian songs to be written down and so could reach wider audiences than the existing repertoires, which until then had been performed by regional singers for regional audiences.

This research considers a specific repertory within the general field of Albanian popular music. I am concerned, for reasons to be explained, only with the 1930s and the repertory of urban lyric song implied by the title. "Urban," as the term is used here, somewhat excludes music from the countryside or mountains (i.e., "rural" music). These songs are, in fact, the popular music of the towns. Although in Albania *këngë popullore* (popular songs) is employed as a general and common term, I have preferred not to use "popular," because in the 1990s the word implies a cultural context more American, or modern, than the songs in question, which are also, after all, part of the folk songs of

Albania. In Albania the term *popullore* (popular), which is closer to the Italian popolare or the Russian narodnaya, is used in a somewhat wider sense to embrace the music that, with the growth of the towns, began to develop distinctive characteristics which tended to be accepted by most Albanians. The repertories covered by popullore songs embrace not only urban songs, but also gypsy songs and sometimes elaborate folk music. If the oral folk music traditions are, more or less, restricted to their immediate areas, the popullore songs or music have, as was stated above, a wider range. By concentrating on "lyric" I hope to isolate a particular aspect of the performance and oral history of the repertory, by which it was developed into something akin to the art song. Because this type of song falls somewhere between the repertories commonly studied (which incline to art music or to allegedly "purer" forms of folk music), this is an area which has not previously received much attention.

A look at Albanian music in the first half of the twentieth century was required, to trace both its roots and the conditions which led to the emergence of urban lyric song. A considerable number of recordings made by three lyric sopranos (one was my mother), a tenor and two baritones (one was my father), as well as recordings by other postwar lyric singers, demonstrate that its first impact on Albanian music was felt during the 1930s and the 1940s. Those early urban songs were inspired by the local environment and everyday events; they were beautifully shaped and rich in emotional expression.

My views differ quite markedly from those of some earlier writers. Doris and Erich Stockman felt that, before the second half of the twentieth century, "the entire musical life of Albania was determined by folk music" (1980: 197). However, urban lyric songs show that, while the musical life of Albania may have been heavily influenced by folk music during the first half of the twentieth century, by 1930 that influence was no longer strong enough to dominate it entirely.

The development of the urban lyric song in the period covered by this article was most directly linked to historical events after the independence of Albania in 1912. It should be emphasized that the Albanian resistance and national unification movement before Albania's independence was directed almost entirely from abroad, mainly by the Albanian Diaspora in Romania, Italy, Greece and Egypt. I come from a family which lived in the Albanian diaspora; on my father's side in Romania and on mother's, in Egypt. Tefta Tashko-Koço, my mother, who was born in Fayum in Egypt and returned to Albania with her family in 1921 when she was eleven years old, recorded several Albanian urban lyric songs for the Columbia Society in Italy in 1937 and 1942.

My father, Kristo Koço, a baritone, came to Albania from Bucharest for the first time in 1938 and was also a member of the group of lyric singers, but was not as active as his wife.

Being orphaned at an early age, I found conversation and discussion with my mother's and father's friends and colleagues a sort of substitute for them. In many cases I have kept notes, for more than thirty years, of these artists' recordings. I knew all the singers and pianists of the 1930s personally and also had contacts with some of the composer–arrangers and poets who lived after the Second World War. I have, therefore, been able to investigate the historical and musical background of Albanian song with personal knowledge of those involved. During my time as conductor of the Albanian Radio and Television Symphony Orchestra (1976–91) I recorded many urban lyric songs, with both professional art music and amateur singers, the latter being accompanied by a small orchestra and I also arranged some of them for both lyric and traditional singers.

Albanian Music Studies

Although the traditional urban song is the most prominent of Albanian musical genres, it has not been studied in depth until now. Traditional urban songs and urban lyric songs since the 1930s are classified into two separate categories: the first is sung by traditional (untrained) and amateur singers, the second by art singers. The Albanian urban lyric song, being on the borderline between the urban traditional song and the lyric song with a strongly recognizable modal flavor, differs in many ways from the rural or mountain song (it is worth recalling that in the 1930s, over 60 percent of the Albanian population lived in rural areas). The core of this study deals with Albanian urban lyric songs (AULS) in the 1930s, as "artistic" versions of traditional urban songs. My main source of information for interpretation of these songs was existing recordings made by art singers of the 1930s, to which I had extensive access.

Whatever the origin of the Albanian urban lyric song, whether Middle Eastern or southwestern Balkan, the composer–arrangers of the 1930s and the lyric singers conceived them as west European Mediterranean vocal and instrumental products.

In 1940, Pjetër Dungu compiled a book called *Lyra Shqiptare* (The Albanian Lyre),[1] published in Italy by the Instituto Geografico De Agostini, Novara. The compilation of the songs was devised by Dungu, but all the songs were also translated into Italian.[2] The *Lyra Shqiptare* contains fifty of the most typical urban lyric songs, with their melodies and texts and it is illustrated with numerous drawings depicting Albanian symbolism. This collection of songs, mainly from Shkodër and Korça and, to a lesser degree from Kosova, Elbasan, Berat and so on, not only served as a table of reference for the AULS, but was also used as a basis for the later elaboration of this genre.

In 1943, Gjon Kolë Kujxhija published in Florence *Dasëm Shkodrane* (A Shkodër Wedding), the first volume of the *Valle Kombëtare* (National Dances), a compilation of wedding songs from the northern Albanian town of Shkodër.[3] Yury Arbatsky published the treatise *Beating the Tupan in the Central Balkans* (1953), a study of the music of the tupan (big drum) as played in eastern Albania, through Macedonia, to western Bulgaria. Arbatsky also discusses the influence of the gypsy peoples in the Balkans, Turkish and Arabic influence, meter and folk musicians.

In the mid-thirties, Kosta Manojlovič, a Slav monk, musicologist and folklorist, harmonized and arranged for mixed choirs and solo voices some Albanian urban songs (AUS). The elements of harmony and counterpoint used in his songs were treated in a skillful way and were used for the later orchestrations of the same urban songs. In the postwar period, research into Albanian folk music was also undertaken by musicologists from other countries, such as Doris and Erich Stockmann, A. L. Lloyd and others.[4]

Jane Sugarman is an ethnomusicologist who specializes in the music of southeastern Europe and the Middle East. She has conducted field research in Albania and the former Yugoslavia, as well as among immigrants in western Europe and North America, with a focus on the participation of musical forms in processes of identity formation. Her 1997 book, *Engendering Song: Singing and Subjectivity at Prespa Albanian Weddings*, analyzes the relationship between singing and gender relations in a diasporic Albanian community. I must admit that I have different views from those expressed by Sugarman where she tries to associate the music and singing of the Prespians[5] with their Muslim religion.[6]

Among the Albanian contemporary ethnomusicologists Ramadan Sokoli is the most eminent to whom scholars of Balkan music should be particularly indebted for his study of Ottoman modes and practices. *The Albanian Musical Folklore* (in two volumes) published in 1965, a valuable book written by Sokol Shupo (1997) and another of the same kind (in four parts) written by Vasil Tole (2001), have substantially enriched our knowledge of Albanian folk and urban music.

Modal Entities

Makam system and practice was a particularly important strand of the Ottoman heritage for the development of northern Albanian urban lyric song. Sokoli defines makams as "modal scales which came from the Turkish-Arabic-Persian culture which the Ottoman invasion had spread by way of folklore both to Albania and other regions of the Balkans. Each of these scales is distinguished by its structure, "ethos" and such other features as its softness and sweetness on the one hand and its passion turning to deepest sorrow on the other" (Sokoli 1965: 25). In the mid-eighteenth century this was the music of the upper classes and is thought to have been played initially in the outer courtyards of the Albanian pashallik-s (Turkish: paşalık),[7] those of Bushati in the north with its capital at Shkodër and of Ali Pasha Tepelena in the south, with its capital at Janina,[8] and performed at private and religious gatherings by well-known professional musicians.

Not all Ottoman makams were used with the same frequency in Albania; some of them were more adaptable to the Albanian ethos and some less. The urban songs of Jare style from Shkodër present the closest parallels to the most significant makams that were originally introduced into Albania. By the end of the nineteenth century, the makam's role in Albanian urban song was progressively modified. Gradually, not only because of the remoteness from the capital of the Ottoman Empire but also through the tendency of Albanian composers to purge their songs of Oriental "excesses," urban songs became less dependent on the highly distinctive features of the original Ottoman makams. The nomenclature changed, also and these modal systems began to be referred to by the Persian word *perde*.

With the Islamization of the villages, which came rather later than in the towns,[9] an interaction of musical features evolved and a greater ethnic and cultural diversity was permitted. The urban song of Middle Eastern modal inclination not only adopted many elements of Ottoman modal scales but also borrowed elements from the local traditional urban and rural song. This simultaneous existence of a typically urban traditional and rural music and the new urban professional songs of the same area created a unique type of Albanian urban song which had a distinctly recognizable regional character. The rural song was inclined to borrow, chiefly in north and central Albania, elements and features of a Middle Eastern musical system already used in the towns, probably because the Turkish monophonic tunes could be absorbed more easily into the monophonic traditional or folk urban and rural (mountain)

tunes of the northern part of Albania. For this reason, Turkish monophonic music found it more difficult to influence the folk music of
south Albania, because of the predominance of multi-part folk music in
that region and secondly because of its affinity with some Greek modalities. However, some of the latter borrowed Middle Eastern elements
and characteristics.

As the Ottoman Empire encroached from the north, Byzantine
secular musical traditions found sanctuary in rural music. It is as if a
"cultural time capsule" was carried away by Albanians who, under Ottoman pressure, left their homeland for Sicily and southern Italy in
large numbers during the fifteenth century. By 1921 there were still
about 80,000 Albanian speakers in these regions. Here they retained
their language and, under papal license, the right to practice the orthodox rites, guarding their inheritance jealously. It is arguable that their
songs embody music that existed in southern Albania before Ottoman
influence.

In southern Albania the archaic musical tradition is predominantly
pentatonic (see figure 1). Often expressed collectively in polyphonic
choral singing with or without a drone, this tradition was able to embrace influence from the Byzantine mainly secular music found in the
Eastern Empire. The southwestern Balkan notion of mode, which includes mainly pentatonic and diatonic modes, is closer, in my view, to
the notion of an echos. A certain "flavor" is imparted to music of Byzantine origin by the fact that it is built up on the same modal scheme or
"echoi," which are not so much distinctive scales as groups of melodies
of a certain type which make up a recognizably *south-western Balkan
mode* entity.[10] To the north, on the other hand, the local tradition was
more homophonic.

Although I referred in the analysis to Ottoman modes and their influence in Albania, this does not mean that these modes preserved in
Albania the same "ethos" and structure, the same intervals and names
as the original Ottoman forms. However, if the surface of some urban
songs is scratched, their modalities may lead to "Ottoman layers"; that
is why it is important, in my view, to refer to the present theory of the
Ottoman Turkish modes (as classified by Signell) and to classify some
of the urban songs according to the makam system. Although the "Ottoman layers" were absorbed into the local idiom, that is, into the urban
and folk culture of the Albanian people, still it is not hard to distinguish, even in a song composed in the 1930s, 1940s or later, the mode
which used to be present as an Ottoman variant.

Instruments and Instrumental Ensembles

It is important to stress that in all parts of Albania where the urban song was cultivated, instrumental urban music was also practiced. The instrumental ensembles in urban areas had their distinctive features, which varied from north to south Albania. Amongst the different types of urban songs, those of aheng played a significant role. Until the end of the nineteenth century, the aheng ensemble of north Albania consisted, roughly, of a saze[11] (long-necked lute, with up to ten strings), a fiddle, a percussive instrument like a dajre or def[12] (tambourine) and a singer; other instruments were added on different occasions, such as the kavall or çapare, a kind of Turkish zil (cymbals).

The bejtexhis,[13] and even dancers, were also part of the aheng ensembles. As time passed, the clarinet was included in the aheng groups and, in addition, the violin and def, which were also included in the southern ensembles. According to Sokoli, around 1905, the instrumental ensembles of Elbasan, in central Albania, consisted of the following: violin, çyr,[14] llauta, clarinet, dajre and one or two other instruments. In Berat, around 1915, according to veteran-musicians, the aheng ensemble of Riza Nebati consisted of a violin (Nebati himself), clarinet, llauta and def, whilst another aheng group (the Qamili brothers) which moved from Përmet to Berat about the same period, consisted of a violin, gërneta (clarinet), llauta and mandoll. The combination of these instruments in specific urban ensembles was an attempt to create the needed balance either for the aheng group solos or for the accompaniment to songs.

Urban instrumental ensembles were particularly common in the most developed mercantile regions and towns of Albania, such as Shkodër. By the end of the nineteenth century and the beginning of the twentieth, the merchants of this town, mainly Christians, made efforts to improve their quality of life by trading with foreign countries such as Austria and Italy. The more elaborate of the imported manufactured instruments, such as the violin and clarinet, were to be found among the merchant class, simply because they could afford them. Towards evening, the townsmen of Shkodër would gather at cafés, locandas for Christians and khans for Muslims and on special occasions they enjoyed their native music played and sung by local urban performers. The urban instrumental ensembles were limited in number and they functioned mainly for special ceremonies such as weddings; the members of these groups, the ahengxhi, did not enjoy any particular social status, and the people who played the instruments or sang in these groups were, generally, looked upon with a sort of contempt. Despite this attitude, these professional or semiprofessional popular musicians played an enormous role in the preservation of popular musical events such as weddings and parties, dances and even live concerts. They were the real carriers of the tradition of urban instrumental and vocal music, in that they followed certain rules which were important for regulating the order of the songs and the order of the events in the aheng parties in general.

Although the aheng practice followed more or less the same rules and performed the same function throughout Albania, local customs and regulations were quite distinct. In Berat, for instance, the instrumental and vocal potpourris in the aheng style, used as introductions to wedding parties, were mainly improvised by the local aheng players, but some elements were also borrowed from other aheng areas. The aheng ensembles of Shkodër, Durrës, Elbasan, Tirana and Berat, all followed Middle Eastern intonations and practices, albeit adapted into local versions, but this was the only point of contact and interchange of the traditional urban music between these towns. This enabled the aheng ensembles to meet the demands of ordinary people all over the Albanian world, at weddings and other festivities and gave them an advantage over rural music, which could not arouse interest beyond its immediate area. The growth of the aheng ensembles in the early years of the twentieth century in a country where three quarters of the population lived in rural areas, made it possible for urban music to reach a much wider audience and for the aheng practice to be introduced into the villages. As they were obliged to participate in some of the rural musical rituals, for example at weddings, the aheng players also included in their repertories the rudimentary traditional music which had been strongly preserved in the rural and mountainous areas as part of the musical identity of the region.

Nationalism

It is obvious that Ottoman influence was reflected in different social aspects of Albanian life and consequently in many urban songs. But the process of the "Albanization" of the songs had started, at the latest, with Kasem Xhurri (born in Shkodër, in the 1830s) "who, after returning to his country, was dedicated to improving the Shkodran aheng, particularly by introducing Byzantine melodies similar to Shkodrane dances and fitting them to the sixth key of Byzantine music" (Gurashi and Sheldija 1961: 213). The newer generations after Muço, Xhurri and Kurti, deliberately attempted to purge the urban songs of "external" elements and to give them a marked local character. Thus, in spite of the Ottoman legacy or Greek affiliation, the entire process of transforming the urban song into an Albanian entity and identity is clearly seen in the way the Middle Eastern modes and sometimes melodies were adapted to the Albanian ethos. The Albanian urban songs fall into three main groups differentiated by mode of transmission:

1. Those of largely unknown authorship, which have been subjected to changes over time in an oral tradition;
2. Songs existing in unwritten form, which have been elaborated and transformed into urban lyric songs through notation by composer-arrangers;
3. Those which are entirely the work of art music composers. The first type of urban song came from aheng music and only rarely existed in notated form in the first half of the twentieth century.[15]

Palokë Kurti was the first Albanian composer to write down songs, most of them based on sharki-s (Turkish: şarki)[16] and peshref-s (Turkish: peşrev).[17] In fact, before and during his time the aheng urban music of his native Shkodër, which was an unwritten music, was heavily under the influence of Turkish music. The urban songs composed by Kurti are clear illustrations of, on the one hand, his association with the aheng songs and, on the other, of his strong individuality as a composer aspiring to create a new type of song. Because of the enormous popularity of Kurti's songs they were readopted by the aheng ensembles, but of course in a more refined form than that of the instrumental tunes which had inspired them.

The second type of urban song, elaborated and transformed into lyric song by means of notated accompaniment, emerged in the 1930s and has been seriously developed since then. Albanian composer-arrangers such as Gjoka, Dungu, Kongoli, Kono and others collected urban tunes and songs from the traditional singers, provided piano or orchestral arrangements and performed them in collaboration with art singers.

In the third type, composers wrote completely new songs. However, these were not claimed as a new and original genre. Rather, the singer-composers were at pains to promote the songs as part of the conventional tradition of the (anonymous) urban, popular song. Through perpetual oral modification and alteration, the original versions of

sions of Kurti's songs have almost been lost, but this does not obscure their authorship. They still play a dual role; firstly as urban traditional music, because as is widely recognized, it "has originated with an individual composer and has subsequently been absorbed into the unwritten living tradition of a community,"[18] and secondly as popular music, because it was originally taken from aheng music and the consciously devised elements have remained unchanged.

In Elbasan, the oral tradition of urban song was transmitted in a different way than that of Kurti. Situated just north of the river Shkumbini, the population of Elbasan belongs to the northern Geg ethnic and linguistic group.[19] The urban songs of this region are also affected by its geographical position and their expression tends to show the melodic freedom which is characteristic of, for instance, the urban songs of Shkodra. The urban songs of the Korça district, in southern Albania, have a character all of their own, and their origin is still somewhat mysterious. It is assumed that some of these elegant songs probably came from Janina in Epirus. They represent the heart of that modal idiom which I have called the southwestern Balkan mode.

Love Songs

Love songs constitute the predominant category of urban songs, regionally distinctive and fiercely guarded by the local people. In the nineteenth century and at the beginning of the twentieth, a composer could not openly dedicate a song to the woman who had inspired it because, in the existing moral climate, a woman's beauty was a taboo subject. However, the love songs became a part of cultural life and the focus of nationalistic feeling, ironically by allowing the people to "forget" the political situation in the pleasure of listening to Albanian urban song as it began its transformation into art song.

The texts of the majority of urban songs are love poems. Their principal theme is the disappointment of love, which often resulted from the rigidity of Albanian society. Women did not appear in public either as creators or as singers but sang mainly indoors; hence the allusions to "the partridge in the cage" and "the poor nightingale." Men, however, could sing at general gatherings, in the traditional coffee-houses or, even more importantly, at urban festivities, among which the dasma (wedding) was the most significant. The male composer-singers generally sang in falsetto, a range later adopted by trained female sopranos. Usually the composer-singer also wrote the verses (bejtexhis[20]).

However, in central and north Albanian love songs of the aheng type, the Middle Eastern influence is obvious. It should be stressed that during the Communist regime in Albania many texts were reworked. The aim was to avoid any versification which did not fit the new socialist ideas, a tendency which was not directed towards refinement or re-creation, but was made purely for ideological reasons.

The Styles of Singing of the AULS in the 1930s

Before the stylized forms of urban music began to emerge around the 1930s, the majority of the Albanian people had enjoyed only folk, traditional urban or popular music, for voice or instruments. Even those living in the towns could not easily digest the so-called urban lyric songs. An effort was required from the artistes to fulfill this genuine public demand. Something was needed to draw a larger audience to the concert halls. The answer might be the inclusion of Albanian songs; at least, in that case, a larger proportion of the audience would understand the words. One could also hear accomplished songs with a fine shape and structure, such as figure 1, *What Are You Asking For, You Poor Old Man*; figure 2, *May God Save Your Beauty*; figure 3, *Looking from the Window* and figure 4, *Nightingale, You Poor Nightingale*.

The interpretation of the lyric singers of the 1930s, which is the strongest factor that made the urban traditional song sound like an urban lyric (art) song, was the key point in the conception and establishment of these songs as cultivated vocal products. There are many details of phrasing and technique common to both art songs and urban lyric songs; these may be seen, for instance, in the way Pavarotti sings a Neapolitan song and in the use made of the same principles by which an Albanian art singer performed an Albanian lyric song. The preferred vocal tone of most Albanian urban lyric songs requires smooth and refined voice production. As was noted earlier, traditional urban songs were not written down. The essential features that made them recognizable as regional or as typical of individual traditional singers' styles had to be learned by the art singers of the 1930s and incorporated into their individual musical styles with care and accuracy. As an art performance, it was the interpreter's presentation which came to be regarded as the work itself. It is possible to identify three marked interpretative approaches which might be described as traditionalist, operatic and melodramatic respectively.

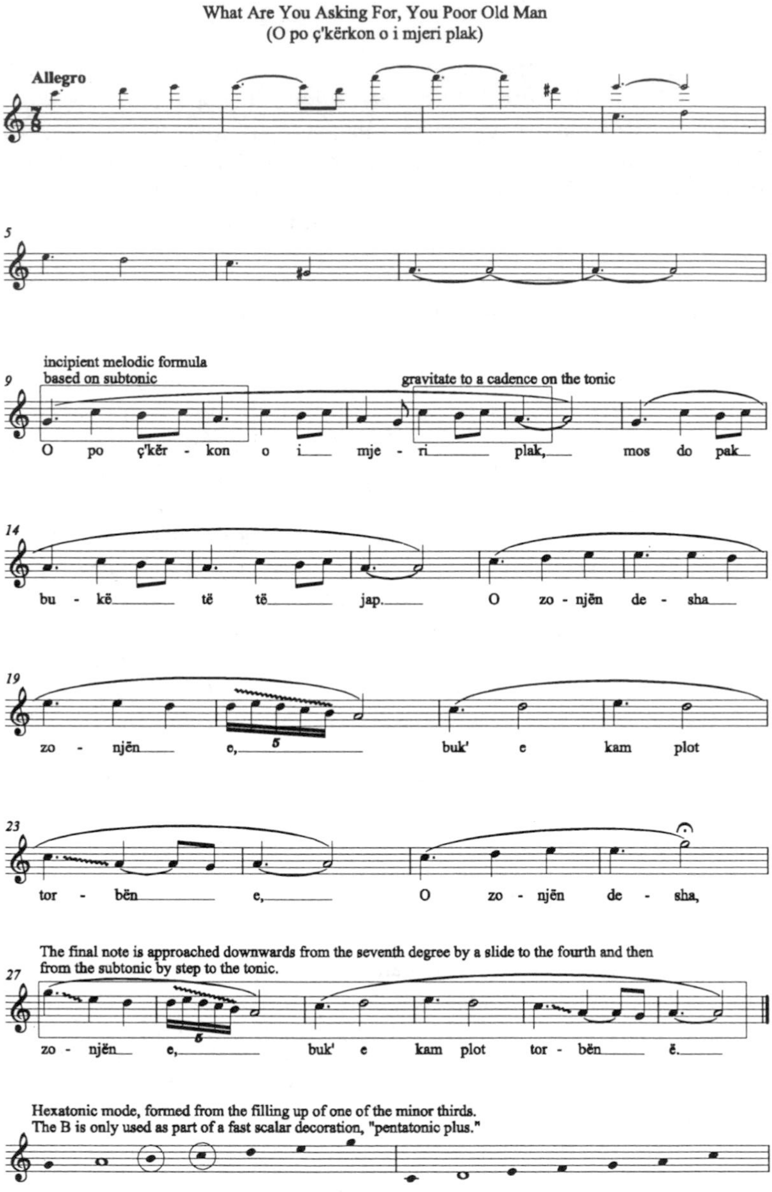

Figure 1. *What Are You Asking For, You Poor Old Man*, Korçare, transcribed by Eno Koço from Kraja's interpretation.

Figure 2. *May God Save Your Beauty*, Skodrane, words and music by Palokë Kurti, transcribed by Eno Koço from Kraja's interpretation.

Figure 3. *Looking from the Window*, Elbasanase, transcribed by Eno Koço from Tashko-Koço's interpretation.

Figure 4. *Nightingale, You Poor Nightingale*, Korçare (Muço?), transcribed by Eno Koço, from Antoniu's interpretation.

The Traditionalist Approach

It is purely by coincidence that the interpretation of the Albanian urban lyric song (AULS) is represented by just one singer from the north of Albania, Marie Kraja, but by five from the south, Antoniu, Truja, Tashko-Koço, Ciko and Kristo Koço. Significantly, only Kraja was inclined to the traditionalist approach, using embellishment and modal elements of both traditional and art music. These elements, as well as her natural vocal timbre and a style of delivery adorned with a "mosaic of tones" (as her voice was described by contemporary music critics), are the essential ways in which she differed from her colleagues of the south. Dozens of trained singers of younger generations followed Kraja's route.

The essence of this style was the imitation of what might be seen as the unsophisticated urban folk singers' delivery; *broken words*, for instance, were a typical feature of the Albanian urban songs. This manner of expression was remarkably well assimilated by regional singers and was transmitted as their own creation, producing an emphatic and passionate communication with the listener. Kraja is said to have shown a great interest in the instruments that made up the ensemble which accompanied the urban song and particularly the violin. Since the embellishments used by this instrument are associated with those of the soprano voice (the vibrato, trill, etc.), Kraja observed that the violin's (qemane's) importance in the ensemble lay not merely in leading the melody or the whole instrumental group, but also in the expressiveness of its playing and its ability to imitate the human voice. Conversely, the violin itself was a point of reference or a model to imitate for the art singers, because of its traditional patterns of playing.

The Operatic Approach

Other singers, such as Tashko-Koço and Antoniu, were also inclined to make the song sound Albanian and, to a certain degree, local. However, they also aimed to bring out the flavor of the song as a whole, according to the structural principles of art song. The essence of musical expression for them was the *cantabile* utterance. "Thus it is the musical line, above all, that the singer must serve and respect. There can be no question of sacrificing it for the benefit of the words" (Bernac 1976). Judging by the recordings of Albanian urban lyric songs (AULS) made in Italy before and during World War II, my mother, Tefta Tashko-Koço, can be said to have been an exponent of the operatic approach. In her interpretation it was the continuity of the vocal line which was of particular importance. The traditional breaks in words or breaths taken mid-phrase or emphatic gaps were treated according to the demands of art singing and the literary text was sometimes sacrificed to the demands of the length of the vocal line. The operatic approach has often been viewed, by traditionalists, as a deviation from the urban composer's intentions. However, in the opinion of the art singers, the true beauty and value of the singing lies in a blend of traditional urban interpretation with vocal performance by trained singers.

The Melodramatic Approach

Kristaq Antoniu is a fine example of this style. The essence of his approach consists in creating an atmosphere and suggesting a drama. The articulation of the poetic text and the contrasting impressions of the narrative modulate from one musical mood to another, from a recitative to a bel-canto line. The song thus represents, on the one hand, the quality of legato singing and, on the other, the preservation of modulations and stresses in the sung text, with rhythmic subtleties that are found in a good spoken monologue. Antoniu, being an experienced film actor, created his own patterns of declamatory singing, his own verbal melody, his own prototypes of ad lib introductions to the songs and his own lineament of sound and rhythm, revealing his sensitivity to the music and words.

Of course, there are no absolute distinctions between these three approaches, particularly between the last two and some overlap is inevitable. What counted in the end, was not just the Albanian art singer's own conception of the song, but, above all, his or her musicianship and personal interpretation.

Concerts and Recordings

Although the concerts of the early 1930s consisted almost entirely of carefully chosen classical pieces, three or four years later the AULS were receiving almost the same critical attention. Looking at some concert-programs of those years, one might be surprised at the diversity of the repertoire and the careful combination of vocal and instrumental pieces.

The climax was reached on the 1 March 1939 (only a month before the Italian military intervention in Albania), when Paluca (Kraja) and Aleksi (Gjoka) gave a concert consisting entirely of AULS. The singers of the later 1930s tried to combine AULS in their programs in different ways; either to intersperse them between classical pieces in different parts of the program, or to put them in a special section of their own. In the early 1940s, when the "veteran" group of artistes was increased by new members, more complex programs were given, some of them in combination with Italian singers and instrumentalists, accompanied by the piano or orchestra.

The climax in the development of Albanian urban lyric song may be considered to have occurred in 1937, with the tour by Albanian artistes to Italy. They were immediately offered recording contracts in Italy. The recording companies played an important role in the dissemination of AULS. In spite of the poor technical quality of the 78 rpm recordings of the 1930s and '40s, which is typical of that period and of some tape recordings which were made in the 1940s and '50s, the songs are a priceless document of the singers' interpretations. It should however be pointed out that all these recordings were made in haste and not always when the singers' voices were at their best.

The first recordings of urban lyric songs were actually made in the 1930s. In 1937 and 1942 Tefta Tashko-Koço recorded for Columbia in Italy forty-five AULS with orchestral accompaniment, as well as Italian and French classical arias. Three Italian conductors, Segurini, Rizza and Consiglio, were involved in her recordings. Her husband, Kristo Koço, recorded two urban songs. Twelve songs are now missing from the set. In 1942 Antoniu recorded for Columbia sixteen AULS. Dungu arranged, orchestrated, accompanied on the piano and conducted the orchestra in Antoniu's set of recordings. The recordings made by Mihal Ciko belong to the period 1942–44, but his main singing career belonged to the 1930s. His piano accompanists were the Italian Mario Ettore and the Albanians Guraziu and Gjoka. Truja's recordings of the urban songs (probably five in all) extended over a longer period of time and were accompanied by piano, always with the same accompanist, the devoted Gjoka. A valuable set of about 300 urban lyric songs was recorded by Kraja in Albania. The majority of these songs are accompanied by piano, chiefly by Lola Gjoka, but others are accompanied by an orkestrina (instrumental ensemble), or even a symphony orchestra. Other performers of AULS, in the early 1940s, at the start of their careers or still studying, attracted favorable critical notices in the local newspapers. Unfortunately some of them never received their due acclaim after the war because of the new political climate in Albania.

These recordings have a special historical value today. The presence of Italian musicians and impresarios proved a considerable stimulus to Albanian art musicians. One outcome, the *Fiera del Levante* of 1937, with the participation of Albanian art singers and pianists, was a platform for displaying the virtues of Albanian urban lyric songs. In these manifestations nearly all trained artists took part, exquisitely dressed in resplendent "folk" costumes and proved that this new stylized type of song was now fully fledged. It was one of the rare occasions on which Albanian artists had crossed the borders as a group to demonstrate their individual and collective talents in the field of urban song. The Italian critics realized what a significant moment this was in the history of Albanian culture.

Conclusions

Although my parents died when I was still in my teens, I was brought up with their voices, their songs and their portraits, which were transfigured in my imagination as purely musical pictures and vocal images. When I started to study music, then graduated and worked in a musical professional field, the abstract images of my childhood stimulated me to make a larger study of the lyric song phenomenon of the 1930s. This occurrence consisted in the fact that by the 1930s, all members of the group of lyric singers were on Albanian soil after a long period of living abroad. A group of gifted people happened to come together at the right time and in the right place and their combined ability to turn the urban song into a glittering concert piece had a marked and lasting impact on Albanian musical culture.

From the beginning, the first recordings of urban lyric songs clearly portended the emergence of a new chapter in the history of Albanian music. Soon after the 1930s, the urban lyric song became a much-loved genre for composers, interpreters, instrumentalists and audiences. It is surprising that although more than sixty years have passed since the first recordings of these songs were released, they still remain models that can be followed, but not matched, for their variety and breadth of interpretation.

Arbatsky was one of the first authors I have encountered to have written on Albanian traditional music. I remember his account that "Albanian traditional music survives on its own" (1953). Despite the chronic political, social and geographical isolation from which Albania has suffered during its recent history, this has not particularly affected the development of the urban song. Not only did the Albanian urban song (AUS), seen as a wholesome and necessary diversion for the urban people, continue to be performed throughout Albania after the 1930s, but the Albanian urban lyric song (AULS), which was first introduced in the 1930s, also went on developing in the post–World War II period on a professional level and new arrangements continued to appear. As these reflections on Albanian urban lyric song in the Mediterranean focus mainly on the 1930s (the period when this tradition was born), there is no scope here for covering the many developments of more recent years, although these are deserving of scholarly attention.

Notes

1. Pjetër Dungu, *Lyra Shqiptare* (Albanian Lyre), notated songs, "Këngë popullore të mbledhura nën kujdesin e Radio-Tiranas" (Albanian [Urban] Songs, assembled under the care of Radio Tirana) Canti popolari albanesi (Stampato in Italia: Instituto Geografico De Agostini-Novara, 1940) 18.

2. The Italian administrative intervention in Albania which had begun gradually in the mid-1930s ended in colonization in 1939.

3. Gjon Kolë Kujxhija, *Dasëm Shkodrane, Nozze Scutarina* (Shkodër Wedding), volume 1 of *Valle Kombëtare, Cori Nazionali Albanesi* (National Dances), (Florence: Tipografia "Il Cenacolo" di Bruno Ortolani, 1943).

4. See Lloyd (1968: 205–22). The Stockmanns deserve special attention, particularly for their investigation on part-singing music of south Albania, the Çam (Cham) singing, the clarinet types in Albania and for their meticulous documentation of Albanian folk music (Stockmann and Stockmann 1960; D. Stockmann 1963; E. Stockmann 1960, 1969).

5. The Prespa people are an Albanian-speaking minority living in the districts around Lake Prespa, in the northeast of Slav Macedonia.

6. The fact that the latter are Muslims has little to do with their music and singing; the musical styles of this region, where three or more different nations are encountered, are specific and innately shared with the Christian Orthodox Albanians and their Slavic and Greek neighbors. During the Ottoman suzerainty when the Prespa community gradually changed its former religion to Islam, its music remained the same as it was in the pre-Ottoman period (allowing for the natural process of transformation) and did not adopt any Ottoman styles. Leav-

ing aside religious and regional identity, it is more important to empha-size that the communities of the southwest Balkans, which include Prespa, to this day still cultivate their local and regional, mainly penta-tonic, drone-based polyphonic singing; this is indigenous and far older than the Ottoman practices introduced into Albania with the arrival of the Turks in the Balkans.

    7. Area governed by a pasha.

    8. Bushati Dynasty of Shkodër, north Albania (1750–1831) and Ali, Pasha of Tepelena, Epirus (1803–21).

    9. "This occurred principally during the fifteenth and seventeenth centuries, that is to say, when the Turks first subjugated the land and when subject peoples who were Moslems became generally eligible for official employment" (Swire 1929: 32).

    10. The term southwestern Balkan mode is my own and I hope it will not be regarded as an arbitrary coinage.

    11. Foreign traditional instrument names, in spite of their origins, Turkish, Persian and Greek, are given in Albanian (e.g., saze and not saz, peshref and not peşrev).

    12. One of the principal membranophone percussion instruments to be found in both southern and northern urban ensembles.

    13. Bards or anecdotists, who in the aheng parties improvise a range of humorous conventional verses; each line is usually composed of seven, eight or more syllables.

    14. A lute-type instrument with a long neck and a pear-shaped body; its (ten?) strings were plucked with plectrum. This instrument is not now in use.

    15. In Albania it is an instrumental ensemble or the music played in the aheng ensembles.

    16. Urban art songs.

    17. A type of instrumental prelude.

    18. The document of the Sao Paulo Folk Music Council Congress, *JIFMC* 2 (1955): 23.

    19. Geg, the northern ethnic group of Albania (Gegëria).

    20. Bejtexhi, Albanian word of Turkish extraction, meaning urban singer, bard.

Bibliography

Arbatsky, Yury. *Beating the Tupan in the Central Balkans*. Chicago:

The Newberry Library, 1953.

Bernac, Pierre. *The Interpretation of French Song*. London: Victor Gollancz, 1976.

Dungu, Pjetër. *Lyra Shqiptare* (Albanian Lyre), notated songs, "Këngë popullore të mbledhura nën kujdesin e Radio-Tiranas" (Albanian [urban] songs, assembled under the care of Radio Tirana), Canti popolari albanesi, Instituto Geografico De Agostini-Novara, Stampato in Italia, 1940, 18.

Gurashi, Kolë. and Gjush Sheldija. "Ahengu Shkodran" (The Shkodran Aheng), *Shkodër Yearbook* (1961): 213.

Kujxhia, Gjon Kolë. *Valle Kombëtare, Cori Nazionali Albanesi* (National Dances)—*Dasëm Shkodrane, Nozze Scutarina* (Shkodër Wedding) 1, Florence, Tipografia "Il Cenacolo" di Bruno Ortolani, 1943.

Lloyd, A. L. "Albanian Folk Song." *Folk Music Journal* 1: 1968.

Shupo, Sokol. *Albanian Musical Folklore*. Tirana, 1997.

Sokoli, R. *Folklori Muzikor Shqiptar (Morfologjia)* (The Albanian Musical Folklore). Tirana: 1965, 25.

Stockmann, Doris. "Zur Vokalmusik der südalbanischen Çamen." *Journal of the International Folk Music Council* 1, no. 15 (1963): 38–44.

Stockmann, Doris, and Erich Stockmann. "Die Vokale Bordun-Mehrstimmigkeit in Südalbanien." *Ethnomusicologie III*: *Wegimont* V (1960): 85–135.

———. "Albania." 197 in *The New Grove Dictionary of Music and Musicians* 1, ed. S. Sadie, London: Macmillan Publishers Limited 1980.

Stockmann, Erich. "Zur Sammlung und Untersuchung albanischer Volkmusik." *Acta Musicologia* 32 (1960): 102–9.

———. "Klarinetten typen in Albanien." *Journal of the International Folk Music Council* 12, no. 1 (1969): 17–20.

Sugarman, Jane C. *Engendering Song: Singing and Subjectivity at Prespa Albanian Weddings*. Chicago: The University of Chicago Press, 1997.

Swire, J. *Albania: The Rise of a Kingdom*. London: Williams and Norgate Ltd., 1929.

Tole, Vasil. *Enciklopedi e muzikes popullore shqiptare*. Tirana: Botimpex, 2001.

Chapter Three

"Humanizing the Masses": Enlightened Intellectuals and the Music of the People

Daphne Tragaki

> We are going to see rebetiko songs . . . raising their voices . . . and living now for interpreting us and now for making us realize our deeper selves.   —Manos Hatzidakis.[1]

Foreword: Rebetiko in the Mediterranean Sea of Musics

The presence of an article on rebetiko song in a book that attempts to explore the notion of "Mediterranean" in music places the ways we think of rebetiko song within a broader network of musical traditions. This promotes new insights in the study of its past and present and inspires new areas of inquiry. At the same time, however, the contextualization of rebetiko within the study of Mediterranean musics may also promote a new stereotype of its cultural identity—that of the "Mediterranean" rebetiko. "Mediterranean," however, is primarily an idea; an imagined entity of cultures, people, landscapes, morals, musics, dances—diverse yet all united by the sea.[2] Such an idea of the "Mediterranean" provided an arena for rhetorics of "otherness" celebrated in studies of local morals, kinship, gender and religious practices echoing an exoticized view of the people inhabiting the southern European coasts—an "otherness" represented in ethnographic accounts forming the so-called "Mediterranean anthropology."[3]

While rebetiko history exemplifies the ways the music was *made* within the flourishing cosmopolitanism featuring the seaports and the overall geopolitical networks of the area, thinking of it as a "Mediterranean" tradition may obscure the ways it interacts with hyper-Mediterranean musical trends and socio-political transformations which also make its history and condition its present. The study of rebetiko in the Mediterranean context embodies, therefore, the pitfalls of revisiting the ideas celebrated by Mediterraneanism and of constituting a musical Mediterraneanism based upon a refreshed assumption of the Mediterranean as a musical region to which the genre belongs.[4] Re-

betiko is traveling in the Mediterranean sea of musics yet it is not confined to it; it also travels within "a complex web of relations between
local, national, international politics and economics" (Herzfeld 1987:
12). Recently, it has been redefined in the context of "world music"
phenomenon acquiring a global appeal of "commodified otherness"
(Feld 1994: 266).[5]

This chapter discusses the ways the so-perceived "Greek," "oriental," "proletarian" and "urban folk" identities of rebetiko fired what was
described as a "holy ideological war" or otherwise "the rebetiko debate" in postwar Greek society.[6] A debate primarily fed by controversies that took place within the urban intellectual circles and which projected tropes of thinking about "Greekness" via exploring the notion of
"folk song." The various discourses were crystallized in writings which
attempted to question the values of dhimotiko traghoudhi—a term
commonly describing the folk song associated with the rural areas—
often in comparison with the values of rebetiko song otherwise generi-
cally termed as laiko traghoudhi (folk song) or, more specifically, as-
tiko laiko traghoudhi (urban folk song). Dhimotiko traghoudhi may
also incidentally be referred to as "folk" song (again used as a generic
term), yet the most commonly used alternative term is that of paradho-
siako traghoudhi (traditional song), which implies its perception as an
age-long musical heritage. In the postwar years the term laiko (folk)
was also used to refer to a particular urban musical style—that developed in the 1960s—which encapsulated elements of the rebetiko tradition.

An Experiment—the Response:
Making "New" Greek Folk Song

In September 1960 the release of the work *Epitaphios* composed by
Mikis Theodorakis stimulated perhaps one the most fervent controversies in the modern history of Greek music among local music experts
and intellectuals about a new record release. For Theodorakis ventured
an "experiment" (Theodorakis [1960b] 1986: 197): to unite in one musical entity, the world of "art"—the poetry of Yiannis Ritsos—with that
of contemporary urban folk song represented in the voice of Grigoris
Bithikotsis accompanied by a bouzouki-based orchestra.[7] The composer viewed his "experiment" as a way of "giving a new thrust to folk
song by giving to it a new content" (197). In fact, *Epitaphios* represented an attempt by a musician who studied under Olivier Messiaen in

the Paris Conservatoire, to compose folk songs, an endeavor that required him primarily to "bow humbly in front of the works of our people, songs and dances, of the songs of the most genuine folk composers" (Theodorakis [1960c] 1986: 188).

The avant-garde nature of *Epitaphios* activated an ardent debate among Greek, mostly left-wing, intellectuals that was described as a "civil war in the music section of our cultural life" (Eleftheriou [1960] 1986: 203). In fact, the central issue that fired the controversy was rebetiko song—a folk song tradition that had developed primarily in the urban centers and cosmopolitan ports of the Eastern Mediterranean in the beginning of the twentieth century—and its use as a source for the making of "neohellenic" folk song. A decade earlier, Theodorakis had already stressed that laiko (folk) song—meaning rebetiko—"teach us how to assimilate creatively the tradition, both of Byzantine and dhimotiko song" for the making of "a genuine folk" and "truly Greek Music School" ([1949] 1986: 169).[8]

The question as to whether the rebetiko song genre was qualified to become the prime paradigm for the construction of "proper" Greek folk music generated further argument over its identity and place in Greek music history; *Epitaphios* was simply the impetus and the sign of a new era for thinking and understanding rebetiko song. Interestingly enough, the experimental *Epitaphios* was preceded by a version featuring the voice of Nana Moushouri, an "art" song singer, released by Fidelity records and orchestrated by the acknowledged composer Manos Hatzidakis.[9] Theodorakis "loved" both versions equally ([1960a] 1986: 179). While the performance of the acclaimed art-song singer (Nana Moushouri) represented, for the composer, a "lyrical Epitaphios," the voice of the folk singer (Grigoris Bithikotsis) becomes the expression "of each one of us who sings with his voice" (179). It becomes a musical metaphor of the Greek levendia, that is, a combination of pride and dignity featuring "our people" (179, 201).

The ambivalent responses to the issue of whether rebetiko was "healthy" music for *laos* (the people) or not, were already displayed in various articles published in the local press a few years before the release of Theodorakis's musical "experiment." For its opponents, it was a genre associated with hashish consumption and the urban criminal underworld; vagabonds, prostitutes, pickpockets, pimps and blackmarketeers. In 1947, Alekos Xenos, a leftist intellectual, expressed overtly his disdain for the "sick atmosphere of rebetiko hashish and pornographic song" ([1947] 1977: 140) by opposing it to the dhimotiko traghoudi genre "that expresses the noblest heroic traditions . . . and becomes a vehicle for the progress of the people." Instead of a symptom of "urban decay," "humiliation" and the music of "the lumpen strata" (Xenos [1947] 1977: 142), the music folklorist, Foivos Anoyianakis regarded rebetiko as the descendant of Byzantine chant and dhimotiko song, "a genuine form of contemporary folk music" (Anoyianakis [1947] 1977: 139). In an article published in the same newspaper, *Rizospastis*—the mouthpiece of the Greek Communist Party— Nikos Politis stressed the element of "passion" in laiko song that "motivates and expresses the folk soul" ([1947] 1977: 144). For the author, leftist intellectuals ought to reflect upon "the obvious gap that divides the people from. the art; there emerges the need to find a point of contact . . . and we will find this in contemporary folk expressions" (145).

The public lecture given in 1948 by the composer Manos Hatzidakis amplified the controversies troubling the progressive artistic circles. For Hatzidakis dared to invite the musicians of the rebetiko dens, the singer Sotiria Bellou and the veteran rebetiko composer and bouzoukiplayer Markos Vamvakaris, to perform in the shrine of progressive intelligentsia, the Mousouri Theatre staging the Athens *Theatre of Art* (Theatro Tehnis). The composer expressed his enthusiastic support for urban folk song "that speaks the truth and only the truth" referring in a sentimental manner to the ways rebetiko encapsulated the "pristine psychic of our folk" and "the intense sentiment of love . . . that ascribes to it a disposition for escaping reality" ([1949] 1977: 153). Moreover he attempted to glorify rebetiko by associating it with well-established musical traditions of the past—Byzantine chant and dhimotiko traghoudhi—an argument that dogmatically justified the Greekness of the genre (154). A few years later, despite Hatzidakis's attempt to vindicate rebetiko, Gardikis rejected categorically the genre any reason for existence, "rottenness does not need caresses: spade and coach. That's what it needs" (1956: 245).[10]

In the numerous zealously and enthusiastically written articles that followed, the authors appear preoccupied with particular issues: the origins and history of rebetiko, the comparison of the genre with the dhimotiko song genre, the moral qualities of urban folk song, the nature of its Greek identity and the assessment of the ideal future for the neohellenic song.[11] The two main arenas where the relevant discourses were developed became the art magazine *Epitheorisi Tehnis* (Art Review) and the *Avghi* (The Dawn) newspaper, both associated with the leftist and progressive urban circles. Beyond a debate in the name of rebetiko, *rebetology* became in those years an allegorical body of discourses that exemplified the concern of local dianoisi (intelligentsia) to determine the music that serves the interests of "our people."[12] This way, the logos (discourse) on urban folk song performs ultimately the agonies and ideological conflicts troubling its agents that echo at the same time, the music-cultural contexts defining them.[13]

The Intellectuals and "the People"

The discourses defining rebetiko debates appear to share certain basic features: they mostly derive from male educated, middle class, leftist or "progressive" authors.[14] These are the people who form a highly influential part of the Greek dianoisi that is socially and culturally distanced in those years from the "people," the people of low economic and educative status seen as those who primarily suffered the postwar devastation. In the debates over the identity and future of the music that is "healthy" for them and is *of* them, namely the laiko song, they, o laos, are absent. The privilege of knowing what serves their interests is thought to be restricted to those who have the access to knowledge, the "thinkers" pictured as somehow gifted individuals who may foresee and, therefore, assess and determine the "right way" for the folk song. Consequently, the agents of knowledge, the intellectuals, appear to occupy by virtue a position above the laos, a condition that describes a priori an asymmetrical relationship between those who, because they *know*, have the power to speak for and indoctrinate those outside the society of the enlightened few.

This monolithic nature of the poetics of rebetiko discourses is reminiscent of Michel Foucault's ideas regarding the interplay of knowledge and power, "We should admit that power produces knowledge . . . ; that power and knowledge directly imply one another; that there is no power relation without the correlative institution of a field of knowledge that does not presuppose and constitute at the same time power relations" (1975: 32).

The politics of leftist rebetology in the 1950s and 1960s exemplifies the correlation of knowledge and power as suggested by Foucault paradigmatically. Regardless whether they express pro- or anti-rebetiko ideas, there is a common sense among the authors participating in the debate that they carry "the duty to promote" music with "a social content useful for the people" (Xenos [1947] 1977: 143). In this way, they imagine themselves as "spiritual leaders" of the Greek people, a charismatic cultural elite whose mission is to prevent the innocent laos from being "deceived" and "corrupted" by malicious exploiters (see Hatzis 1961: 341). The relevant writings illustrate the "people" as a naïve and unsuspicious child, an object of manipulation by "dark powers" (Theo-

dorakis [1961b] 1986: 242) who is often also regarded as "not responsible at all" for its musical orientations (Anoyianakis [1947] 1977:
141). For Kouzinopoulos, "the love of the people [for rebetiko song] is
not always a criterion for evaluating how correct is the course taken by
the people with respect to its own interests" (1961: 612).

In fact, "the people" are referred to in various ways as betraying
the author's ideological bias. Seen as the ingenuous and unspoiled
agent of folk song culture, they become "our people" (Anoyianakis
[1947] 1977; Maheras 1961: 92; Dromazos [1961] 1986: 231; Theodorakis [1961b] 1986: 240; Leivaditis [1961] 1986: 222). As the heroic
human force who bravely fought in the Resistance during World War
II, they become "the Greek people" (Theodorakis [1949] 1986: 158,
164; Xenos [1960] 1986: 218). As the lowlife dwellers of the city who
are impassively indoctrinated by capitalist exploiters, they cease to be
referred as "people"; they are "the mass" (Gardikis 1956: 245; Hatzis
1961: 339), or "the proletarian masses" (Vournas [1961] 1977:180), or
"the proletarians of the cities" (Skouriotis 1956a: 151), or "the lumpen
strata" (Xenos 1947: 142). Finally, as the "unhealthy" part of the laos
who are drawn to crime and illegal activities—thought mostly to define
the guilty past of rebetiko song—the "people" are debased to the status
of "the underworld," the "marginal groups" of the society (Maheras
1961: 88; Dromazos [1961] 1986: 229; Tahtsis 1964: 203).

By exhibiting the duty to "humanize the masses" (Gardikis 1956:
245) and "block the perversion of Greek music" (Orfinos 1956: 432),
the intellectual projects himself as a chivalrous and thoughtful persona
operating in the service of the music that people "really need" (Hatzis
1961: 341). "The debt of the poets and the musicians is to fight. To find
the ways and the means for disseminating a kind of folk art that is going to express the psychological needs, the patriotic heartbeats and the
broader humanistic spirit of our days for a free and peaceful world"
(Xenos [1960] 1986: 219–20).

This supposed benefactor and supervising figure corresponds to the
ideal of "universal" intellectual mainly promoted by the philosophical
tradition of the Enlightenment. For Foucault, the "universal" intellectual is the subject self-proclaimed to be free from superstitions and
various fixations that may mystify his/her so-perceived prophetic pretensions. It is a universality embedded in the intellectual's role as a
missionary for humanity unveiling deceit and hypocrisy, attacking false
hierarchies and combating injustices and inequalities. Beyond his/her
humanistic concern for articulating the "truth," such an "enlightened"
figure enjoys, more than anything else, a legislative role purposefully
appropriated (see Dreyfus and Rabinow 1982: 202). Inevitably, then

"the universal intellectual . . . plays power's game because he fails to see this point" (203).[15]

In the case of the leftist rebetology the authority of knowledge is moreover performed in the intellectual's so-perceived ability, often confidently expressed, to predict the future of folk song. The majority of the relevant writings clearly articulate or connote a realization that "we live at the beginning of a new period for neohellenic song" (Maheras 1961: 99). The threshold to a new era is understood as a state of transition that folk song is thought to currently undergo defined by the political and social changes following the industrialization and urbanization of Greece in the postwar years. It is precisely the rhetoric that described this formative period of instability that justified the urgent intervention of intellectuals. On this basis, "the holy ideological war" performed in the rebetiko discourses erupted (Vournas [1961] 1977: 164) because Greek music history was troubled by an era of "musical anarchy" (Avgheris [1961] 1986: 210).

In this vein of thought, rebetology attempts to establish itself as a body of discourses whose agents consciously portray themselves as being in advance of their own time. The appropriation of such a supervising attitude by the leftist and progressive intelligentsia largely corresponds to the ways the notion of a cultural elite was promoted by the French Revolution and the Marxist-Leninist theory of the Communist party as being the revolutionary avant-garde of the proletariat (see Calinescu 1987: 104, 114). In the Greek case, this militant notion of avant-garde is invested in a "movement for the new form of neohellenic song" (Leivaditis [1961] 1986: 223) where the protagonists are basically Western-educated composers seen as the more or less successful "reformers," "refiners" and thus "civilizers" of folk song (Vournas [1961] 1977: 183; Maheras 1961: 94; Avgheris [1961] 1986: 210; Dromazos [1961] 1986: 228; Leivaditis [1961] 1986: 223).[16]

Contesting Rebetiko: Socialist Visions and the Challenge of Modernity

In several, mostly anti-rebetiko writings, the prophecies declaring a crucial passage in local music history stand side by side with rhetorical constructions of musical eschatology that evoke the growing decadence of Greek music,[17] a decadence that appears inevitable unless the leftist intellectuals manage to take control of the situation—and "the people"—changing folk music history.[18] This decay is primarily associated with rapid urbanization, the emergence of the urban "underworld" and the fashionable entertainment aesthetics, the commercialization of folk song promoted by the media (in those days radio broadcasting) and the music industry. Musical decadence thus is understood as a symptom of the urban condition that is sensed as the locus of modernity par excellence defining the cultural dystopia—a historical endpoint—where the contemporary musical poetics of folk song are performed.[19] For Bohlman, "Modernity poses a threat, which becomes increasingly real because the conditions of modernity accelerate time and history. The alternative to the global spread of modernity and its decreasingly human forces is escape from the historical present" (2002: 8).

Postwar rebetiko perceived as the exemplary music culture of the Greek city becomes, for intellectuals, the metaphor of the "new musical reality" where the modern identity for neohellenic song is formulated (Dromazos [1961] 1986: 228). It refers to the era that Greek music is regarded as entering, leaving behind the age of dhimotiko song, a generic term which broadly describes the rural folk song styles that developed during the Ottoman years. Rebetologists experience, therefore, this music-historical passage at least with aporia. In fact, it is considered as a transition embodying discontinuities: a process that consolidates the already developing cultural shift from "tradition"—projected in dhimotiko song culture—to "modernity" that dictates the music politics in the city personified in rebetiko song.[20] The sense that Greek music is changing inspires reflections on the nature of dhimotiko—thought of as the exemplary folk song of the past—and generate a need to detect analogies with the folk song that defines the present and, most possibly, envisages the future.[21]

This comparative approach concluded in the rhetorical construction of the binary scheme that opposes or differentiates rebetiko song—the sounds of urbanity and modernity—from dhimotiko song—the sounds of the ancient traditions that flourished among the rural communities. The antithetical conceptual schemes promoted by the relevant discourses were crystallized to stereotypes still "haunting" popular ideas on folk music history: the music of the nature that serves the heroic ideals featured by a will to struggle and the hope for a better world is contrasted with the music of the polluted city that bears the depression of the lowlife urban groups and promotes sensualism and passivity. Urban music is associated with commercialization and individuality, while rural music is seen as the collective, spontaneous expression of the "anonymous" oral tradition. "Dhimotiko songs have the space of Greek sky, the fresh air of the high mountains, the levendia of common people. Rebetiko songs have the closed, cloudy sky of the cities, the stifling atmosphere of the dens and the factories, the misery and bended soul of contemporary man" (Christianopoulos [1961] 1977: 160).[22]

On the one hand the value of dhimotiko song is beyond any doubt; it is celebrated as a splendid paradigm of local folk music (Skouriotis 1956a: 152; Orfinos 1956: 431; Kouzinopoulos 1961: 613; Maheras 1961: 98; Anoyianakis [1961] 1977: 186; Hatzis 1961: 338). On the other hand, the overall biological history of rebetiko—its birth, flourishing and decay, or states of development—is narrated like a story conditioned by a telos; rebetiko is destined either to decay or to evolve. Besides, the authors hardly show any concern for substantiating their statements and arguments. The relevant texts appear as sentimentally charged rebetiko truisms that aim at persuading enthusiastically about what is regarded as the "right" history of rebetiko.

For the rebetophiles, rebetiko encapsulates the dhimotiko song tradition and beyond that the musical forms of the Byzantine chant. It represents, therefore, a stage in the evolutionary unilinear progress of Greek music history that assimilated creatively the sacred traditions of the past; as such, it deserves to be regarded as "true" folk song.[23] For the opposite side, any kind of comparison between the two genres is regarded as "sacrilegious" (Samouilidou 1956: 228): being detached from the dhimotiko song genre, rebetiko is denied a mythology that justifies the time-depth of its musical heritage. Its Greekness is erased, canceled and, subsequently, its "truly" folk qualities are seriously undermined.[24]

The agonizing whether to award or deny rebetiko a place in the pantheon of "sacred" local musics—such as the dhimotiko and Byzantine chant—implies a broader concern for local cultural identity that is invested, in certain cases, with an ethnocentric bias. In the case of the rebetophile discourses "our genuine folk song is a live branch of the Greek music tree" (Theodorakis [1961a] 1986: 212). It "directly derives from Greek music tradition and more particularly, the Byzantine" (Leivaditis [1960] 1986: 221). For its opponents, rebetiko "is formulated out of the leftovers of the Turkish conqueror" (Xenos [1947] 1977: 142; also [1961] 1986: 217–18). Bouzouki, the instrument that became the synonym of rebetiko genre represents a "bad heritage . . . a remaining of the slavery" (Hairopoulos [1961] 1986: 249) that uses musical modes which are not "genuine and pure Greek modes," in contrast to those featured in Byzantine chant (Papadimitriou [1949] 1977: 150). In this vein of thought, to prove that rebetiko is "original" Greek music further proves that it is "genuine" folk music.[25] The musical authenticity of rebetiko song is defined, therefore, by a disemia that embodies harmonically both claims for national ("Greek") and social ("folk") identity.

The Greekness that the majority of the authors are mainly preoccupied with is that described as romiosini, connoting a Greek identity associated with the Byzantine and Ottoman years of Greek history.[26] The romiosini of rebetiko is essentialized in the ways the genre capitalizes musically the song traditions perceived as the hallmarks of those eras, namely dhimotiko song and Byzantine chant. The agents of romeiko song are the romioi (pl.)—broadly thought of as the heroic Greeks who fought against the Ottoman rule. Vournas, for instance, declared that "there is nothing in our music, except for rebetiko, that comes out of the *romeiki omonoia* (concord)" and sings "the *romeiki levendia*" (Vournas [1961] 1977: 175). As an exemplary vehicle of musical romiosini, rebetiko is thought to be "the lyrical expression of a proud, agonistic, democratic and peaceful people" (184). In the same spirit Dromazos stressed that the Byzantine chant[s] that "survived" together with dhimotiko song in the body of rebetiko express the "multifaceted character of the romiosini's soul" ([1961] 1986: 230). For the opposite side:

> The songs of the people express their struggle with an optimistic and brave common feeling . . . Because these songs are the positive response to life, namely to "us" . . . Rebetiko song, however, express the problems of the people who live in the margins of the society . . . who don't believe in "us" . . . the musical phrases (of rebetiko) conclude to a sigh full of pressure, which . . . crumbles at the depths of frustration. (Maheras 1961: 90)

"Frustration," "pessimism," "fatalism," "melancholy", "depression" are states of being—propagated by the anti-rebetiko discourses—that oppose to the essence of romiosini as projected in rebetiko writings. The songs that ideally picture the romeic heart considered as "the true neohellenic songs" should be "full of hope for a new peaceful and great epoch" (Maheras 1961: 99) and awaken "the patriotic debt" to struggle for a better society (Xenos [1961] 1986: 218). To that extent the definition of romeiko song within the leftist intellectual discourses meets the socialist visions for the urban folk people. This is a romeiko rebetiko song that embodies "the unconscious dynamism of working class man" (Sofoulis 1956a: 153,) that instigates him to fight for his rights against the social injustice imposed by a "class structured state" (Dromazos [1961] 1986: 233–34).

Moreover, the historical connotations of romiosini identified in rebetiko connect[s] the genre with the broader Balkan and "Oriental"
(mainly denoting Eastern Mediterranean) countries—the area once
identified as kath'imas Anatoli that is "the Orient nearby us." This musical romiosini is thought to have developed within a cultural world
Greeks used to be part of, defined by the Byzantine and, subsequently,
the Ottoman Empire. The "Oriental" past of rebetiko is defined either
as a primitive stage in rebetiko history (see Theodorakis [1961c] 1986:
263) which the genre has currently overcome—often associated with
drug consumption—or as an element that justifies its participation
within a so-called great musical civilization (Anoyianakis [1961] 1977:
197). For the strictest rebetiko critics, this "Oriental" rebetiko nature
justifies its "antisocial content" served by "the heavy oriental tunes full
of melancholy, fatalism and disenchantment" (Maheras 61: 88).[27]

In certain cases, the Orient imagined as "our" exotic past is sentimentally idealized side by side with the association of rebetiko music
with the ancient "golden" age (Tsarouhis [1963] 1977: 201; Tahtsis
[1964] 1977: 202; Spanoudi [1952] 1977: 156). Tsarouhis, for instance,
at the same time he identified ancient Thrace as the birthplace of
zeibekikos dance,[29] stressed the multicultural origins of ancient Greek
modes declaring that they survive today within the music cultures they
derived, concluding, "the anemic Greek music was always fed from
abroad" (Tsarouhis [1963] 1977: 201).[29] In this case, the search for
rebetiko origins back to the glorious classical era understood in connection with the area of kath' imas Anatoli appears detached from the ethnocentric bias mainly featuring rebetological discourses. Placing the
"golden" age (the hellenic) next to "our" familiar Orient (the romeic) is
rather here defined by a nostalgia for an age-long magnificent civilization—encompassing both the so-perceived ancient and the oriental
heritage—Greek music once used to share.[30]

The notion of romiosini celebrated in rebetiko discourses furnished
with socialist ideas for the "healthy" urban working class, constitute the
arena where the concept of "neohellenic" song is interpreted. In this
case, the term refers to the identity of Greek folk song following the
Occupation years and the aftermath of the Civil War (1946–49). In that
sense, the concept of "neohellenic" song becomes an allegory of the
ways the "new"—postwar—Greekness meets modernity, generally
seen as the vehicle of musical novelty and cultural trends. As such, the
"new" Greek folk song is thought to embody ways in which the identity
of "our" music is redefined within the current modern condition; it is
the sound of the dialogue of Greekness with modernity.

Interestingly, both sides appear to face modernity with embarrassment and suspicion. It represents a cultural condition superimposed on
Greek reality from abroad and more specifically the West (denoting
western Europe and especially the United States). Western imperialist
cultural politics are seen to dictate the condition of modernity following
a catastrophic plan to assimilate and "corrupt" the so-far "unspoiled"
Greek music culture against the "real" will of the "people." The making
of the "true" neo-hellenic song stands therefore as the response of "the
oppressed masses" against a somehow demonized West portrayed as an
agent of musical "degeneration" (Vournas [1961] 1977: 181).

Ironically, the discourses on this "truly" neohellenic song are
themselves essentially modern; they represent what Lyotard would call
a "grand narrative," that is grand stories about the world featuring the
modern era which sustain and legitimate the exercise of power.[31] Postwar rebetology as an authoritative discourse is, therefore, inherently
modern yet with antimodernist pretensions; it is a modern meta-
narrative on modernist music culture.

While there is a common disapproval of the modernist West, leftist
discourses display a dispute over whether rebetiko is indeed the appropriate musical weapon against it. On one hand, rebetiko is considered
as a symptom of the "alienation" that Greek culture is, in those years,
thought to have suffered from. For Xenos, "the musical products
corrupting for the psychology of the people, rock 'n roll, cha-cha,
rebetiko, were disseminated under a fashionable populism by every
means and were supported in every way" ([1960] 1986: 219). In this
case, the "best source for inspiration" (Maheras 1961: 96) for the making of neo-hellenic song is considered the dhimotiko genre "the capital
of the folk music" (Hatzis 1961: 341) that "truly expresses the desires,
the joys and the pains of our people" (Maheras 1961: 98).[32]

For the opposite side, rebetiko becomes a musical metaphor of the
working-class resistance against the alienating forces, "Our national
radio . . . bombards ungratefully our people with all these popular musical under-products of the mechanical civilization. Nevertheless, the
resistance of this people is analogous with that of other great eras of our
national rebellions!" (Theodorakis [1960c] 1986: 187).

As a song of "the truth" (Hatzidakis [1949] 1977: 153) rebetiko is
thought to essentialize a local counter-history that may subvert Western
history: it is "the most unspoiled song genre" (Leivaditis [1961] 1986:
221), which expresses a "revolutionary outbreak" (Sofoulis 1956: 153).
Rebetiko authenticity thus is carefully treasured and protected as a
value that encapsulates a primordial musical truth existing ever since
the genesis of Greek music. As such, the value of authenticity fortifies

folk song against modernity that is charged with hybridity and an undesirable heterogeneity which challenges the very essence of rebetiko musical "truth." This "true" rebetiko is imagined as the soundscape of a musical utopia: it embodies the fantasy of an alternative society that is found nowhere. In fact, it is the sound of the utopia leftist rebetologists are dreaming of—the placeless, ideal topos where the visions of the socialist ideology come true.[33]

Musical modernity as the vehicle of "foreign-derived" (xenoferto) trends is, furthermore, often understood in relation to the politics of the music industry and the growing tourist development of the country: "this is an era of industrialized rebetiko that is a big business that directs the taste of the audience" (Xenos [1960] 1986: 216; see also Maheras 1961: 89).[34] Tahtsis, a rebetophile, describes the ways bouzouki music became in the 1960s a tourist attraction and was exoticized as the sound of the Greek soul:

> A paranoiac situation prevailed where the tourist and the urbanite [denoting the middle-class groups] go to see the people and the people go to see the tourist. The tourist admires the products of the economical degradation, which he could only aesthetically sympathize and from aloof and flatters the people for who, at the same time, he became an object of wonder and amusement. (Tahtsis [1964] 1977: 208)

The tourist exploitation and commercialization of folk music are condemned as by-products of the "enterprising interests" (Hatzis 1961: 339) and the "degrading tactics of capitalism" (Xenos [1947] 1977: 142). On this basis, contemporary urban folk song is thought to be determined by the postwar process of industrial development and the technological advancement of the mass media, which they considered as the instruments of the capitalist politics aiming at patronizing the musical taste of the people. In this way, leftist rebetologists view contemporary urban folk song as happening within an era of progress; an era when things are changing by moving forward.

The sense of rapid and somehow uncontrollable change inspires feelings of nostalgia for an idealized past when Greek people used to sing and dance "healthy" music—the times of dhimotiko songs and the agricultural communities of the village. For rebetophiles, rebetiko may stand as a safeguard of Greek music securing its Greek identity in the face of progress, since it incorporates the heritage of "our" glorious musical traditions. Extreme anti-rebetiko discourses, on the other hand, perform this nostalgia coupled with a strong repulsion for the music of the "polluted" city culture, that is seen as an "infectious" "social gutter" (Skouriotis 1956a: 152). In this case, the defense of the "local" is empowered in the sounds of dhimotiko song which is invested with rhetorics of "purity" and "cleanness" that are contrasted to the rhetorics of "stench" and "dirt" employed for rebetiko.[35]

In fact, both pro- and anti-rebetiko discourses attempt to interpret urban folk song via a rigorous Marxist theoretical model that places the genre "under the influence of 'the laws of historical causality'" (Vournas [1961] 1977: 183). Within this analytical context, rebetiko music is considered as a musical culture that directly reflects the socioeconomic changes dictated by the capitalist politics: a music mirroring the growing urbanization and industrialization of Greek society and the subsequent emergence of "lumpen proletariat" (Skouriotis 1956a: 151).[36]

Moreover, leftist intellectuals appear concerned to evaluate the moral values of the folk song that is "proper" for the proletarians. On one hand, rebetiko is imagined as a corrupted and alluring female that seduces the proletarians leading them to the land of pleasures: it is "pornographic" and "sick" (Xenos [1947] 1977: 141) and "promotes sensual excitement" (Orfinos 1956: 432) that serves "the dominant ideology which attempts to impose on the masses an ideological deadend" (Dromazos [1961] 1986: 232). The sensual excitement and the need to escape from reality—associated with drug songs—inspired by the rebetiko sounds are disapproved as harmful for the morality of the people and alienating for their agonistic consciousness. Rebetiko "perverts" and "harms the healthy mass, especially the youth" (Hatzis 1961: 339) leading to "vagabondism, prostitution and crime" (Skouriotis 1956a: 151).

To that extent, the discourses over the morality of urban folk song embody puritanical nuances that attempt to debase rebetiko song by stressing its "corrupting" nature. Bearing in mind that the agents of the relevant discourses are mostly male authors, the relevant rhetorics speak allegorically of the moral ideal of the proletarian woman or, more generally, of the Greek woman. It is an ideal projected in the ways they express a strong repulse of the "prostitute," "pervert" and "vagabond" character of rebetiko song that is contrasted to the "immaculate" and "pristine" nature of dhimotiko song. This very ideal of female morality is also connoted and antithetically sustained by the rebetophile rhetorics that glorify the "modesty," "chastity" (Leivaditis [1961] 1986: 221), "sentimental purity" (Spanoudi [1952] 1977: 157) and "pristine psychic" (Hatzidakis [1949] 1977: 153) of rebetiko song.

Ultimately, the postwar leftist rebetology becomes an allegory of "the troubles and adventures and the fate of the progressive movement during the last years in Greece" (Kouzinopoulos 1961: 612).[37] Following the recent defeat in the Civil War (1946–49), the Greek Communist Party (K.K.E.) was urged to reassess the political scope of the movement. In fact, the broader concern with the nature of contemporary urban folk song embodies a concern with the character of the "folk people" seen as the agents of the socialist vision. On this level, rebetological discourses are defined by an all-pervading demand for "uplift" (anatasi) and "reformation" (anamorfosi) of urban folk song— that further implies the uplift and reformation of the left movement. By prescribing the criteria for a "healthy" folk music, leftist intellectuals aspire to create the song destined to reinforce the anticapitalist spirit of the "people." In this way, rebetological debates perform the anxiety of the communist party to maintain the support of laos in the fight against its "exploiters" and prevent them from abandoning the struggle for "the ideal of freedom" (Dromazos [1961] 1986: 232).

It is important to bear in mind that the agents of the "holy ideological war" experience in the years they write the effects of destitution and devastation Greek society suffered following World War II. Beyond the socialist dogma to "humanize the masses," there appears the persona of the politically sensitive and subversive leftist intellectual who is driven by a sense of responsibility to fight for "a better world." On this basis, the public discourse on urban folk song becomes a vehicle of political action the "spiritual leaders" of the people understand as a debt they decisively undertake within an era defined by a socioeconomic crisis that demands such initiatives (see Theodorakis [1961d] 1986: 266).

Furthermore, it appears that middle-class intellectuals imagine rebetiko as a sonic land of an 'other' world defined by the adventures of mangas, heroic figures, the alluring females and the troubles the folk suffer in this "unfair world." For Christianopoulos, "there is always inside us a strange curiosity for rebetiko" (Christianopoulos [1961] 1977: 158). To that extent, rebetiko becomes the sound of difference, in this case a music-cultural difference which is appealing for middle-class authors as a pathway for escaping from the so-perceived bourgeois boredom. Tahtsis's confessional rhetorics reveal the ways the intellectual quest for escapism is coupled with leftist subversive awakenings, "For a long time, I identified myself with them (rebetiko songs) . . . not only as a Greek, but both as a person (*sic*). In those days, I started protesting against all the lies I was told from my birth and these songs were protest songs . . . they protested against life itself . . . and were mourning the failure of the movement" ([1964] 1977: 206).

Nonetheless, the basic musical vision celebrated by the subversive dianoisi is that of the "true" Greek folk song that is nurtured by the grand traditions of the past while, at the same time, it corresponds to the "real" needs of the people in the present. For several authors, the making of such an ideal folk song is placed in the hands of responsible "civilizers"—the aspiring composers "who create upon the existing rebetiko song the modern neohellenic folk musical character based on our traditional elements which come from the only historically legitimate way, the way of survival" (Vournas [1961] 1977: 183). Such ideological pretensions define the context where the ambivalent responses to Theodorakis's musical experiment, *Epitaphios*, took place.

Epitaphios represented a primary paradigm that exemplified a mode for realizing the variously disputed neohellenic visions of folkmusic—an attempt to give to the socialist "grand narrative" a musical substance. In fact, it encompassed the domain of the "folk" (laiko) and the "art" (entehno) song, becoming a precursor of the so-called entehno laiko genre, the "art-folk" music style.[38] For the opponents of the musical experiment, its "mixed" identity was disapproved of as a paradox: "art" personified in Ritsos's poetry does not deserve the penies (strokes) of bouzouki considered as "totally strange" to it (Arkadinos [1960] 1986: 190; Avgheris [1961] 1986: 210–11). In this way, the works of "art"—the music of the knowledgeable composers—are distinguished as superior from the works of "the people," seen as products of the folk instinct embodying a charming naivety. On the contrary, the composer himself aestheticized this very folk "muse" (Theodorakis [1960a] 1986: 177), "folk musical wisdom" and "sharp musical instinct" ([1960b] 1986: 193). *Epitaphios*, therefore, *sounds* the ennoblement of the impulsive and passionate "folk" that is elevated in the hands of the reformer to the status of the "art"—a project disapproved by his critics as "populism" (Xenos [1960] 1986: 217).[39] In fact, he follows his polemics in the ways he conceptualizes the notion of "art" as a sophisticated and spiritual expression compared to that of the soperceived primitive—and thus "true"—"folk music" he aestheticizes as "the music that connects the man with his roots" (Theodorakis [1960d] 1986: 184).

This quest to rediscover the primordial musical forms of folk song again recalls the ways relevant ideas were celebrated in the ranks of the cultural elite in the age of Enlightenment. The disenchantment felt for the "contemporary" defined by the effects of the industrial revolution generated a growing distrust towards the ideal of progress and technological "miracles." Dissatisfied by what they saw as an increasingly dehumanized society, the bourgeois people promoted the notion of "return to the roots" as a way to reclaim the ideal of an uncontaminated humanity. In the case of leftist rebetology, the discourses over folk song are conditioned by a similar disenchantment with an alienating and miserable urban society. Urban living sensed as a fatal fall from paradise becomes furthermore an allegory of the failure of the leftist movement to prevent and control this "fall"—the prevalence of capitalism.

In the following years, the need to re-discover the music of the "people" was moreover *performed*: local people of the letters and arts sought to play, sing and enjoy the "authentic" urban folk song.[40] In the echoes of the French May '68 and the hippie movements the progressive dianoisi and student groups supported a counterculture that celebrated their subversive ideals in the name of rebetiko song. In the 1970s the revival of the underworld sounds performed the opposition to the dictators' music politics that condemned rebetiko song as "dangerous" for the morale of the youth.[41] Whether on the level of discourse or on that of the performance, rebetiko song in the postwar years became the forum for the poetics of Greek music history that generated tropes of thinking about "our music," contesting identities, assessing and re-inventing Greekness: it provided the pretext to *make* the knowledge of the present and imagine prosperous musical futures.

Notes

The present chapter is the outcome of a broader study on rebetiko song culture which I started in 1997 as a doctoral research student. My thesis is an ethnography of contemporary rebetiko revivalist performances in the city of Thessaloniki (northern Greece) based on fieldwork. My main concern there is to discuss the rhetorics and aesthetics that define the current "other-ing" of rebetiko song within the ongoing postmodern transformations of Greek music culture associated with the phenomenon of "world music." The ideas presented here are mostly based on the study of historical sources rather than upon the "lived experience" of rebetiko culture. The text is not a verbatim reproduction of a part of the thesis.

1. Manos Hatzidakis, from a lecture given in 1948. Reprinted in Holst (1977: 155).

2. See, for example, Braudel's (1977) holistic notion of the "Mediterranean." More recently Bohlman has pointed out that "we construct

approaches to the music of the Mediterranean that emphasize connect-
edness and contradiction" (2002: 1).

3. For a critique of Mediterranean anthropology, see Llobera
(1986), Herzfeld (1987), Pina-Cabral (1989) and Kavouras (1995).

4. The term *Mediterraneanism* was coined by Herzfeld.

5. See Tragaki (2003).

6. The adjective *mesogiakos* (Mediterranean) does not appear in
the relevant writings. In terms of its geo-cultural identities rebetiko was
primary discussed within a bipolar Oriental/Greek conceptual scheme.

7. The leading bouzouki player was Manolis Hiotis, the famous
virtuoso bouzouki player of the 1960s who contrived the four-string
bouzouki. His wife and acclaimed arhondorebetiko singer, Mairi Linda,
also participated in the recording of *Epitaphios*.

8. Theodorakis uses alternatively the terms *folk song* (laiko traghoudhi) and rebetiko song in his writings. The term *Greek Music
School* coined by himself describes his ideal of modern Greek folk-
song style in terms of the musical traditions it ought to encapsulate.
The term was never broadly adopted by local scholars, music experts
and researchers.

9. An "art" song singer uses the bel-canto singing style with clearly
articulated tones and the employment of melodic dynamics (within the
piano–forte range) deriving from Western art singing techniques. "Art"
singing is therefore differentiated from "folk" singing characterized by
the nasal and throat-produced vocal qualities and the absence of melodic dynamics.

10. This is the way they used to collect human bodies who died
from starvation and from the cold winter weather during the Nazi
occupation.

11. See also Gauntlett (1989). Stokes discusses the ways Ottoman
art music was the subject of an "ideological onslaught in the 1920s and
1930s in the hands of modernizing Kemalist elites" (Stokes 1996: 1).

12. In Greek, *rebetologhia* (rebetology) is a term that broadly describes the study of rebetiko song. The term appears in Hatzidakis
([1978] in Petropoulos (1996). *Rebetologhia* is also the title of one of
Petropoulos's accounts (1990).

13. Denisoff discussed a similar phenomenon regarding the use of
folk song as a protest song by the American left celebrated in the folk
music revival during the 1930s and 1940s (1971). See also Denisoff
(1969: 51–65, 1972); Lund and Denisoff (1971: 394–405); Reuss
(1971: 259–79, 1975: 89–111); Becker and Franco (1988); Lieberman
(1989); Porter (1991: 113–30) and Reuss and Reuss (2000).

14. The term *progressive* (in Greek proodeftikos) is broadly used to describe open-minded ideologists who may not directly adhere to the Communist Party.

15. For Foucault, the role of the intellectual is "to struggle against the forms of power in relation to which he is both object and instrument: within the domain of 'knowledge', 'truth', 'consciousness' and 'discourse'" (Foucault and Deleuze [1972] 1973: 104). Such intellectuals may form a revolutionary force, because they are in a position to control and disable the power–knowledge interplay (Foucault [1977] 1984: 67–69). Similar ideas are advocated by Edward Said in his *Representations of the Intellectual* (1994). For Edward Shils (1972: 3) the intellectuals represent a minority of persons "with an unusual sensitivity to the sacred, an uncommon reflectiveness about the nature of their universe and the rules which govern their society." The sociology of intellectuals represents a body of literature that discusses the intellectuals' social and cultural status following mainly three different approaches:

(i) intellectuals as "class-in-themselves," that is a class detached from any practical interests and preoccupied with the knowledge and pleasure of art or science (see Benda [1927] 1928).

(ii) intellectuals as "class-bound," that is a class "organically" attached to the interests of a particular social group (see Gramsci [1932] 1971) and

(iii) intellectuals as "class-less," that is a "socially unattached" group that transcends class (see Mannheim [1929] 1985). For an overview of the sociology of intellectuals from the 1920s up to the beginning of the twenty-first century see Kurzman and Owens (2002).

16. Several writers also describe the rebetiko composer Vasilis Tsitsanis as a "refiner" of folk song. He personifies the "second" era of rebetiko that culminates in the 1950s when rebetiko song was "ennobled"; that is, it ceased to be associated with the performance contexts defined by the criminal underworld (see Spanoudi [1952] 1977; Maheras 1961: 94; Tsarouhis 1966; Tahtsis [1966] 1996 and Christianopoulos [1961] 1977: 160).

17. Xenos ([1947] 1977: 141, [1960] 1986: 219); Papadimitriou ([1949] 1977: 151); Orfinos (1956: 433); Gardikis (1956: 245); Skouriotis (1956a: 152); Triantafyllou (1961: 615); Dromazos ([1961] 1986: 232); Maheras (1961); Vournas (1961 [1977]: 169); Kouzinopoulos (1961: 612).

18. The Marxian revolutionary intellectual movement rests in this respect on a much older intellectual tradition, the "apocalyptic" or "millenarian" tradition. "The belief that the evil world as we know it, so full of temptation and corruption, will come to an end one day and will be replaced by a purer and better world, originates in the apocalyptic outlook of the prophets of the Old Testament" (Shils 1972: 19).

19. The term *dystopia* refers to a utopian society where the social order is relentlessly harsh, destructive and miserable; an ideally immoral, catastrophic, merciless society—a perfect hell. The first use of the term is attributed to the English philosopher and economist John Stuart Mill (1868), who criticized Victorian ethics as a profound problem of mankind (*On Liberty*, 1859).

20. It is interesting that the Marxist-biased sociologist Anthony Giddens (1990: 4) described the consequences of modernity as "a set of discontinuities." Giddens is particularly concerned with "the darker side of modernity" associated with globalization, industrialization, the politics of the nation-state and the military powers and the consequent re-ordering of the social relations.

21. It is noteworthy that the origins of rebetiko represented one of the main questions posed by the inquiry initiated by the *Avghi* newspaper in 1961. The newspaper formed a set of questions (on the origins of folk song, its development and possible association with other local genres, its "moral" content and the role of mass media in its formulation), which were addressed to eleven local intellectuals who subsequently published their responses.

22. The term *levendia* refers to a set of moral characteristics combining bravery, pride, manliness, generosity and dignity. Levendia is traditionally considered as a male characteristic.

23. Anoyianakis ([1947] 1977: 139, [1961] 1977: 191); Vournas ([1961] 1977: 173–74); Sofoulis (1956: 153); Christianopoulos ([1961] 1977: 160); Theodorakis ([1961a] 1986: 213); Leivaditis ([1961] 1986: 222); Papadimitriou ([1961] 1986: 225); Dromazos ([1961] 1986: 230).

24. Xenos ([1947] 1977: 142); Papadimitriou ([1949] 1977: 150); Kouzinopoulos (1961: 613); Skouriotis (1956a: 151); Maheras (1961: 90); Gardikis (1956: 245); Hairopoulos ([1961] 1986: 249).

25. See also Andriakaina (1996: 225–57).

26. Herzfeld distinguishes the notion of romiosini to that of ellinismos as a couple of stereotypes representing "the double image of Greek cultural origins" (1987: 101). Romiosini refers to the Greek identity associated with the Byzantine past of Greek history, while ellinismos describes the Greekness formulated within the ancient classical era. Despite the schematic conceptualization of the terms by

Herzfeld, "Hellenic" and "romeic" are neither opposite terms—
"Hellenic" may acquire various other, more generic uses—nor do they
represent a binary set of criteria describing Greek cultural identity.

27. To that extent, rebetiko music is either seen to have supported
the Resistance movement (Vournas [1961] 1977: 181; Tahtsis [1964]
1977: 202) or, for the opposite side, to have been associated with
groups who "deprived national consciousness" (Maheras 1961: 92).

28. The term *zeibekikos,* that is, a $\frac{9}{8}$ rhythmic pattern, describes both
the relevant dance and song style and is closely associated with the
rebetiko genre.

29. It is noteworthy that the contribution of Tsarouhis, Tahtsis,
Christianopoulos and Hatzidakis in rebetophile discourse exemplifies,
apparently not by accident, a special intellectual reality, namely that of
gay leftist or progressive intellectuals. The mythical image of the working-class, strong and brave man who displays his masculinity in dashing zeibeikikos dance movements was transformed in the eyes of the
avant-garde gay intellectuals to an appealing male ideal. This way, the
exoneration of rebetiko worked as a metaphor of gay aesthetic aspirations. Gay rebetologists appear to capitalize upon ancient Greek morality—where public homosexuality is socially accepted—in an attempt to
validate further their social gender (see Tragaki 2003: 132–35).

30. Such an understanding of rebetiko origins and history features
mostly the recent revival of the genre associated with the contemporary
interest in the "world music" movement (see Tragaki 2003: 383–93).

31. See Lyotard ([1979] 1984).

32. See also Papadimitriou ([1949] 1977: 146); Orfinos (1956:
432); Skouriotis (1956a: 152); Gardikis (1956: 245); Kouzinopoulos
(1961: 612).

33. Ricoeur, who suggested that "all utopias . . . are treated by
Marxism as ideologies" (1986: 6), identifies in utopia "a constitutive
role in helping us rethink the nature of our social life" that works as
"one of the most formidable contestations of what it is" (1986: 16).

34. Rebetiko was already "industrialized" from the end of the nineteenth century in the United States (see Smith 1991: 143–51; 1995:
125–35) among the Greek diasporic communities in New York. Ber-
liner, Grammophone, Odeon, His Master's Voice and Columbia were
among the labels who recorded rebetiko songs during the first couple of
decades of the twentieth century. In 1931 Columbia established its record factory in Athens. Among the first recordings undertaken was a
rebetiko song (with a bouzouki-based instrumentation, see Kounadhis
2000). Ever since, the genre was broadly commercialized and popular-
ized. In the postwar years it was no longer a "marginal" musical style;

it was a popular music favored by people of various social groups all over the country.

35. Gardikis (1956: 245) one of the strictest anti-rebetiko authors stated characteristically, "We decently complain about the daily attack of the rebetiko stench against our breath." Papadimitriou describes rebetiko metaphorically as a symptom of "withering" ([1949] 1977: 151).

36. The strong Marxist bias is also evident in the use of particular terminology, such as "the proletariat," "the folk mass," "the urban class" and "the capitalist interests." Relevant ideas are also found in Karl Mannheim's notion of "relationism" that suggests the determination of consciousness by the social location of the individual (in *Ideology and Utopia: An Introduction to the Sociology of Knowledge* ([1936] 1985) and in Max Weber's *The Protestant Ethic and the Spirit of Capitalism* ([1930] 1976).

37. Politis also refers to "the aftermath of the resistance movement" ([1947] 1977: 145).

38. Theodorakis's experiment had inspired several Greek composers who used rebetiko as a musical tradition of reference in their work (see Tragaki 2003: 146), while a year earlier Hatzidakis composed *The Boys from Peiraus* (Ta Paidia tou Peiraia) for the soundtrack of the film *Never on Sunday*, which became ever since the most popular Greek tune abroad.

39. Theodorakis ([1960b] 1986: 201) stressed that he taught the rebetiko folk singer, Grigoris Bithikotsis, how to sing the acclaimed poetry of Yiannis Ritsos.

40. Folk song revivals are basically middle-class phenomena (see Rosenberg 1993).

41. For rebetiko revivals see Tragaki (2003, chapters 6 and 7).

Bibliography

Andriakaina, Eleni. "I Diamahi gia to Rebetiko: I Ellinikotita os Isorropia Loghou—Pathous." 225–57 in *Rebetes kai Rebetiko Traghoudhi*, edited by Nikos Kotaridis. Athens: Plethron, 1996.

Anoyianakis, Foivos. "To Rebetiko Traghoudhi." *Rizospastis*, 28th January 1947, reprinted in Holst 1977: 139–41.

———. "Gia to Rebetiko Traghoudhi." *Epitheorisi Tehnis* 79 (July 1961), reprinted in Holst 1977: 184–200.

Arkadinos, Vasilis. 1960 "I Mousiki tou Miki Theodoraki ston Epitafio tou Y. Ritsou: Mia Prospatheia gia Ananeosi tou Laikou mas

Traghoudhiou." *Avghi*, 8 October 1960, reprinted in Theodorakis 1986: 188–91.

Avgheris, Markos. "Apantisi." *Avghi*, 22 March 1961, reprinted in Theodorakis 1986: 208–11.

Becker, Jane S., and Barbara Franco., eds., *Folk Roots, New Roots: Folklore in American Life*. Lexington, Ma: Museum of Our National Heritage, 1988.

Benda, J. *The Treason of the Intellectuals*. Translated by R. Ardington. New York: William Morrow, [1927] 1928.

Bohlman, Philip V. "Music, Myth and History." *Ethnomusicology Online*, www.research.umbc.edu/eol/3/bohlman1.htm

———. "World Music at the End of History." *Ethnomusicology* 46, no. 1 (2002): 1–32.

Braudel, Fernand. *La Méditerranée, L'Espace et L'Histoire*. Paris: Arts et Métiers graphiques, 1977.

Calinescu, Matei. *Five Faces of Modernity: Modernism, Avant-Garde, Decadence, Kitsch, Postmodernism*. Durham: Duke University Press, 1987.

Christianopoulos, Dinos. "Istoriki kai Aisthitiki Diamorfosi tou Rebetikou Traghoudiou." *Diaghonios* 1, 1961, reprinted in Holst 1977: 158–64.

Denisoff, Serge R. "The Proletarian Renaissance: The Folkness of the Ideological Folk," *Journal of American Folklore* 82 (1969): 51–65.

———. *Great Day Coming: Folk Music and the American Left*. Urbana: University of Illinois Press, 1971.

———. *Sing a Song of Social Significance*. Bowling Green, Ohio: Bowling Green University Popular Press, 1972.

Dreyfus, Herbert L., and Paul Rabinow. *Michel Foucault: Beyond Structuralism and Hermeneutics*. Brighton, Sussex: The Harvester Press, 1982.

Dromazos, Stathis. "Apantisi." *Avghi*. 5 May 1961, reprinted in Theodorakis 1986: 228–34.

Eleftheriou, A. "Epistoli." *Anexartitos Typos*. 29 December 1960, reprinted in Theodorakis 1986: 203–4.

Feld, Steven. "From Schizophonia to Schismogenesis: On the Discourses and Commodification Practices of 'World Music' and 'World Beat'". 257–89 in *Music Grooves*, edited by Charles Keil and Steven Feld. Chicago: The University of Chicago Press, 1994.

Foucault, Michel. *Sourveiller et Punir: Naissance de la Prison*. Paris: Gallimard, 1975.

———. "Truth and Power." 51–75 in *The Foucault Reader*, edited by Paul Rabinow. New York: Pantheron, [1977] 1984.

Foucault, Michel, and G. Deleuze. "The Intellectuals and Power." *Telos* 16 ([1972] 1973): 103–9.

Gardikis, D. "To Rebetiko," *Epitheorisi Tehnis* 21 (1956): 245.

Gauntlett, Stathis. "Orpheus in the Criminal Underworld: Myth in and about Rebetika," *Mandatoforos* 34 (1989): 7–48.

Giddens, Anthony. *The Consequences of Modernity*. Cambridge: Polity Press, 1990: 4.

Gramsci, Antonio. "The Intellectuals," 5–23 in *Selections from the Prison Notebooks of Antonio Gramsci*. Translated by Q. Hoare and G. Smith. New York: International Publications, [1932] 1971.

Hairopoulos, K. H. "Epistoles," *Apoghevmatini*, 19–21st July 1961, reprinted in Theodorakis 1986: 247–51.

Hatzidakis, Manos. "Ermineia kai Thesi tou Laikou Traghoudhiou." *Elliniki Dimiourghia,* March 1949, reprinted in Holst 1977: 151–55.

Hatzis, Kostas. "To Laiko Traghoudhi." *Epitheorisi Tehnis* 82 (October 1961): 337–45.

Herzfeld, Michael. *Anthropology through the Looking Glass: Critical Ethnography in the Margins of Europe*. Cambridge: Cambridge University Press, 1987.

Holst, Gail. *Dhromos gia to Rebetiko kai Arthra gia to Rebetiko Traghoudhi apo ton Elliniko Typo*. Translated by Nikos Savvatis. Athens: Denise Harvey, 1977.

Kavouras, Pavlos. "To Aigaio os Eniaia Politismiki Periohi: mia Kritiki Anthropologiki Prosengisi." 17–36 in *Axones kai Proypotheseis gia mia Diepistimoniki Erevna* (Praktika B' Symposiou gia ton Politismo tou Aigaiou, Samos). Athens: Pnevmatiko Idryma Samou, "Nikolaos Dimitriou," 1995.

Kounadhis, Panauiotis. *Eis Anamnisin Stighmon Elkystikon* (In Memoriam of Engaging Moments). Athens: Katarti Press, 2000.

Kouzinopoulos, Lazaros. "To Telos tis Sizitisis gia to Laiko Traghoudhi." *Epitheorisi Tehnis* 84 (December 1961): 612–13.

Kurzman, Charles, and Lynn Owens. "The Sociology of Intellectuals." *Annual Review of Sociology* 28 (2002): 63–90.

Leivaditis, Tasos. "Apantisi," *Avghi*. 28 March 1961, reprinted in Theodorakis 1986: 220–24.

Lieberman, Robie. "My Song is My Weapon": People's Songs, American Communism and the Politics of Culture, 1930–1950. Urbana: University of Illinois Press, 1989.

Llobera, Joseph. "Fieldwork in Southeastern Europe: Anthropological Panacea or Epistemological Straitjacket?" *Critique of Anthropology* 6, no. 2 (1986): 25–33.

Lund, Jens, and Serge R. Denisoff. "The Folk Music Revival and the Counter Culture." *Journal of American Folklore* 84 (1971): 394–405

Lyotard, Jean-Francois. *The Postmodern Condition: A Report on Knowledge.* Manchester: Manchester University Press, [1979] 1984.

Maheras, E. I. "To Rebetiko kai to Synhrono Laiko Traghoudhi." *Kainourghia Epohi* (Summer 1961): 84–99.

Mannheim, Karl. *The Sociological Problem of the "Intelligentsia"* [1929], reprinted in Mannheim, [1936] 1985: 153–64.

———. *Ideology and Utopia: An Introduction to the Sociology of Knowledge.* New York: Harcourt Brace [1936] 1985.

Mill, John Stuart. *On Liberty.* London: Penguin, 1979.

Orfinos, Petros. "Dhimotiko Traghoudhi kai Mousiki Aghoghi." *Epitheorisi Tehnis* 17 (May 1956): 431–33.

Papadimitriou, Vasilis. "To Rebetiko kai oi Simerikoi Thiasotes tou." *Elefthera Grammata*, February 1949, reprinted in Holst 1977: 145–51.

Petropoulos, Ilias. "Rebetologhia," *Ihneftis* 51 (January 1979): 12–30.

———. *Rebetika Traghdoudhia.* Athens: Kedros, [1979] 1996.

Pina-Cabral, João de. "The Mediterranean as a Category of Regional Comparison: A Critical Review." *Current Anthropology* 30, no. 3 (1989): 399–406.

Politis, Nikos. "Epistoli sto Rizospasti." *Rizospastis* (23rd February 1947), reprinted in Holst 1977: 143–45.

Porter, James. "Muddying the Crystal Spring: From Idealism to Realism and Marxism in the Study of English and American Folk Song." 113–30 in *Comparative Musicology and Anthropology of Music,* edited by Bruno Nettl and Philip Bohlman. Chicago: University of Chicago Press, 1991.

Reuss, Richard A., "The Roots of American Left-Wing Interest in Folksong." *Labor History* 12 (1971): 259–79.

———. "American Folksongs and Left-Wing Politics: 1935–56." *Journal of the Folklore Institute* 12 (1975): 89–111.

Reuss, Richard, and Joanne Reuss. *American Folk Music and Left-Wing Politics, 1927–1957.* Lanham, Md: Scarecrow Press, 2000.

Ricoeur, Paul. *Lectures on Ideology and Utopia.* New York: Columbia University Press, 1986.

Rosenberg, Neil. *Transforming Tradition: Folk Music Revivals Examined.* Urbana: University of Illinois Press, 1993.

Said, Edward. *Representations of the Intellectual.* Pantheon, 1994.

Samouilidou, Erifylli. "To Dhimotiko Traghoudhi." *Epitheorisi Tehnis*

22 (October 1956): 227–28.

Shils, Edward. *The Intellectuals and the Powers and Other Essays.* Chicago: Chicago University Press, 1972.

Skouriotis, Yiannis. "To Dhimotiko Traghoudhi apo Koinoniki Apopsi." *Epitheorisi Tehnis* 20 (August 1956a): 148–52.

———. "To Dhimotiko Traghoudhi." *Epitheorisi Tehnis* 23–24 (November–December 1956b): 461.

Smith, Ole. "Rebetika in the United States Before World War II." 143–51 in *New Directions in Greek American Studies,* edited by Dan Georghakas and Charles Moskos. New York: Pella, 1991.

———. "Cultural Identity and Cultural Interaction: Greek Music in the United States, 1917–41." *Journal of Modern Greek Studies* 13 (1995): 125–35.

Sofoulis, Kostas. "Epistoli," *Epitheorisi Tehnis* 20 (August 1956): 152–54.

Spanoudi, Sofia. "Oi Kosmoi tis Laikis Tehnis, o Tsitsanis." *Ta Nea* (1 February 1952), reprinted in Holst 1977: 155–58.

Stokes, Martin. "History, Memory and Nostalgia in Contemporary Turkish Musicology." *Music and Anthropology* 1 (1996), www.research.umbc.edu/eol/MA/index/number 1.

Tahtsis, Kostas. "Zeibekiko, 1964: Ena Mikro Dokimio." *Pali* 2–3 (1964), reprinted in Holst 1977: 202–9.

———. "On Tsitsanis." *Eikones* (7 October 1966), reprinted in Elias Petropoulos, *Rebetika Traghoudhia,* Athens: Kedhros, [1979] 1996: 259.

Theodorakis, Mikis. "To Synhrono Laiko Traghoudhi." *Simerini Epohi,* 1 (9 October 1949), 2 (23 October 1949), 3 (7 November 1949), reprinted in Theodorakis 1986: 157–69.

———. "Report." *Avghi* (6–8 October 1960a), reprinted in Theodorakis 1986: 172–80.

———. "Epistoli." *Epitheorisi Tehnis* 73–74, no. 13 (21 October 1960b), reprinted in Theodorakis 1986: 192–202.

———. "Epistoli." *Proto* (October 1960c), reprinted in Theodorakis 1986: 185–88.

———. "Interview." *Dhromoi tis Eirinis* 35 (October 1960d), reprinted in Theodorakis 1986: 180–85.

———. "Apantisi." *Avghi* (23 March 1961a), reprinted in Theodorakis 1986: 212–13.

———. "Lecture in Metropolitan." *Athinaiki* (15 July 1961b), reprinted in Theodorakis 1986: 239–43.

———. "Ap' to Laiko Traghoudhi stin Opera." interview, *Dhromoi tis Eirinis* (July 1961c), reprinted in Theodorakis 1986: 256–64.

————. "I Thesi tis Laikis Mousikis kai oi Efthines gia ton Ekpoliti-smo." *Tahydhromos* 382 (July 1961d), reprinted in Theodorakis 1986: 265–67.

————. *Gia tin Elliniki Mousiki, 1952–1961.* Athens: Kastaniotis Press, 1986.

Tragaki, Dafne. "Urban Ethnomusicology in the City of Thessaloniki (Greece): The Case of Rebetiko Song Revival Today." Ph.D. dissertation: Goldsmiths College, University of London, 2003.

Triantafyllou, Vlassis. "Epistoli." *Epitheorisi Tehnis* 84 (1961): 613–15.

Tsarouhis, Yiannis. "Mikro Sholio gia to Zeibekiko." *Theatro* (1963), reprinted in Holst 1977: 201.

————. "On Tsitsanis." *Eikones* (7th October 1966), reprinted in Petropoulos, [1979] 1996: 259.

Vournas, Tasos. "To Synhrono Laiko Traghoudhi." *Epitheorisi Tehnis* 76 (April 1961), reprinted in Holst 1977: 164–84.

Weber, Max. *The Protestant Ethic and the Spirit of Capitalism.* New York: Charles Scribner's Sons, [1930] 1976.

Xenos, Alekos. "Epistoli sto Rizospasti." *Rizospastis* (4 February 1947), reprinted in Holst 1977: 141–43.

————. "Apantisi." *Avghi* (24 March 1960), reprinted in Theodorakis 1986: 214–20.

Part 2
Broadcasting and New Media

Chapter Four

Robert Lachmann's *Oriental Music*: A Broadcasting Initiative in 1930s Palestine

Ruth Davis

Introduction

This chapter grows out of a project based on a series of twelve radio programs entitled *Oriental Music,* written and presented by the comparative musicologist Robert Lachmann for the Palestine Broadcasting Service in its inaugural year, 1936–37. The programs, focusing on musical traditions of Palestine, were illustrated by live studio performances by musicians and singers from Jerusalem and its surroundings, simultaneously recorded onto metal disc. My edition of *Oriental Music* will present Lachmann's twelve lectures with transcriptions of the musical examples and their texts, translations, an introduction and commentary and a compact disc of the digitally remastered musical recordings.[1]

In the following pages I introduce Lachmann's radio programs within the wider context of his research in Palestine in the late 1930s. Drawing on his largely unpublished writings from this period,[2] I consider Lachmann's ideology and vision for the new medium of broadcasting and its potential role in promoting traditional music and musical scholarship. In the strife-ridden social and political climate of the time, Lachmann believed that by adopting a musical policy that reflected the tastes of all the indigenous groups, not just the Westernized sector, radio could play a vital role in fostering human, as well as musical understanding; such a policy, he suggested, could have significant political, as well as artistic advantages.

The Palestine Project (1935–38) and its Aftermath

In September 1933, Robert Lachmann, musicologist, linguist and pioneering scholar of Middle Eastern music, was dismissed by the Nazi authorities from his position as music librarian in the Berlin State Library, because he was Jewish. After over a year of negotiations, relating primarily to financial constraints, Lachmann accepted an invitation by Dr. Judah L. Magnes, president of the newly established Hebrew University of Jerusalem,[3] to found and direct an Archive of Oriental Music there. Lachmann arrived in Jerusalem on 29 April 1935 accompanied by his technician from Berlin, Walter Schur and his own state-of-the-art recording equipment. In addition, Lachmann brought copies of his personal collection of some 500 wax cylinder recordings, derived largely from his field work in North Africa in the 1920s and copies of some fifty wax cylinder recordings made by Abraham Zvi Idelsohn in Jerusalem in 1913, to form the basis of the new Archive.[4]

Between June 1935 and May 1938, Lachmann made 959 recordings in Palestine, documenting sacred and secular repertories of various Eastern Jewish and Christian communities, Samaritans and Muslim Arabs.[5] In many instances, he recorded the same repertory several times, performed by the same and different musicians. His immediate aim was "to secure representative items of every kind of music extant among the different groups of the population" as quickly as possible before the traditions became "transformed or altogether destroyed by growing European influences."[6]

Lachmann's insistence on recording all the religious groups: Christian, Muslim and Samaritan as well as Jewish, gave rise to misunderstandings and criticisms from both Muslim and Jewish quarters and it alienated potential sponsors, interested only in the Jewish element. In response to the latter, Lachmann argued that comparative study with the neighboring traditions was indispensable for understanding the true nature and identity of Jewish music. Ultimately, however, his vision overrode both partisan and purely scholarly interests: by involving all the different ethnic groups of Palestine Lachmann believed that his work could "be made to contribute, however modestly, towards . . . a better understanding between Jews and Arabs."

Lachmann's professional correspondence and diaries from the Palestine years describe an unrelenting stream of obstacles relating to inadequate and insecure finances and lack of institutional support. All too often, the responses to Lachmann's initiatives, whether from British, Arab or Jewish sources, reflect misunderstanding, indifference and occasionally, downright opposition. With World War II on the horizon, increasing Jewish immigration from Nazi Europe fueling Jewish nationalist aspirations and Arabs staging a general strike (1936) and revolt (1936–39), Palestine was in the grips of social, political and economic turmoil. Evidently, the times were not auspicious for convincing potential sponsors, whether in Palestine or abroad, of the potential sponsors, whether in Palestine or abroad, of the value and urgency of his unique and eclectic project. Chronic illness led to Lachmann's hospitalization in September 1938 and eventually, to his death in May 1939, aged only fortysix.

After the partition of Palestine in 1948, Lachmann's Archive remained on the deserted University site on Mount Scopus in East Jerusalem, now part of the Hashemite Kingdom of Jordan. In 1964, the entire collection was transferred by military convoy to the new University campus in west Jerusalem, Israel, where it was incorporated into the newly founded National Sound Archive (Phonoteca). A catalogue of the Archive was prepared by the Israeli musicologist and former student of Lachmann, Dr. Edith Gerson-Kiwi.[7] In addition to Lachmann's Palestine recordings and his collections from Berlin the Archive includes about 180 commercial records of various North African, Middle Eastern and other Asian repertories, Lachmann's recording diaries, miscellaneous music and text transcriptions and translations, photographs of musicians and musical instruments, copious personal and professional correspondence and various unpublished lectures and articles.[8]

Among the latter are the twelve radio programs entitled *Oriental Music,* transmitted by the Palestine Broadcasting Service (PBS) in approximately fortnightly installments between 18 November 1936 and 28 April 1937. Launched just eight months after the PBS was inaugurated in March 1936, Lachmann's programs clearly reflect the broadly educational orientation of the new service, modeled on the BBC. His stated aim was to acquaint his European listeners "with the main aspects of the present day music of the Near East and with the principles underlying it"; thus, he would provide them with "ways towards understanding . . . as many and as various specimens of unadulterated Oriental music as possible."

Lachmann illustrated his programs with a total of forty musical examples. Of these, thirythree were live studio performances by local musicians, simultaneously recorded on metal disc. The live performances are entered in Lachmann's recording diaries where they are identified by the rubric "Radio" or "Palestine Radio." In all cases, Lachmann notes the dates of the recordings, titles of the repertory and names of the performers; in some, he also includes remarks on the technical quality of the recording, the instruments, voices and other aspects of performance practice, the quality of the performance and references to other recordings of the same or similar repertory. The remaining seven examples, representing traditions from elsewhere in the Middle East and Asia, were taken from Lachmann's personal col-

lection of commercial recordings; these are listed in a separate catalogue.

When Lachmann's Archive was incorporated into the National
Sound Archive (Phonoteca) in 1964, the specialist equipment needed to
play the wax cylinders and metal discs was no longer available in Israel. The recordings languished, inaudible, in a cupboard until 1992
when a project was launched by the Jewish Music Research Centre,
funded by the Vienna Friends of the Hebrew University, to transfer the
collection onto audio tape. The project was carried out in Jerusalem,
using specialist equipment and technical expertise from Vienna.

Lachmann's recordings were originally intended to serve primarily
as a basis for research (i.e. transcription and analysis); cut onto metal of
inferior quality, their use for demonstration purposes, even by the technical standards of the time, was, as Lachmann himself recognized,
problematic. More than half a century later, the discs were found to be
in a bad state of deterioration with hiss, clicks and stylus jumps mask-
ing the performances to a greater or lesser degree. The recordings belonging to "Oriental Music" have been repaired and much of their ex-
traneous noise removed in collaboration with the Department of
Engineering, University of Cambridge, using the CEDAR process.[9]

Lachmann's Ideology and Vision for Music Broadcasting in Palestine

The Palestine Broadcasting Service (PBS) was established by the British Mandate administration in March 1936. The station, based in Jerusalem, operated on a single channel divided into separate English, Hebrew and Arabic departments. Broadcasting was initially confined to a
total of five hours daily, from about 5:30 pm, with the English programs receiving prime time airing in the latter part of the evening (Hirshberg 1996: 141).

Lachmann's writings stress two interrelated goals for his Palestine
project as a whole:

  (i) the systematic collection, preservation and study, from a
       multi-disciplinary perspective, i.e., historical, sociological,
       ethnological and philological, of the oral musical traditions of
       the Near East; and

(ii) the promotion, by means of these activities, of understanding between peoples of European and Near Eastern descent. He considered both goals as urgent.

His vision for broadcasting was, from the outset, based on his belief that the interests of radio and the music scholar were fundamentally compatible. In as much as the radio station wished to provide high-quality music programs with wide appeal across the various sectors of the population, it could achieve its aim most effectively, Lachmann proposed, by collaborating with music scholars concerned with recording, preserving and promoting indigenous music. In the fragmented, strife-ridden social climate of late 1930s Palestine, moreover, a programming policy that reflected the musical tastes and values of all the indigenous peoples could, he believed, have significant political advantages.

In a document entitled "Remarks on broadcasting music from the Jerusalem station" dated 2 June 1935 (i.e., some nine months before the inauguration of the PBS) Lachmann proposes criteria for the selection of particular kinds of music and musicians. His central premise is that the new medium will have an educational purpose and that it should aim therefore not only to please, but also to guide the taste of its listeners. For Lachmann, the two goals are inseparable: "The more the audience and especially the younger generation, become aware of what pure and unspoiled tradition is, the more there is hope that they will become impatient with the mixtures and sham productions which crowd the market. In fact, the stronger appeal of the 'real thing' to the audience is unmistakable whenever genuine music is recited in concerts side by side with imitations of it."

The question of what is "genuine" in music and what is not is, for Lachmann, inextricably bound up with the problem of musical hybridization; thus he rejects all "attempts at hybridizing Eastern and Western music in a way which harms both and does not do any good to either." He specifically objects to

(i)   adding Western harmony to Eastern tunes; and
(ii) performing Eastern music on European instruments, in particular, those of fixed tuning, such as the piano, which cannot produce the variable intervals of the Arab modal system and whose use therefore "should be stopped definitively."

Noting that the high tension of the violin strings and the tone color of this and other European instruments such as flutes, clarinets, oboes and drums, are incompatible with "the delicate shades of Oriental urban melodies," Lachmann advises that these instruments too should be "excluded from Eastern bands, as least as far as the authority of the broadcasting station goes."

In his Palestine document, Lachmann was clearly echoing the views he himself expressed, along with the other comparative musicologists, at the First International Congress of Arab Music held in Cairo in 1932.[10] Three years later, however, his attitude appears both more flexible and more cautious. Whereas his speeches to the Cairo Congress had stressed only the negative aspects of European musical borrowing, here Lachmann acknowledges, at least in principle, that there may be "valuable and . . . hopeful productions using Western as well as Eastern elements and one must take care not to stop these along with the worthless ones." In particular, Lachmann is cautious about prejudicing against attempts that are yet to be realized, particularly in an environment of such diverse ethnic composition and intense social flux as present-day Palestine. "Young Jewish or Arab composers may find, one day, a new way of expressing themselves . . . in a musical language somewhere, possibly, between the Western and the Eastern tradition." Certainly, he considers it "advisable to examine every individual case, instead of barring the way to new possibilities by rash generalizations."

As for "the mixtures and sham productions which crowd the market," Lachmann is clearly referring to commercial recordings of Egyptian and other foreign Arab urban music such as those he described in a letter to Magnes later that year. In his letter, Lachmann specifically cautions against the use of such products for local broadcasting, not least because they are already "heard in cafes, shops, private houses throughout this country," and their artists "are easily accessible by listening to the broadcasting stations of Cairo and Istanbul and are heard, as a matter of fact, by large masses of the population." He continues, " I have witnessed concerts of this kind at Nablus, at Haifa and at the Damascus Gate, Jerusalem, where they are transmitted in Arab cafés by means of loudspeakers" (letter dated 13 November 1935, quoted in Katz 2004: 118–19).

In rejecting such music, Lachmann was effectively rejecting the mainstream style of urban Arab music promoted by the commercial record, film and broadcasting industries. Centered in Cairo, this pan-Arab style was rapidly becoming the dominant variety throughout the Middle East. Characterized by ensembles combining violins, cellos and frequently other Western instruments with traditional Arab ones and melodies colored by Western harmonies and rhythms, it featured the

very kinds of musical hybridization Lachmann considered "harmful."
Yet his main objection to the use of such music for broadcasting was
based not so much on musical aesthetic and ideological criteria, such as
those outlined in his introductory talk, but rather on what he considered
to be its "limited appeal" to the majority of the local population. "There
is little hope for any enthusiasm to be raised by reproducing [such]
discs. . . . The audience would of course much rather hear local music
from their favorites, who are known to them personally, than the urban
music of Egypt etc. on which they are being fed to weariness. As for
the singers and players, urban, rural and Bedouin, of this country . . .
they would, I am sure, be deeply disappointed at being invited to hear
records from other countries instead of being given a chance of displaying their own abilities." Lachmann concludes, "Would it not be a more
gratifying task for the Jerusalem Station to support the original music
existing in this country and thereby to promote its development instead
of offering their audience records bought from elsewhere . . . ?"

Lachmann concludes his report by singling out certain types of
music that deserve special attention. In particular, he points to "the special value hidden both in Arab and Jewish folk music," whose attraction, he explains, is not solely aesthetic; indeed, this aspect may be difficult for urban audiences, accustomed to different standards (whether
European or Arab), to comprehend. Rather, the special value of folk
music relates more directly to its expressive function, peculiar to the
individual peoples to which it belongs. "If it is worthwhile becoming
acquainted with the character and emotions of the Bedouins, the short-
est way to them is to listen to their song which is their most typical and
spontaneous expression and reveals a beauty of its own to anybody
who cares to attend to it." However, Lachmann cautions that such music should not be broadcast too often, or to audiences that are unpre-
pared and he suggests that "recitals of it should be preceded by short
explanations as to its origin and meaning."

For certain listeners, Lachmann observes, the broadcasting of traditional Jewish folk music from all over the world and especially from
Eastern communities, will have a particular significance. Not only will
exposure to this music help resolve the question, so topical at the time,
as to what is typically Jewish in music; the traditional tunes might also
provide a basis for new attempts at Jewish folk song. Finally, he rec-
ommends broadcasting recitals of the various sacred musical traditions.
In the current climate of innovation and experimentation in both Jewish
and Christian liturgical music, such recitals, he proposes, would help
clarify the boundaries between sacred and secular genres, "and in particular, keep alive, or revive, public consciousness of the true aim of

sacred music which is not prettiness [as may be the case in secular mu-
sic] but concentration of mind. Their very monotony . . . has enabled
ancient music liturgies to survive to the present day."

Lachmann's Oriental Music

Oriental Music was directed primarily towards European listeners, not
generally known for their receptivity towards, still less their enthusiasm
for Eastern music. Rich in musical, historical and ethnographic data,
the twelve programs present a variety of approaches towards the understanding of specific musical traditions of diverse religious and ethnic
communities of Palestine, including Bedouin and village Arabs, Jews
of Yemenite, Kurdish and Iraqi descent, Copts and Samaritans.

The series opens with an introductory talk, without musical illustrations. In this, Lachmann dismantles certain conventional attitudes
towards Eastern music, including some widely held prejudices. He
challenges the popular notion that music, while apparently a natural,
spontaneous form of expression, is somehow an international language,
instantly accessible to all; on the contrary, he insists, it takes a special
effort to understand and appreciate foreign music. Thus the tendency
among Europeans to regard Eastern music as "inferior" and at "a lower
stage of development" than Western music stems not from any intrinsic
qualities in the music itself but rather, he suggests, from their ignorance
and failure to understand it.

Certain Europeans, he acknowledges, have adopted a more positive
approach; however, their motives tend to have little to do with understanding Eastern music itself. Thus Lachmann expresses his doubts
about those orientalist composers who seek to exploit this music merely
for its exotic effects; while their products "may be interesting as part of
the composer's work," such pieces "have no resemblance with their
alleged originals and even the general exotic impression that they must
have conveyed has faded away in the course of time." Indeed, he observes, "the very qualities which distinguish [the creative musician] as
a composer make him unfit for helping us towards a better understanding of foreign music."

Likewise, Lachmann dismisses that misguided class of "reformers," both European and Oriental, who seek to "improve" Oriental music by reproducing it with Western harmonies and in equal temperament; to this end, they have introduced Western instruments such as the
piano, or harmonium, distorting at once the scales, tuning and timbre of

Oriental music. As a result, "instead of the real thing, we obtain a hybrid production, typical neither of East nor West and shallow like ditch water."

Lachmann concludes his introductory talk by urging his listeners to approach Oriental music on its own terms, "leaving all European prejudice behind." Only thus "we may hope to penetrate to its core," thereby acquiring vital understanding both of the music itself and of the people who produce it. "In no other country, perhaps, the need for a sound understanding of [its music] and the opportunity of studying it answer each other so well as they do in Palestine. For the European, here, it is of vital interest to know the mind of his Oriental neighbors: well, music and singing, being the most spontaneous outcome of it, will be the surest guide, provided he listens to it with sympathy instead of disdain."

Yet Lachmann cannot resist throwing in an ulterior motive of his own. In common with other comparative musicologists, he regarded the oral traditions of the Middle East as somehow timeless and unchanging, potentially offering direct evidence of the musical practices of antiquity. "It is almost impossible to discuss Eastern music without being led into the past. In fact, this is one of its highest claims to our interest; through the mouth of a present day musician we may hear tunes which have charmed audiences of a thousand years and more ago. . . . Present day Bedouins, in playing the fiddle, follow rules established by musicians at the court of the early Abbasid Khalifs; negroes of the Sudan can correct our notions about how the lyre of Ancient Egypt was handled; and who knows how much may possibly be learnt from Oriental Jews of today about the singing at the ancient temple in Jerusalem."

Nine of the eleven remaining programs (nos. 2–9 and 12) are each devoted to one or more types of music of a particular ethnic or religious group or subgroup of Palestine; these are illustrated by live studio performances by local musicians and singers. Programs 2, 3, 4 and 6 concentrate on liturgical repertories of Yemenite Jews, Copts, Kurdish Jews and Samaritans; programs 7 and 8 describe the contrasting wedding rituals of Yemenite Jewish men and women and program 12, those of Arab village men. Program 5 presents a Bedouin Arab singing epic songs, accompanying himself on the rababa (fiddle with rectangular body and one string). Only one program (no. 9) is devoted to urban art music: this features the Jewish 'ud (Arab lute) player Ezra Aharon, a recent immigrant from Baghdad whom Lachmann had recorded at the 1932 Cairo Congress. Programs 10 and 11, based on commercial recordings from Lachmann's own collection, place the local traditions in the context of a broader spectrum of Middle Eastern urban secular repertories.

Listed below are the musical contents of Lachmann's programs.

Program 1, 18/11/36—No music.

Program 2, 2/12/36—Synagogue cantillation and song of the Yemenite Jews of Jerusalem, sung by Sa'adiya Nahum, Rafael Nadav, David Nadav.

Yemenite cantillation is characterized by "a simple and archaic style," and by the "intense strain and religious fervor" of its delivery. Examples i, ii and iii are each sung to a different melodic mode, corresponding to the particular biblical passage:

(i)   Exodus 14:30–15:16. *Sirat ha-yam* (Song of the Sea).
(ii)   Esther 9:29–10:3. End of the Book of Esther, sung to a special mode of its own.
(iii)   Proverbs 1:1–10. Sung to the mode of the *Song of Songs*.
(iv)   Non-liturgical song (sira) with hand clapping.

Program 3, 16/12/36—Cantillation and hymns of the Coptic liturgy, sung by the Coptic Bishop of Palestine and four priests from the Coptic Monastery of Jerusalem.

The Coptic liturgy is divided into three melodic modes corresponding to the three Masses.

(i)   Hymn based on the mode of the Kyrillus Mass, sung on solemn occasions when the bishop or other dignitary enters the church; accompanied by triangle and cymbals.
(ii)   Hymn in honor of the Virgin Mary from the middle of the Basilius Mass; accompanied by triangle and cymbals.
(iii)   Extract from the Gregorius Mass chanted in free rhythm; without percussion.

Program 4, 6/1/37—Synagogue cantillation of the Kurdish Jews of Jerusalem, sung by Eliahu Yahye Mizrahi.

Kurdish cantillation is distinguished from the Babylonian tradition, to which it is akin, by "its straightforward delivery and its male robust vigor." Each of the following passages is sung to a different melodic mode:

(i)   Exodus 20:2–17. "The Ten Commandments," in which the Lord's voice speaks through Moses to the community. This passage has a special mode of its own.

(ii)   Judges 5:1–11. *Sir Deborah* (Deborah's song) sung to the mode of *Sirat ha-yam* (Song of the Sea)

(iii)   Jonah 1: 1–10. From the afternoon service of Yom Kippur (the day of atonement).

(iv)   *Patach Eliahu ha Navi* (Open up! Elijah the Prophet). Passage from the *Zohar* (chief book of cabbalistic doctrine) sung at the beginning of each service.

Program 5, 20/1/37—Bedouin Arab songs, sung and played on the rababa (fiddle with rectangular body and one string) by Bajis Hanna Ma'addi from Taiba, Ramallah district.

(i)   Song in measured rhythm, from a narrative about two Bedouin tribes involved in a territorial feud. The territory, represented as a bride, chooses between the two tribes.

(ii)   Song in free rhythm composed by a Bedouin chief who married a girl from a hostile tribe; she died after a short, but happy marriage. Every day, throughout the following year, he composed a song to express his grief. This is one of them.

Program 6, 3/2/37—Liturgical cantillation and secular song of the Samaritan community of Nablus, sung by High Priest Taufiq Kohen, his brother Ibrahim Kohen and Amran Kohen, son of the former High Priest.

Samaritan cantillation is based on eleven melodic modes, referring to the different parts of the Pentateuch (the Samaritan scriptural canon) sung on different types of occasion.

(i)   Exodus 15:1–19. *Sirat ha-yam* (Song of the Sea).

Examples ii, iii and iv represent three melodic versions of the two lines of Moses's song in Deuteronomy 32:3: *Ke-ev-sem* (For in the Name of the Lord). These two lines precede every liturgical reading, sung to the corresponding melodic mode, reduced to a concise formula:

(ii)   Precedes the cantillation on festive occasions, such as the celebration of the birth of Moses.

(iii)   Precedes dirges.

(iv)   Precedes the cantillation referring to the miracles performed by Aaron before Pharaoh.

(v)   Convivial song in Arabic.

Program 7, 17/2/37—Men's songs from a Yemenite Jewish wedding in Jerusalem, sung by Sa'adiyya Nahum, Yahya Nahari and Hayyim Mahbub.

(i)   *Nasid.* Song for the bridegroom's henna ceremony.
(ii)   *Hidduya.* Song for the bridegroom's head-shaving ceremony.
(iii)   *Nasid.* Sung before the marriage ceremony in the bride's house.
(iv)   *Zaffa.* Sung by the groom's companions as they escort him to the bride's house on the morning after the marriage ceremony.

Program 8, 3/3/37—Women's songs from a Yemenite Jewish wedding in Jerusalem, sung by two unidentified women, with frame drum and tambourine.

(i)   Song for the bride's henna ceremony.
(ii)   Song for the cutting of the bride's front locks on the day preceding the marriage ceremony.
(iii)   Sequence of three songs accompanying dancing.

Program 9, 16/3/37—Arab urban music: taqasim (solo renderings in free rhythm of individual melodic modes, or maqamat*)*, performed on the 'ud (Arab lute) by Ezra Aharon, a recent immigrant from Baghdad whom Lachmann had recorded at the 1932 Cairo Congress.

(i)   Taqsim in maqam hijaz .
(ii)   Taqsim in maqam saba.
(iii)   Taqsim in maqam sika.

Program 10, 31/3/37—Arab urban music: "the Western style," commercial recordings.

(i)   Odeon 93324: Tunisian song (missing).
(ii)   Odeon 93571: Algerian song.
(iii)   Baidaphon 093364: Moroccan song.

Program 11, 14/4/37—Arab urban music: "the Eastern style," commercial recordings.

(i)   Odeon O-5168b: Egyptian song.

(ii)   Orfeon 10524: Turkish piece for tambur.
(iii)   Odeon O-5168a: Persian popular song from the series *Musik des Orients* compiled by Erich M. von Hornbostel (missing).
(iv)   Odeon 95113: Hindustani song (missing).

Program 12, 28/4/37—Songs from an Arab village wedding in Central Palestine, sung by Muhammad Abu Musallem of the Bani Murra tribe, from 'Ain Yabrud, Ramallah district; 'Abd al-Fattah al-Sahada of the Bani Malik tribe, from Qatanna, near Jerusalem. Ahmad Samir from Qatanna plays the shabbabah (reed flute).

Examples i. and ii. are sung before an open fire in the evening(s) following the agreement of the marriage until the marriage itself, which may take place one or several days later:

(i)   *Sahja*. Moderately paced dance song performed by old men.
(ii)   *Tashji'*. Sung by all the men, old and young, followed by a dahhiyya (this word is repeated rapidly, almost breathlessly).

Examples iii, iv and v are sung on the marriage day:

(iii)   *Zaffa hamasiyya* Sung by the young men, before and after the groom's bath.
(iv)   *'Ala dal'una—dabke* Circle dance with solo singer and shabbabah (reed flute).
(v)   *'Al-hama* Sung by the groom's companions to announce his arrival at his house, where his bride awaits him.

Conclusion

For ethnomusicologists today, the significance of Lachmann's programs lies not only in their unique musical and ethnographic content, but equally, in the methods and ideas they represent. The talks are uncompromising in their erudition, illustrating Lachmann's personal belief, in the early years of broadcasting, that the new medium had a serious educational role to play. Written in fluent, albeit idiosyncratic English, in an engaging, informal style, the twelve lectures present, in a relatively accessible format, ways of studying and thinking about music normally confined to the (mostly German) scholarly literature. Altogether, the programs illuminate the methods and scope of Lachmann's Palestine project as a whole.

Steeped in the intellectual and ideological traditions of the Berlin school of comparative musicology, certain of Lachmann's preoccupations are clearly products of their time. Others, however, are startlingly contemporary in their outlook and significance. His assumption that present-day practices provide direct evidence of the remote past; his mission to discover the common roots of Jewish and Christian chant and ultimately, to establish a chronology of all the Eastern chant traditions; his preference for pure, "unadulterated" traditions and his tendency to view Western influences as decadent and destructive, clearly rank among the former. In contrast, his discussions of musical ethnicity and identity and of contrasting social attitudes towards music and musicians, and his recognition that certain types of music can only be properly understood in relation to their social function and context, are no less topical today.

The talks themselves are studded with wide-ranging, crosscultural comparisons, transcending geographical and historical boundaries. Thus in program 6, the liturgical cantillation of the Samaritans is discussed with reference to the Japanese *No* drama; in program 4, the liturgical cantillation of Eastern Jewish communities is related to the healing practices of an American Indian tribe; and in program 5, the singing of the Bedouin Arab accompanying himself on the rababa is compared with contemporary practices in the Balkans; while these in turn are held to shed light on the way both Anglo-Saxon and ancient Greek epic poetry were performed.

Lachmann's research in Palestine was preceded by that of the Lithuanian cantor Abraham Zvi Idelsohn, who recorded and transcribed a wide range of sacred and secular traditions performed by Jewish musicians and singers during his stay in Jerusalem between 1906 and 1921. The results of Idelsohn's project are published in his ten-volume monumental study *Hebraisch–orientalischer Melodienschatz* (1914–32). However, while Idelsohn's recordings concentrate on Jewish male singers and musicians, Lachmann insisted on collecting repertory from all the religious, ethnic and gender groups; thus his recordings of the Coptic liturgy, the wedding songs of the Yemenite women and the wedding and narrative songs of the Bedouin and village Arabs belong to the earliest documentation of these traditions.

As a compendium of methods and ideas by a seminal figure in the history of ethnomusicology, Lachmann's programs provide a window on the discipline both at the close of its formative phase in Europe and at its birth in Israel. Ultimately, through his recording, research and teaching, Lachmann established the study of non-Western music at the heart of musical scholarship in Israel; the principles that guided his research, based on comprehensive collection, transcription and analysis, were continued by his students and his Archive became the foundation and model for the research activities of the Jewish Music Research Centre and the National Sound Archive (Phonoteca) of the Hebrew University of Jerusalem.

Notes

1. My edition is in preparation for A-R Editions in the series Recent Researches in the Oral Traditions of Music.

2. I am grateful to Dr. Gila Flam, director of the Music Department of the National and University Library, Hebrew University of Jerusalem, for making these writings available to me. Since carrying out my original research, some of these writings have been published in Katz 2003. See note 6, below.

3. The Hebrew University of Jerusalem was officially inaugurated in 1925.

4. Lachmann had deposited his masters with the Berlin Phonogram Archive. Founded in 1900, this Archive had developed a unique technology for copying recordings: from 1906, all incoming music recordings were galvanized to produce copper negatives of the original wax cylinders. Since the negatives, called galvanos, were considered a superior medium for preserving musical information, these were normally kept by the Archive and the wax copies were returned to the collector. The galvanos themselves were never played; rather, they served as matrices for further copying as the cylinders would normally have to be replaced after about ten playings (Ziegler 1994). In Jerusalem, Lachmann copied his entire cylinder collection onto metal disc by means of a special "pick up" designed by Walter Schur.

5. No more than two years of this period were actually spent in Palestine. Since his income was insufficient to support his work and living expenses in Palestine continuously, Lachmann established an annual pattern of spending the summer months in Europe (Berlin and London) supported by a pension from his former employment in Berlin. Terminal illness prevented him from resuming work on his return to Jerusalem in the autumn of 1938.

6. Unless otherwise indicated, my quotations from Lachmann are taken from his unpublished correspondence held in the Music Department of the National and University Library. See note 2, above.

7. This work is summarized in Gerson-Kiwi 1974.

8. Selected manuscripts by Lachmann, edited by Gerson-Kiwi (Lachmann 1974, 1978) and Katz (2003) have been published posthumously by the Magnes Press of the Hebrew University, in the Yuval Monograph Series.

9. Acronym for Computer Enhanced Digital Audio Restoration. I am grateful to Dr. Gila Flam and Mr. Avi Nahmius, sound engineer at the Phonoteca, for providing me with digital copies of the forty musical examples used in *Oriental Music* and to Dr. Simon Godsill of the Department of Engineering, University of Cambridge, for carrying out the sound restoration.

10. The objection to borrowing from Western music stemmed from a fundamental belief, shared by the comparative musicologists, that music embodies "the spirit of a nation" and as such, can change "only when such change emanates from the depths of the very source of that music" (KMA'A 1933: 439; cited in Racy 1992: 80).

Bibliography

Gerson-Kiwi, Edith. "Robert Lachmann: His Achievement and his Legacy," *Yuval* 3 (1974): 100–8.

Hirshberg, Jehoash. *Music in the Jewish Community of Palestine, 1880–1948: A Social History.* Oxford: Oxford University Press, 1996.

Idelsohn, A. Z. *Hebraisch-Orientalischer Melodienschatz* 1–10 (Leipzig: Breitkopt and Hartel, 1914–32)

Lachmann, Robert. *Zwei Aufsatze: Die Musik im Volksleben Nordafrikas. Orientalische Musik und Antike*, Yuval Monograph Series, edited by Edith Gerson-Kiwi, no. 2. Jerusalem: Magnes Press, 1974.

————. *Gesange der Juden auf der Insel Djerba*, Yuval Monograph Series, edited by Edith Gerson-Kiwi, no. 7. Jerusalem: Magnes Press, 1978.

Katz, Ruth. *The Lachmann Problem: An Unsung Chapter in Comparative Musicology.* Yuval Monograph Series 12. Jerusalem: The Magnes Press, 2003.

KMA'A. *Kitab al-mu'tamar al-musiqa al-'arabiyya* (Book of the Arab Music Conference). Cairo: al-matba'a al-amiriyya, 1933.

Racy, Ali Jihad. "Historical Views of Early Ethnomusicologists: An East–West Encounter in Cairo, 1932." 68–91 in *Ethnomusicology and Modern Music History*, edited by Stephen Blum, Philip V. Bohlman and Daniel M. Neuman. Urbana: University of Illinois Press, 1992.

Ziegler, Susanne. "The Collection of Wax Cylinders (former Berlin Phonogram Archive)." Paper read at the IASA conference. Bogensee, 1994.

Chapter Five

Outside-In: Music, New Media and Tradition in North Africa

Tony Langlois

Introduction

This chapter will consider the ways in which contemporary media and musics in particular, are used in everyday life in Morocco and Algeria. It will examine the tensions existing between the cultural associations, or content, these media bear and traditional conceptions of home and community. I will do this firstly by describing, in broad terms, what these traditional values are, then by considering the nature of the music and the other media that are enjoyed in the home. I will then look at the consequences and negotiations that ensue when these interact in context.

Before embarking on this discussion, however, I freely acknowledge that such generalized descriptions of social discourses cannot account for the multitude of ways in which these will be expressed in practice. Certain cities, quarters, streets or even families will be more "liberal" or "conservative" than others, just as differences between life in a small Berber village and a major Mediterranean city will be vast. Nation-states themselves shape dominant moral and political values, alongside one's age, gender, class and ethnicity. And without intending to expand the possible manifestations of these principles infinitely, the concept of "North Africa" can itself be reasonably stretched to include émigré communities around the world, who share a great deal of the language, music, values and social codes with the Maghreb.[1] As Marranci discusses just such developments in a later chapter in this volume, however, I will not pursue this digression further.

Morality and Urban Space

In order to appreciate the impact of media consumption practices upon
contemporary life it will first be useful to describe the concept of
houma—a notional community or neighborhood and the obligations
this concept imposes.

In almost any town or city in North Africa you may find that people have a strong sense of the neighborhood in which they live. Cities
built along traditional architectural lines, such as Fez or Seffrou in Morocco (see Geertz 1968 and Rosen 1978), are often composed of distinct quarters, with at least one neighborhood mosque, a communal
bakery and hammam, the public steam bath. Bakery and hammam are
often found together, as the same furnace that bakes each family's
homemade bread may well heat the steam for bathing. Many quarters
have their own well, possibly a saintly shrine and access to local markets where essential foodstuffs can be bought. In addition, regular migration patterns from rural villages to major cities have, over time, developed quarters with common ethnic backgrounds, certain specialized
trades and extended familial links. As Morocco alone boasts several
very different regional languages in addition to the official Arabic the
potential cultural diversity of a large city is great. So, for example, it is
common to find one family split between village and metropolis, with
brothers trading and migrating back and forth along the same route; a
pattern described well by Waterbury (1972) in his book *North for the
Trade*.

Even in outwardly "modern" cities like Oran in Algeria, where
French colonizers imposed an entirely Western urban structure, one
finds very similar migratory patterns based upon familial and economic
links to the hinterland and beyond. This phenomenon contributes to the
generation of largely self-supporting neighborhoods that are ethnically
distinguishable. So here we have a very pragmatic basis to a strong
collective feeling—and as close business relationships tend to be limited to the immediate community, each quarter is to some extent in
competition with its neighbors.

Another driver for this strong awareness of houma is the principle
of female sequestration. Although the practice is often much more relaxed than the ideal, the basic premise is that young women make the
best matches in marriage when they are believed to be chaste. Before
an engagement is arranged, investigations as to the moral character of
the intended bride are made throughout the quarter—and particularly at
the women's sessions in the hammam.[2] As serious suggestions of im-

morality, or perhaps rather, of indiscretion, could embarrass both families, it is considered important that between their teen years and wedding that girls observe certain norms. These include: not being seen out
after dark, especially alone or with a strange man and not spending
more time than necessary outside unless accompanied by female relatives. In theory, the "ideal" female habitus is framed in time and space
by moral boundaries, though the actual practice can be quite variable.

The role of the men in this arrangement is to occupy the public
space of the quarter, either as they work in it, sitting in cafés or simply
socializing on street corners. Young boys are introduced to this role
early in life by being sent for water, to the bakery or the local hanout
(corner shop), whilst girls tend to help their mothers inside the home.
Because all the families in a quarter know each other, any unusual activity or visitors will be obvious and appropriate action taken. So communities tend to be self-policing as well as economically independent
and here too there is potential for antagonism between adjoining
neighborhoods. In the course of my research in Oran (Algeria) and Oujda (Morocco) I asked people to draw maps of the quarters in town and
describe the kind of people who lived in each. Almost invariably men
considered adjoining quarters to be hostile to various degrees, especially after dark and associated each with particular ethnic groups.
Women seemed less conscious of these distinctions, but as many had
come into the quarter from the neighborhood of their parents, they
knew particular parts of the city much better than others. To women,
everywhere outside the home was potentially dangerous, particularly at
night, when they would feel highly conspicuous.[3]

Self-help is important in North African societies, where governments have neither the resources nor the infrastructure to provide social
welfare and manage only the most essential health care. Both Algerian
and Moroccan states subsidize the price of staples like flour and pow-
dered milk, but many areas still experience deficiencies in electricity
and even water supply. Consequently, I have seen whole apartment
blocks in Oran mobilized with buckets and hoses to bring water from
one functioning standpipe to all its residents. Likewise it has been
common for such blocks to share access to satellite television dishes,
spreading the cost of the equipment and deciding democratically which
stations they wish to access. (See also Hadj-Moussa 2003, for a description of such arrangements.)

So for very pragmatic reasons North African communities have a
strong local sense of identity, of self-regulation and interdependence
and these cultural values appear to be important, if not always strictly
maintained, by émigré Maghrebis around the world. Conceptually then,

the home is considered a feminine space (as discussed, amongst others, by both Bouchara-Zannad and Virolle 1989). According to traditional design, both rural and urban houses are built around courtyards, providing shade in the summer months and space for family gatherings, but which also afford privacy and security within the home. Narrow alleys between houses allow and control, access in the older cities and though newer developments provide roads for vehicles, much the same principles are applied to domestic architecture. Small barred windows face public space, whilst the inside is often open, leafy and colorful.[4] By this same binary logic, public space within a quarter tends to be a male domain of negotiation, association and commerce—a protective barrier around the home. Beyond the quarter and beyond the houma, are areas of danger, immorality and adventure.

Music

Music has had an interesting role in both marking and transgressing the boundaries of this moral universe, not least because in many Islamic societies music itself has strong moral connotations.[5] Because the limits of male and female space are so sharply defined, certain musics can be found in North Africa that are almost uniquely associated with women, their domestic contexts and with the "folk" forms of religious practice they are more likely than men to be involved with.[6] Female musicians, some semi-professional, play b'nader (plural of bender—a large-frame drum strung with gut snares) and sing songs to accompany visits to local shrines, pre-wedding parties and other life-cycle events. Some of these medahatte performances (particularly those taking place before weddings) reputedly include sexually suggestive songs and dances, though the repertoire also contains love songs and others drawn from popular maraboutic Islam.[7]

Music associated primarily with men can also fall into the categories of sacred or profane. Sufi musical practices are tolerated by orthodox Islam, in fact the two overlap and in some important areas, but rarely do they receive official approval. Through a variety of ascetic disciplines, often involving music and lengthy ritual, men seek psychic unity with Allah. Although the techniques of each sufi brotherhood are distinct, each following the example of their founding shaykh, they differ in important ways from women's ecstatic practices, with which, in keeping with other social practices, they never mix.

Perhaps precisely because of the tension existing between male and female cultural domains, the nightclubs, bars and "hotels," where these barriers are relaxed, constitute a moral space at the opposite end of the spectrum from sufi practices. Correspondingly, these clubs tend to be situated outside residential areas—in the basements of hotels on the edge of town or, as in Oran, in small resorts some way along the coast from the city. Raï music is typical of this niche in Algeria and eastern Morocco, but various forms of cha'abi fill an identical role elsewhere in the region.[8] Until the 1990s raï songs sometimes contained fairly explicit references to alcohol, hashish and sex and though these themes are now rare, the performance context itself continues to evoke these connotations. Men who can afford to are free to visit nightclubs, where they can drink, dance and meet women beyond the surveillance of their own neighborhood and without trespassing in anyone else's houma. No woman caring for her reputation would be seen anywhere near these clubs, as they are associated with prostitution.

So in principle there is a clear distinction, at times a conflict, between moral conceptions of the home and the outside world and this maintains community boundaries, the privileged status of older men and networks of control within it. Interestingly, the one context in which these moral domains are allowed to merge is during weddings, when raï and cha'abi musicians are brought into the heart of the community to enable dancing and celebration. Naturally the texts of the songs are almost entirely innocuous in these circumstances, but the very fact of this notorious music being performed within the houma contributes to the excitement of the event. Very often the bride will come from outside the immediate neighborhood and traditionally she is brought to the groom's household in procession. In some cases this takes place on foot, accompanied by musicians, but more often this procession involves lines of noisy, decorated cars, with a percussion band playing in the back of a pickup.[9]

In effect this exuberant display of change of status involves an inversion of the moral gravity that normally applies to the houma. It dramatically marks a transition in the lives of the couple, establishing publicly the new rights and responsibilities that are to prevail from then on. It does so in part by invoking the dangerous and sexualized domain that is normally kept well outside the community, bringing the "outside" in and rendering the forbidden visible. Naturally it does so in a highly controlled form. For fear of unruly behavior, young people from different neighborhoods are rarely left unsupervised by responsible adults, public drinking is not permitted and songs never become too risqué.

Nevertheless dancing does usually carry on till the early hours of the morning and for a short time many normative boundaries are let down.

This catalytic role of music and musicians is far from unique to this situation. The rwaïs musicians of the Atlas mountains perform a very similar symbolic role (see Schuyler 1985) as do the Roma wedding musicians of the Balkans (Buchanan 1996). In each of these cases it is not simply a matter of needing music to dance to, as a recording could provide this. And as many dance musics are without words, or at least without words that are in themselves very meaningful, I would argue that it is not the explicit content so much as the music's associations which excite the imagination of the audience. Although such contexts are inevitably unique and complex, I suggest that it is often the physical presence of morally suspect "outsiders" themselves, in the center of the most tender space in the community, that stimulates such an affective response. It is this pinch of "profanity" that allows this stylized brush with chaos and pretty soon, in keeping with familiar descriptions of communitas, the reestablishment of familiar social structures.[10]

Boundaries and Modern Media

So far I have sought to demonstrate a principle by presenting a simplified model of the relations existing between urban spaces, music and moral concepts. Although I am satisfied that such a notional model still exerts influence upon North African social practices, contemporary lifestyles present challenges to the operation of this principle. Electronic media in particular allow recorded or broadcast material to be accessed in increasingly unpredictable and uncontrollable contexts. In some respects this has brought about a transgression of moral boundaries—not only within the community but also at a transcultural level. This section of the chapter will outline developments in electronic media in Algeria and Morocco and it will be followed by a discussion of the consequences of these changes.

Radio and television have been popular sources of information and entertainment in North Africa since they were made available. Gramophone recordings of music, whether indigenous, from the eastern Arab world or Europe, have been a part of everyday life since early in the last century. Up until fairly recently, however, these media were easily controlled by governments and/or international record companies. Given that vinyl record production requires expensive pressing factories, and TV and radio broadcasts an even heavier investment, it is clear that powerful institutions would have the biggest influence on their output. In the 1960s the newly independent countries of North Africa employed these resources to develop a new sense of national identity that coherently marked a departure from the culture of preceding colonial regimes.

This nation-building imperative, combined with a centralized technological infrastructure guarenteed that many of the diverse musics that existed in North Africa went unrecorded. At the time they were considered unsophisticated, too coarse, or they were only thought to appeal to a minority regional market in a period where cultural unity was privileged. The favored indigenous recordings through the 1960s and early '70s were chosen to reflect positive aspects of national cultures; for example, the "classical" Andalus schools or the related Moroccan melhoun and Algerian hawzi traditions.[11]

In this postcolonial context, it is understandable that these genres, which are clearly non-European but nevertheless with the aura of a distant "golden age," should have been given elevated status. Andalus was promoted in schools, urban conservatories and broadcast on state television and radio broadcasts, particularly at times (such as the anniversary of the king of Morocco's coronation) when a sense of national solidarity is invoked. Such top-down efforts to influence taste are, however, seldom completely effective and on the whole it has been the educated middleclasses who have identified most with Andalus. In the 1960s, Algeria's generally ill-fated adaptation of Eastern-bloc socialism only rendered the cultural diet more monotonous and of course people did not adopt these musics en masse but listened instead to live local musics, to Jacques Brel and the Beatles.

Between independence and the 1980s many social and political changes had taken place in North Africa. Enthusiasms for socialism, pan-Arabism and pan-Africanism had dimmed with the experience of economic realities and ineffective management. The single-party states that dominated Tunisia and Algeria were facing widespread criticism, and attempts had even been made on the life of the king of Morocco. Significantly, the migration route to Europe was rapidly closing, leaving expanding young populations with nowhere outside their countries to improve their circumstances.

In the late 1970s, in the midst of this growing political pressure, cassette production technology arrived in North African cities. Equipment was cheap and small and although sound quality was poor, it became possible to record a song one week and buy it on street corners the next, without any government control whatsoever. Very soon, raï music from the nightclubs of Oran and Oujda, replete with local slang, current in-jokes, suggestive imagery and bearing immoral associations, was on the streets, in cars and, very soon, in homes. This posed a challenge not only to the authority of the Algerian state but to the innocence of domestic space and for some time was a matter of considerable public concern (see Daoudi and Milliani 1996). To those who promoted high moral "national culture," raï was the worst of all combinations. Its vernacular was highly local yet modernized with foreign electric instruments. Based upon a very low form of entertainment to begin with, many songs were derived from women's "folk" Islam, whilst others referred to sex, drink and hopelessness. Even worse, these were performed in derija, a colloquial form of Arabic spattered with foreign and Berber words, a language which is considered far from the ideal fs'ha or classical forms. As Frank Tenaille (2002) suggests, this was a bastardized form of music, devoid of the heritage and refined, poetic expression of Andalus.

After initial and ineffective attempts to ban the music, the Algerian government eventually allowed a much tamer version of raï to be broadcast on state television and radio.[12] This was partly because legitimizing the music meant it could be taxed and also because the government was by then under pressure from Islamic reform movements and hoped to present a more liberal face to the country's disaffected youth. Domestically, raï had a similar impact, as family patriarchs attempted, often in vain, to ban cassettes from the house. Algerian men I knew were sometimes embarrassed when I noted the raï cassettes they held in their collection. Though many admitted to enjoying some of the music, they would not dream of listening to it in the presence of their elders or sisters. Girls often had to listen to cassettes secretly then, and even after the songs gradually became more acceptably sentimentale in the 1990s, the genre's dubious associations remained. Eventually the more outspoken singers left the country to work abroad and domestic raï focused on increasingly romantic themes, though still with a fatalistic, despondent tone. Despite these changes, young women in particular were discouraged from listening *openly* to certain songs and always turned the music off when older men entered the house. If the man was their father or an elder brother they may have been reprimanded; if it were a stranger, association with the music may well have formed a bad impression of her character, something which unmarried women avoided at all costs. During this decade, the growth of militant Islamic movements in Algeria rendered raï even more controversial and the "toning down" of the songs may have well been a response to this new situation.[13]

Though consumption practices continue to be shaped by domestic norms, more recent technological developments have further deregulated *access* to musics of all kinds. Many "record shops" now use the Internet and computer hardware to download music and "burn" compact discs for their customers. On a recent visit to a shop in Morocco, the proprietor could provide me with a CD containing a personalized mixture of local musical genres, all selected from a vast playlist on his computer. Every kind of music from North Africa, including those in minority Berber languages, were available, so reflecting and accommodating the ethnic mix of the region. Although, I was told, he could also provide Western musics on request, this would take longer as he had to download the album from the web. The demand for Western pop music was so small that very little was kept in stock, even on the computer's hard drive. Given the scale of the unofficial economy in both Algeria and Morocco it is not in the least surprising that such "piracy" abounds, though it will be interesting to see how this affects the local music business. As even with cassette technology, musicians' work was routinely copied without payment, it is possible that they consider wide exposure more beneficial to their performing careers than royalties.

La Parabole: An International Context

Since the 1990s, widespread access to satellite television (la parabole) has had an enormous influence upon the consumption of all kinds of information, including music. However, because the overwhelming preference remains for indigenous genres and Arabic language pop songs, the most significant impacts of this development have been in the areas of current affairs and entertainment programming.[14] As these clearly have a bearing upon the construction of a moral of community, I will briefly outline them here.

In order to understand the importance of global media in the area of current affairs, one should know that in North African countries it is never wise and not always possible, to openly criticize the government. In principle Algeria enjoys freedom of speech, but many journalists and editors have been intimidated or killed during the last decade of political strife and it is seldom clear which political factions have been responsible. Only fairly recently has Morocco adopted a more relaxed media policy, though many topics still remain taboo. Despite growing political cynicism, television news tended to reflect government perspectives until at least the 1990s. With the advent of satellite broadcasts, North Africans were suddenly able to access alternative versions of news about their own country, about Middle Eastern issues and "The West." Although these perspectives were not necessarily more credible than domestic news, viewers became sophisticated readers of the media, comparing reports from gulf Arabic and French stations to their own national networks.[15]

Unlike other Islamic countries it was never feasible for governments to ban reception of these broadcasts. The black economies in both Algeria and Morocco are so pervasive that attempts to regulate the medium would be hopeless—and early attempts to do so, as in Fes in 1991, contributed to outbreaks of serious rioting. Instead, both governments attempted to turn the matter to their advantage, presenting a liberal government face whilst imposing a duty on reception equipment. Public interest in international affairs (such as the intifada or the gulf wars) also served to attract attention away from contentious issues closer to home. I have come across the view several times in both Algeria and Morocco that their respective government was irresponsible in allowing access to satellite broadcasting; it was reckless to put such temptation in people's way. Interestingly, such commentators tended to justify their views by expressing concern for the morality of women and children at home, regardless of the material they watched themselves. By opting for a liberal approach, governments placed responsibility for regulation directly upon the consumers, that is, the family and thus gained revenue in sales tax without being liable for the content. In fact, most subscription channels are "cracked," that is, the code that enables access is used illegally, so the use of immoral material is clearly deliberate and unapproved by the authorities.

Broadly speaking I have found that men and women tend to watch different kinds of television, especially during early evenings, when most women are at home but men socialize elsewhere. At cafés, which are primarily a male domain in North Africa, satellite televisions are ubiquitous and likely to be showing current affairs or sports channels. The women of a household seem to prefer soap operas and films.[16] National news programs, however, tend to be fairly popular with everyone and viewers will switch from other formats to the local service for hourly or evening bulletins.

VCDs

An area of considerable recent growth in the areas of media consumption is that of video compact discs, or VCDs. These discs contain visual material, such as films or music videos, using the most basic technology available.[17] Compared to DVDs these discs tend to be of poor visual quality, with none of the supplementary "features" and viewing options available on this medium. They are nevertheless very simple to produce and can be played on a range of different formats, from computers to cheap VCD players. In 2004 these discs cost fourteen Moroccan Dhirham (the equivalent of £1 sterling). The visual material contained on VCDs includes the latest Hollywood films, kung fu movies from Hong Kong and Indian Bollywood productions. Such a large proportion of these discs, however, feature performances by local musicians. Some have been copied directly from national or satellite television, though many appear to have been produced by the musicians themselves as a musical/visual product in their own right. Though the production quality of VCDs is variable, a wide range of musical styles can be found on sale at market stalls, making diverse regional genres available to both rural and urban audiences. Most music VCDs are considered to be acceptable for family viewing, but as they are largely watched inside the home are, in practice, more likely to be used by women than by men.

Some of the more remarkable discs, from the ethnographic point of view, feature 'ripped' visuals from popular films and music videos, to which Moroccan popular songs have been overdubbed. One example shows Michael Jackson and the characters from *Shrek* dancing in time to *cha'abi* songs; others employ dance routines from Indian films or Disney's *The Jungle Book*. From the lively response these performances receive when played at street kiosks, the ironic juxtaposition of music and visuals is clearly found to be amusing. The objectives here may be simple entertainment rather than political satire, but nevertheless this illustrates both the creative use of affordable digital technologies and a decidedly local response to global media. Just as 1970s raï employed cheap cassette technology to combine traditional and international musical styles, so contemporary "pirates" are cutting and mixing digital material in ways which are both imaginative and unpredictable.

Consequences and Negotiations

As I have suggested already, North Africans have become sophisticated users and readers of the media over the last twenty years. Unlike typical consumption patterns in Europe, North African paraboles are regularly turned to foreign language satellites and so in many respects may access a wider range of cultural perspectives than the average Western viewer. As women's literacy rates are not high, especially in rural areas, one might have expected that this new access to all kinds of information might have brought about significant changes in social attitudes. In fact its impact has been more subtle, partly because patterns of media consumption are themselves influenced by gendered tastes and the notion of the houma.

To take an example, the Al Jazeera Arabic language news service is very popular in cafes and its very graphic, daily coverage of conflicts in Israel and Baghdad inevitably present these as cultural "front lines" with "the West" in a general sense and with America in particular. However, even where families have their own satellite television access, Al Jazeera seems to be less popular in the home, possibly because its content is not considered suitable for the domestic environment. So the tendency for men to watch sports and current affairs programs with their friends in a public space is consistent with other discourses relating to masculinity and the "wider world." At home women prefer to watch films, VCDs and Egyptian dramatic serials, frequently relating to more emotional, psychological and interpersonal relationships. So just as there remains a conceptual distinction between male/public and female/domestic space, so tastes also tend to reflect gender-based preferences.[18]

Given my original proposal that the houma is conceptually a space of moral virtue, how is it that the introduction of thoroughly worldly material, both visual and musical, has not brought about a crisis of core discourses?

Firstly I would suggest that these notional structures are still so central to social life that they are maintained by a certain degree of mutual sleight of hand. So long as women remain physically in the home environment, especially at night and perform the domestic roles required of them, then men turn a blind eye to what they watch or listen to. In order to make this possible, women often change the station or CD when men return home at night. Perhaps new pressures have been placed upon normative structures of morality and gender, but this does not change the fact that most women remain largely dependent upon their husbands and fathers, not only for resources, but for a social identity in the community. A man's own good standing in the houma depends in turn upon a successful performance of maintaining appropriate boundaries. So long as indiscretions are not visible this status is not threatened. The outside "immoral" world can be *viewed* from the security of the home, but it is not in the interests of men or women to allow this to challenge the status quo.

Secondly, to both male and female audiences, the "outside world" remains a distant place which is viewed through a highly local prism. A minority of individuals have firsthand experience of Europe, the United States or even other Muslim countries, so foreign soap operas and Al Jazeera alike create exotic worlds of drama, sexuality and violence that are more mythical than real.[19] Whatever the rhetoric about the influence of media upon morality, all parties understand that there is a huge difference between a recording of a raï singer and his physical presence. To take another musical example, in the appropriate context, a maraboutic musician may cause fainting fits amongst his female listeners— this simply does not happen with recordings of the same music. Likewise, although men in North African cafés enjoy discussing international politics and the (usually inferior) cultural attitudes of others, these remain largely theoretical debates. Viewers may become incensed about the Gulf War or the Gaza Strip but very rarely encounter material that criticizes their own governments, either on local or international channels. As perceived though the local optic, "the West" constitutes at best an amoral "other," and this is demonstrated by its own media to be manifestly materialistic, murderous and sex-obsessed. It is also a world with which North Africans have little close engagement. On the other hand, debate within the domestic public sphere is limited, suggesting perhaps that, as with the domestic status quo, a close inspection might threaten the credibility of value systems that are too cherished to put at risk.

Whilst local media do not broach thornier issues (which become instead the subject of extensive rumors), they are nonetheless enabling much greater awareness of the ethnic variation existing *within* North African countries. Nation-building involves the consolidation and promotion of core cultural elements and, in Algeria, this has meant subsuming regional ethnic differences into a single national identity. As serious friction with Berbers from the Kabyle region has demonstrated, this process of homogenization has not been without its critics. Throughout the region, access to cheap recording technologies has enabled minority cultural perspectives to be expressed in music and regional languages despite government programs of "Arabization." At the time of this writing, both Moroccan and Algerian governments appear to have made concessions to these interests, allowing broadcasts of regional musics on national radio and television and most importantly, the local use of Berber languages in state education. Each Saturday evening Moroccans watch musical performances from different parts of the country, performed in languages and styles which often sound more exotic than Western music. This fairly recent acknowledgement and acceptance of internal cultural diversity is a departure from previous attitudes and through broadcast media will inevitably influence the ways in which citizens formulate notions of the state and their relationships with "others," both inside *and* out.

Notes

1. It can be argued that the concept of houma has different significance between generations; that it represents parental values which are not shared by young people today. I would suggest that such changes are in no small part due to the transgressive influence of modern media, but that contemporary attitudes are formed in relation to inherited moral values. I am grateful for conversations with Becky Schulthies, of the University of Arizona, which have contributed to my understanding of this and related issues.

2. A subject described by Susan Schaeffer-Davis in her book, *Patience and Power* (1983).

3. Such moral boundaries are not merely sustained through a culture of surveillance but are also supported by commonly held supernatural beliefs including the "evil eye" (el aïn) of strangers and possession by spirits (djinn), both of which are considered more likely when alone in unfamiliar or public spaces. Thus complementary institutions control the social use of time as well as space.

4. Gilsenan's (1990) discussion of the structure and use of domestic architecture in Lebanon bears useful comparison with North African arrangements. Bourdieu's early work on Algeria (1977) considers the change in habitus brought about by the introduction of Western industrial practices to primarily agrarian, kin-oriented North African society.

5. See Rouget (1985) and Al Faruqi (1985) for elaboration on the theme of music's inherent morality. Rouget argues that it is as much the way of listening as the music itself which renders it sacred or profane. Al Faruqi summarizes the legal distinctions made between music that encourage virtue or sensuality.

6. Langlois (1999) discusses the religio-musical practices of Moroccan women. Maraboutic Islam privileges the role of saintly lineages. Charismatic individuals claim descent and often supernatural powers, from an ancestral holy personage, whose shrine they often maintain. For female adherents, practice typically entails offering gifts at shrines

for intercession and ecstatic rituals. See also Gellner's (1969) *The Saints of the Atlas*.

7. The songs of Umm Kulthum and other classic sharqi (Eastern) singers are also highly esteemed, but these are difficult for amateurs to sing and are most popular as recordings.

8. Raï music is most associated with Oran, where it developed from a rural wedding genre, to an entertainment in the bars of Colonial Algeria, to an eclectic "world music" within a few decades. Cha'abi is a generic term for indigenous popular musics throughout North Africa. Moroccan cha'abi is musically distinctive and is the mainstay of both urban nightclubs and radio broadcasts. Amongst several excellent books on raï, its songs, history and original social setting, I would recommend, Virolle-Souibes (1995), Schade-Poulson (1999), Tenaille (2002) and Daoudi and Milliani (1996). For a discussion of raï's negotiation of global and local influences see Langlois (1996).

9. Different musics may be employed for particular aspects of a wedding. Whist raï or cha'abi remain the preference for dance parties, acoustic percussion ensembles, occasionally accompanied by trumpet or ghraita (oboe) and sometimes in the style of maraboutic g'nawa troupes, are common for processional aspects of the event.

10. See Victor Turner (1969) for his classic anthropological understanding of the dynamics of social structure.

11. The Andalus tradition, supposedly derived from the courts of the Islamic Spanish caliphate, had a complex history, including use in both Sufi and "nightclub" contexts, before being appropriated as a privileged genre by independence movements in Algeria and Morocco. With political autonomy Andalus schools (of which there are four distinct traditions) filled the niche previously occupied by Western classical musics and in some cases European techniques for learning and performance were also applied to the genre. See Ruth Davis (1997) for a study of such developments in Tunisian ma'luf (the local form of Andalus). For more detailed description of these genres, refer to Guettat (1980) and Poche (1995).

12. It proved impossible to ban raï for three reasons. Firstly it was very popular locally and production knitted well with the already highly developed black market in Algeria. Secondly, the music was also produced and broadcast a few miles across the border in Morocco, where it wasn't perceived as a threat to their national identity. Thirdly, the recordings were quickly picked up by expatriate North African communities in Europe and America, finally reaching the mainstream "world music" market. For a useful comparison with the impact of re-

cording technology on India, see Peter Manuel's *Cassette Culture* (1993).

13. Many raï singers were intimidated and several key figures in the scene assassinated, but the music industry in Oran, like the black economy generally, managed to adapt to and survive the political turmoil afflicting the nation.

14. Music-video channels are very popular domestic viewing, though the bulk of the Arabic language programming comes from Egypt. The production quality of this visual material is high and videos often take a narrative form, adding a story line to the theme of the song. Few locally produced music videos are as sophisticated and they never appear on Egyptian channels, yet if radio play is an indication of national preferences, they are much more popular. MTV, which in the early 1990s attracted considerable attention in cafes, seems to be much less popular than Levantine satellite channels, though it is hard to know if this is because of its visual or musical content.

15. During the 1990s, Algerians often came across more informative news about their own country on French-language stations than on their national networks. This caused considerable discussion, as viewers were aggrieved by critical representations of Algeria, especially when originating from an ex-colonial power. At the same time, video and audio cassettes were also in circulation which promoted distinctly anti-Western and antigovernment sentiments. Faced with such contradictory information (supplemented by a lively rumor mill) many Algerians I knew at the time gave credence to very little they heard or saw.

16. Hannah Davis (1989) provides a valuable description of Moroccan women's local interpretation of global television programs and the role of Egyptian TV dramas in structuring domestic narratives is considered by both Abu-Lughod (2002) and Armbrust (1996).

17. VCDs are simply compact discs which use MPEG 1 compression to store up to eighty minutes of visual and audio information. The quality of a good VCD is comparable to that of a VHS, but most are slightly more blurred, especially when already copied from a television broadcast. Sound quality, however, is good and as output can be directed to domestic stereo equipment, this medium has become a popular means of consuming music within the home.

18. These programs are shown around 1pm, when families are often resting following their midday meal and in the early evening, when men are most likely to be outside the home. Abu-Lughod (2002) and Armbrust (1996) both discuss the impact of these series upon domestic discourse in Egypt itself. In Morocco and Algeria these moral tales, told in perhaps twenty daily episodes, are extremely popular and are

broadcast on national (terrestrial) stations. Other significant imports include soap operas from South America and Spain, though these are not shown at peak viewing times. The suggestive content of some Mexican soaps in 2003 raised public concerns about moral values, but although it is certainly possible to regulate domestic transmissions, the range of different media currently available have made banning almost impossible at the national level.

19. Hannah Davis (1989) elegantly describes ways in which Moroccan women "read" Western soap operas in terms of local beliefs and values. I have found that Western presentations of romantic love are popular amongst North Africans. Movement away from extended family control is attractive and supports desire to marry maghrebis who are European passport holders.

Bibliography

Abu-Lughod, Lila. "Egyptian Melodrama: Technology of the Modern Subject?" 115–33 in *Media Worlds*, edited by Ginsburg, Abu-Lughod and Larkin. Berkeley: University of California Press, 2002.

Al Faruqi, I. "Music, Musicians and Muslim Law." *Asian Music* 17, no. 1 (1985): 3–36.

Armbrust, W. *Mass Culture and Modernism in Egypt.* Cambridge: Cambridge University Press, 1996.

Bouchara-Zannad, T. "Espaces humides feminins dans la ville. Le dar el Arbi et la hammam. Etude de cas: la Medina de Tunis." 233–40 in *Espaces Maghrebins: Pratiques et Enjeux*, edited by Nadir Marouf. Oran: Universite d'Oran, Editions ENAG, 1989

Bourdieu, P. *Algeria 1960.* Cambridge: Cambridge University Press, 1977.

Buchanan, Donna. "Wedding Musicians, Political Transition and National Consciousness in Bulgaria." 200–30 in *Retuning Culture*, edited by Slobin. London: Duke University Press, 1996

Daoudi, Bouziane and Hadj Milliani. *L'aventure du Raï.* Paris: Editions Seuil, 1996.

Davis, Hannah. "American Magic in a Moroccan Town." *Middle East Report* 19, no. 4 (1989): 12–17.

Davis, Ruth. "Cultural Policy and the Tunisian Ma'luf: Redefining a Tradition." *Ethnomusicology* 41, no. 1 (1997): 1–21.

Geertz, C. *Islam Observed: Religious Developments in Morocco and Indonesia.* New Haven: Yale University Press, 1968.

Gellner, E. *The Saints of the Atlas*. London: Wiedenfield and Nicholson, 1969.

Gilsenan, M. *Recognising Islam*. London: I. B. Tauri, 1990.

Guettat, M. *La Musique Classique du Maghreb*. Paris: Sindbad, 1980.

Hadj Moussa, Ratiba. "New Media and Politics in Algeria." *Media, Culture and Society* 25 (2003): 451–68.

Langlois, Tony. "The Local and the Global in North African Popular Music." *Popular Music* 15, no. 3 (1996): 259–74.

———. "Heard but Unseen: The Female A'issawa Musicians of Oujda, Morocco." *Music and Anthropology* 4 (1999), web journal www.muspe.unibo.it/period/MA/index/number4/langlois/lang0.htm.

Manuel, P. *Cassette Culture—Popular Music and Technology in Northern India*. Chicago: Chicago University Press, 1993.

Poche, C. *La Musique Arabo-Andalouse*. Paris: Cite de la Musique /Actes Sud, 1995.

Racy, A. J. "Arabian Music and the Effects of Commercial Recording." *World of Music* 78, no. 1: 47–58.

Rosen, L. "The Negotiation of Reality: Male–Female Relationships in Sefrou, Morocco." 561–85 in *Women in the Muslim World*, edited by Lois Beck and Nikki Keadie. Harvard: Harvard University Press, 1978

Rouget, G. *Music and Trance*. Chicago: Chicago University Press, 1985

Schade-Poulson, Marc. *Men and Popular Music in Algeria: The Social Significance of Raï*. Austin, Texas: University of Texas Press, 1999.

Schaeffer-Davis, S. *Patience and Power: Women's Lives in a Moroccan Village*. Cambridge: Schenkman, 1983.

Schuyler, P. "The Rwais and the Zawia: Professional Musicians and the Rural Religious Elite in Southwestern Morocco." *Asian Music* 17, no. 1 (1985): 114–31.

Tenaille, Frank. *Le Raï: De La Bartardise a la reconnaissance International*. Paris: Cite De La Musique/Actes Sud, 2002.

Turner, V. *The Ritual Process*. London: Pelican, 1969.

Virolle-Souibes, M. "Une Figure de la Limite: Le Seuil domestique." 241–54 in *Espaces Maghrebins, Pratiques et Enjeux*, edited by Nadir Marouf. Oran: Universite d'Oran, Editions ENAG, 1989.

———. *La Chanson Raï: De l'Algerie Profonde a la Scene Internationale*. Paris: Karthala, 1995.

Waterbury, J. *North for the Trade: The Life and Times of a Berber Merchant*. Berkeley: University of California Press, 1972.

Part 3
Men and Women

Chapter Six

Performance on a Mediterranean Theme: Musicians and Masculinity in Crete

Kevin Dawe

"Come outside," he said. "The *santuri* isn't at home between four walls. It's wild and needs open spaces." We went out. The stars sparkled. The Milky Way flowed from one side of the sky to the other. The sea was frothing. We sat down on the pebbles and the waves licked our feet. "When you're broke, you have a good time," said Zorba. "What, us give up? Come here, *santuri!*"

—Nikos Kazantzakis.[1]

Taximi[2]

In Kazantzakis's novel, Alexis Zorba traveled the Aegean and into the Balkans with his beloved santuri. Nowadays, Mediterranean musicians, especially the superstars of Mediterranean music, move well beyond Mediterranean shores to travel the world. Khaled, Amr Diab, George Dalaras, Paco de Lucía and many others are perhaps the new breed of Mediterranean musician, living at home and/or abroad and in their music drawing at once on very local sounds as well as those from well beyond the Mediterranean. The Mediterranean and its musicians come well within the reach of global media, international music industry and that mighty enabler of self-redefinition "world music." Notions of a "Mediterranean music" are clearly articulated by the "world music" industry (see Plastino 2003), even if musicians from the Mediterranean area do not always acknowledge similarities and influences in their work. However, groups like Radio Tarifa and Bustan Abraham or individual artists like Ross Daly and Luís Delgado continue to explore musics across the Mediterranean. Many locally based musicians regularly crisscross the Mediterranean on tour, in concert or on recording sessions, and there have been extensive collaborations between them.[3]

I have a series of basic questions to ask of all of these musicians. How have the many traveling Mediterranean musicians, like Cretan lyra players, who are entangled in very local Mediterranean musical worlds managed during a time of radical social and musical transformation in the region? With all the changes that have affected very different Mediterranean societies in an era of modernization and globalization, professionalization and pop charts, Internet and MTV, how do musicians negotiate what might now be seen as their "between worlds" existence? How do musicians make a living in a changing local musical world, hanging on to more traditional work patterns, long-established roles and systems of exchange, whilst responding to new opportunities offered by a well-established music business? Most of all, how have local and older notions of musicianship fared? How do we define the Mediterranean local musician in a globalizing soundscape? Most of all, how is he or she defined locally? Are long-held notions and models of musicianship now irrevocably lost? These questions are, of course, relevant to all musicians in the Mediterranean (as elsewhere). But these were some of the questions I began to ask of Greek musicians in the autumn of 1989 and those which I have tried to address since then working, in particular, with musicians on the Greek island of Crete.

Theme 1: The Musician and Society

> Even in social formations where, as in Kabylia, the making explicit and objectifying of the generative schemes in a grammar of practices, a written code of conduct, is minimal, it is nonetheless possible to observe the first signs of a differentiation of the domains of practice according to the degree of the codification of the principles governing them. (Bourdieu, 1977: 20)

Musicians' activities become embroiled in many different kinds of power relations that come into play between themselves and their patrons and audience; whether on the wedding circuit in Crete or on a tour of Greek-arts clubs in Australia. These arrangements depend on more than contractual obligations. Issues of class, gender, race, ethnicity, identity and "otherness" feed into notions and definitions of 'the musician' in the contexts in which he or she tries to make a living and shape how that living will be made. For the musician, even in today's globally mediated world, the intimate relation between musical structure and social structure can be empowering and "being a musician" is to take on a role that usually embodies a range of extramusical values, duties and obligations. Each culture has established roles for musicians to play and will value them accordingly. To a great extent, musicians' performances are a reaffirmation of these values in society and, accordingly, a re-creation and legitimization of their role. Most professional musicians I have met are devoted to their art; but whether gifted or not, survivors have one thing in common: the tenacity to keep on going against all odds. Technique is not everything but it helps; however, foresight, planning and the ability to make the right connections and moves are skills and talents that also have to be honed and developed as part of "the business" and as obligatory career moves. After all, a nightly club or hotel gig that supports the musician and his family might not be there forever as the size, tastes and demands of audiences change along with fluctuations in the local economy. The club or hotel management can also change overnight. The work might be seasonal.

I have found the problems of professional musicians to be particularly acute in island contexts, such as Crete.[4] Here competition is often far greater. Opportunities exist but within a smaller area and within a limited number of venues. Less able musicians may also try to muscle in (for example, playing for tourists). Well-established musicians fill the securer niches and the local musical economy is often controlled by a limited number of powerful musicians, producers, clients, patrons, families, or officials, residents and nonresidents (such as record-company executives based in cities far away). It can be difficult for young musicians to break into the local scene. The available niches provide precious sources of income, and they often depend on family and kinship ties and connections, systems of reciprocity, reputation and perhaps a one-hit record or television appearance. All of these aspects of a musician's background enable him or her to keep a foothold in a particular venue, where the proprietors, their clientele and the musician develop a symbiotic relationship. If musicians manage to break into the international market, there might also be the added and sometimes lucrative injection of capital back into the local community and the possibility of local celebrity status.

The values and standards of performance practice are often thrown into question as tourism and tour operators offer new and/or extra work and start to dictate the ways in which performances should be organized for the consumption of tourists and others (e.g., businessmen and women). Traditional repertoires are played alongside an international set and, in my experience of Greek-island "bouzouki nights" neither type of music seems to benefit. Amidst the plate smashing and the innuendo one hears an age-old melody that can reduce a local audience to tears, but here its meaning is irrevocably lost. Some musicians turn their back on "tourist music" and specialize in different sectors of the available market. Some of their activities overlap but nevertheless specialists develop within a niche market.

Veteran musicians in Crete have honed their musical and business skills, reworking local notions of value and exchange into an effective and upgraded modus operandi. This has enabled them to maintain a niche in the local musical economy and use it to move into national and international networks. Some of the virtuosi are well traveled. They have played for Greek and other audiences in the United States, Canada and/or Australia for many years. They are plugged into a network that gains them work in a remote mountain village one week and then, via a flight to Brisbane, work in the Cretan diaspora the next. This does not happen all the time but occasionally it does for the better-known or well-connected members of the musical community. Musicians in Crete are no strangers to making a living in an island context and exploiting their island connections to the fullest extent in a world market. In Crete and in places (as one local put it) "more Cretan than Crete" the Cretan musician epitomizes the island, its people and all they stand for.

Link 1: Lyra Music

In Crete, the lyra-laouto ensemble[5] retains its power and influence as emblematic of "the heartland" and "the body politic," as men's/shepherd's instruments and as the 'national' instruments of Crete. Music impacts on Cretan life largely through the apparatus of a local recording industry and a live-music circuit. For many musicians these offer a rare opportunity to make money from music, and there is never any shortage of young, willing and able musical entrepreneurs ready to participate. However, away from the club and tourist end of the market, it is the virtuosi who find a reasonably steady but never fully reliable niche locally through the recording and performance of lyra music. These were observations that I was able to confirm fairly quickly during my first months of fieldwork.

Theme 2: Performance and Masculinity

> There is less focus on "being a good man" than on "being good *at* being a man"—a stance that stresses *performative excellence*, the ability to foreground manhood by means of deeds that strikingly "speak for themselves." (Herzfeld, 1985: 16)

Given the multidimensional nature of any performance event and the usually crucial role of musicians at them, many of the social and musical ideas prevalent within a society may coalesce with and be traced within the resultant organization of musical materials, for example, in the musician's choice of themes, their phrasing and dynamics and the interpretation of repertoire by the performer in relation to the unique flow of events at each and every performance. The musician depends on his musical activities as "deeds that strikingly 'speak for themselves.'" But he also has to monitor their success and sometimes *make* his music speak. Schuyler (1984) documents the work of professional Berber musicians in Morocco by looking at the ways in which musical materials are organized as suitable to meet the demands of particular types of performance contexts, such as weddings. For Schuyler then, the ethnography of performance provides a promising "meeting ground" for approaches that tend to study the "cultural system" and the "music itself" (Schuyler 1984: 91; but see also Herndon and McCleod 1980; Behague 1984; Sugarman 1987).

Musicianship can be seen as a set of musical and social practices constructed in response to the needs of particular societies, a means of getting the job done but also being sensitive to the aesthetics of the community. "Musicianship" might therefore be seen as a state of being based on regulated improvisations, where individuals are alert to the demands of the particular social circumstances in which they find themselves. After some time, I saw the possibility of linking my observations on Cretan men's musical practices to the practices defining masculinity or manhood written about by Mediterraneanists in classic village-based ethnographies and regional surveys. My reading of Michael Herzfeld's *Poetics of Manhood* had already prepared me for the rich parade of manly performances I might see in Crete.[6] But how might such practices unfold around, in and as *musical* performance? In general terms it was clear to me, as one might expect, that musical practices were clearly reinforcing individual/community understanding, based on agreed upon ways of "being" and "doing" in the world. In fact, I drew on another Mediterraneanist to make the connections for me. Bourdieu's "dispositions," are conducted in relation to "known" structures which in themselves are ways of "knowing." This relates clearly to Bourdieu's notion of habitus, which is made up of "systems of durable, transposable dispositions, structured structures predisposed to function as structuring structures, that is, as principles of the generation and structuring of practices and representations which can be objectively "regulated" and "regular" without in any way being the product of rules" (Bourdieu 1977: 72).

It is the potential for *transposition*, as well as the durability of and play within the system that I see as usefully mapping onto musical

ways of "being" and "doing" in the world, where musical improvisations are more than just experiments with sound. The frequently ob-
servable trends in musical performance practice are clearly *regulated*
by non-musical practices, and it is difficult to see any boundary between them. As illuminated by studies of performance, music is clearly
not a separate activity but becomes a creative interplay with domains of
activity which are normally considered to lie outside of music. Musicians have to be good at managing diversity, surprises and contradictions; in Crete this is an essential attribute of masculinity.

Studies in the Mediterranean area have been particularly revealing
regarding constructions of manhood in society (see Gilmore 1990). On
both sides of the sea, there exists a culturally sanctioned stress on
manliness: toughness, aggressiveness, stoicism and sexuality. These
studies have also revealed gender as problematical. It is problematical
for men in the Mediterranean area because some are better placed than
others to achieve manhood. Some men are financially better off than
others, some men, though not rich, have a number of opportunities to
foreground their manliness in the community (for example, the shep-
herd who steals a sheep). To be rich does not mean that one has attained the ultimate "manly" state, but at least one is on the way as an
independent operator. If you are poor, you may be dependent, but at
least you can try and persuade others that you are a man of independent
means. The culturally constructed, idealized male self therefore informs
numerous aspects of an individual's life.

The lyra musicians I met in Crete were as good at negotiating and
procuring fees as they were at playing instruments and singing. They
were as good at verbal improvisation (off-the-cuff remarks, rhetoric,
hyperbole) as musical improvisation, as good at engaging appropriate
musical themes as they were at engaging the audience. Gilmore (1990:
36) discussed the "agential modality" of being a man, where the individual is expected to demonstrate a "gregarious engagement" in the
public arena of acts and deeds and visible, concrete accomplishments. I
wanted to try and discover how manhood ideals were sustained and
how and why men endeavor to sustain such an image or role that holds
power and prestige—against what are they negotiating?—but, above
all, I wanted to find out how Cretan men as musicians maintain their
position in a highly competitive and patriarchal social environment (but
where women rule the home).

It became clear that this required phenomenal skills at improvisation. As Herzfeld puts it in his study of Cretan villagers: "improvisation, dominance and competition are all aspects of single-male selfhood" (Herzfeld, 1985:136, see also Herzfeld, 1991). This definitely

could be seen in the work of musicians. As my later research revealed, non musicians encounter these "aspects of a single male selfhood" in different spheres of activity, in everyday activities, but musicians constantly work in the glare of the spotlight and public eye where they are open to challenge and scrutiny even more than other men. Whilst other men rely on the use of musical references to perform in daily recurring social situations, musicians are responsible for upholding their manly tradition and the dominant position of manhood whilst championing the tradition of music, poetry and dance. I have argued elsewhere (Dawe 1996) that Cretan music is influenced by the ideals, rhetoric and imagery that help to sustain the dominant position of men in Cretan society. But the situation is even more complicated. Musicians are professional employees paid to get on with the work at hand and traditionally they are of low status. Musicians must negotiate and overcome this further challenge as a part of the particular power struggles that dominate Cretan life. Herzfeld's model of manhood in a Cretan mountain village seemed to work well as an aid to understanding the hidden and the not-so-hidden meanings of Cretan lyra music. Clearly, musicians were upholding a tradition rooted not just in celebration but crucially in the celebration and re-creation of masculine ideals. Improvisation, for instance, took on a whole new meaning here as musicians fought for their musical as well as social and family lives.

Link 2: The Celebration

Cretan celebrations are fast and furious events that are intensely challenging and grueling for even the most experienced musicians. I have written elsewhere about the ways in which musicians work musical and verbal structures (musical themes and rhyming couplets) up into extended improvisations that facilitate and accompany dance (see Dawe 1996; 2004a). Musical skills are pushed to the limits with increasing intensity as the speed and rhythms of the dances are alternated in rapid succession; the virtuoso improvisations of the lyra player feed off the acrobatics of the dancers and the verbal interjections of guests. There is a movement away from known melodic material accompanied by an intensification of melodic and rhythmic invention whose "highs" are punctuated with cries of encouragement, whistles and gunfire. The musical strategies of the musicians, their manipulation of musical themes, tempi, improvisations and poetry occurs in a way that takes into account and manages the moods and sounds of the total environment in their attempts to orchestrate a successful performance—that is, a performance that is convivial for participants (dancers, guests who want to intone poetry, those listening) and profitable for musicians. The essential interplay between all these elements can be seen to create a community of machismo at the celebration.

Theme 3: Improvisation on a Mediterranean Performance

Anoyiá Village, Crete, 29 June 1991

The wedding procession

The musicians arrived from Crete's capital city, Iraklion, at four o'clock in the afternoon and proceeded to set up their equipment on a raised platform in the area reserved for such occasions. The area lay behind a small church set sideways onto the higher square in the Pasparákis's neighborhood. The bandleader was Dimitris Pasparákis (based in Iraklion), and the wedding was between a member of the Pasparákis family (the groom) and the Skoulas family (the bride). During the next hour, the musicians made four trips between this neighborhood in the higher part of the village and the Skoulas neighborhood in the lower part of the village, including a visit to what would become the house of the newlyweds. The purpose of the first procession through the village, involving all the male members and friends of the Pasparákis family, was to collect part of the dowry gifts for the groom from the bride's family.

> As a key rite of passage through which a man and a woman, each in different ways, acquires full adulthood in the community, marriage is largely about gender and sexuality and the ways in which these are organized for the reproduction of the family, community and the state. (Cowan 1990: 89)

The procession signaled to villagers that the wedding had started and—apart from enemies gained in sheep rustling—all could join in. Rather, all men could join the procession, women could watch. The procession actively draws lines through the village, choosing neutral routes and those able to offer the best acoustic spaces (the lyra player leading the procession, accompanied by two laouto players *must* at least try and be heard above the singing of the men). The steep and winding steps and alleyways of the village were traversed as the procession meandered down to the lower square where a crowd had gathered outside the Skoulas's house. After ten minutes, the musicians emerged from the house with the bridal banners being carried before them and the baskets containing the dowry gifts being carried behind them. The bandleader began to play the "melody for the groom" as the procession wound its way back up the steep hill.

The wedding service in a large church located in the lower part of the village began at six o'clock that afternoon. The musicians sat outside and waited. When the newlyweds emerged, the musicians began playing the protos syrtos dance for the bride and groom, joined by close relatives and more distant relatives (by now in village costume). This open circle dance demonstrated to the whole village that the two families were now joined.

The Evening Dance

The evening dance began at eight o'clock. Here, in the upper square of the village, the musicians and celebrants made full use of the available space. There is no doubt that the incantations of the lyra and laouta create an intense, exciting and challenging performance dynamic at the evening dances, which make up the longest part of Cretan wedding celebrations. The focus at these celebrations is upon the activities of men, musicians, dancing (highly complex, varied and physically demanding), the recitation of poetry, the firing of guns and other displays of bravura and eating and drinking. In the public arena men are in control; even though women take up the dance, it is to the tune of a lyra-playing male.

The lyra player comes to epitomize the control men have in these contexts; the sound and appearance of the instrument are worked by musicians as they intervene in and oversee the proceedings; both man and instrument become symbols of authority, masculinity, village identity, Cretanness and "tradition." The incantations of the lyra bring the past into the present, expectations are met, and the revelry and excitement that is precipitated is on a Dionysian scale. Ultimately, the lyra itself becomes the focus of attention as man and instrument appear to become one. The unique and unmistakable sound of the lyra—aided and abetted by mini mixing desks and a PA system—cuts through the cacophony and reverie of the celebration, framing the event, pulling in the community and reinforcing a sense of the liminal but keeping everything under control.

> The entire art of the musician resides in his choice of musical formulas that, depending on their configurations call for either smooth gliding or unbridled leaping. Too much jumping would exhaust the dancers; but if there isn't enough the dance would be boring. (Lortat-Jacob 1995: 10)

Inextricably linked to the instrumental improvisations that drive the performance dynamic described above are the verbal improvisations of the lyra player and male guests, as well as whistles, cries and gunfire.

> Improvisational skills in dance, song and banter signify the very excellence as Glendiots that they also demonstrate at the immediate level of the performance. Self-regard, eghoismos, is a social value, not an individual trait. (Herzfeld 1985: 26)

Figure 1. Themes and linkage material from the *Anoyianés kondiliés* suite as performed by D. Pasparákis (Anoyiá village, 29 June 1991).

The essential interplay between all these elements creates a community of machismo at the celebration—a sense of solidarity, as well as a flirtation with the liminal, where a crossing of accepted social boundaries is enacted, played with even, but always contained. The lyra is at the epicenter of this complex performance dynamic and its sound the prime mover. The instrument and its repertoire have evolved with and are inextricably linked to, the intricate rituals, spectacle and display of the celebration.

The music stopped with the first hints of sunrise in the leaden black sky. The mauve hue that gradually appeared and spread over the countryside eventually became strong enough to reveal the debris covering the area of the celebration. An exhausted crew of musicians made their way unsteadily off stage at six o'clock that morning. But their duties were not over. They walked to the house of the newlyweds, who had by now consummated their marriage and began singing rhyming couplets called *mantinades* for the next two hours.

Coda: Reflections on a Mediterraneanist's Performance

Clearly, musical performance presents a multifaceted series of events whose thematic and linking structures are carried by more than just "the music itself." Musical structures surely reflect broader concerns but is it as neat a model as I have presented it here?. Is there an eghoismós ("self-regard") at work in the construction of Cretan social life, acting as a guiding principle in the work of musicians and in the activities of musicians as Cretan men? Some would rather point to the notion of anthropiá (feeling towards one's fellow humans) as a "discourse in which other concepts are foregrounded" (Loizos 1994: 78), the former notion gleaned from studies of mountain village pastoralist life, the latter expressed by other agriculturalists and coastal inhabitants. Yet, musicians now move between these and other worlds as never before. One reaches out to the classics of Greek ethnography in any consideration of the ways in which domestic power is distributed in Crete, but in a consideration of performance on a Mediterranean theme, the links to other places and peoples in this book and elsewhere are clear. It is also clear that such notions may be as contested in Mediterranean performance as they are now debated within the academe.

> "A Macedonian song of your own country, Zorba," I said. "A Cretan song of your own country!" said Zorba. "I'll sing you something I was taught in Candia; it changed my life." He reflected for a moment. "No, it hasn't changed my life really," he said, "only now I know I was right." He placed his finger on the *santuri* and craned his neck. He sang in a wild dolorous voice. (Kazantzakis [1961] 1988: 184)

Notes

1. The santuri is a trapezoid-shaped, hammered dulcimer or zither.

2. Taximi (Gr.) is an unmetered improvisation usually found at the beginning of a composition. It introduces the modal structure and mood of the piece to the audience.

3. More recent collaborations include Ross Daly with Bustan Abraham, George Dalaras with Paco de Lucía, Amr Diab with Angela Dimitriou and Luís Delgado with musicians from Morocco.

4. See Dawe (1998, 1999, 2000, 2003a, 2003b, 2004a, 2004b, 2004c).

5. The lyra (plural = lyres) is a three-stringed, upright, bowed lute; the laouto (plural = laouta) is a four-course (eight strings grouped in pairs), plucked, long-necked lute. The ensemble is sometimes augmented with a second laouto or mandolin. The lyra player is usually but not always the lead singer within the group.

6. Music rarely receives a mention in the classic Greek village ethnographies, even if weddings and other social gatherings involving celebration are detailed. See, for example, Campbell (1964) or du Boulay (1974). However, themes of honor and shame, family and patronage may be played out in music too. I have already referred to what I believe to be Herzfeld's *musical* book on manly performances. Later writings make such connections explicit though pave the way for the questioning of monolithic conceptions of "Mediterranean genders." See, for example, Sugarman (1987), Cowan (1990), Stokes (1992), Dawe (1996) and Magrini (2003).

Bibliography

Bourdieu, Pierre. *Outline of a Theory of Practice.* London: Cambridge University Press, 1977.

Campbell, John. *Honor, Family and Patronage: A Study of Institutions and Moral Values in a Greek Mountain Community.* Oxford: Oxford University Press, 1964.

Cowan, Jane. *Dance and the Body Politic in Northern Greece.* Princeton, New Jersey: Princeton University Press, 1990.

Dawe, Kevin. "The Engendered *Lyra*: Music, Poetry and Manhood in Crete," *The British Journal of Ethnomusicology* 5 (1996): 93–112.

———. "Bandleaders in Crete: Musicians and Entrepreneurs in a Greek Island Economy." *The British Journal of Ethnomusicology* 7

(1998): 23–44.

———. "Minotaurs or Musonauts?: Cretan Music and 'World Music.'" *Popular Music* 18 (1999): 209–25.

———. "Roots Music in the Global Village: Cretan Ways of Dealing with the World at Large." *World of Music* 42, no. 3 (2000): 47–66.

———. "Between East and West: Contemporary Grooves in Greek Popular Music (c.1990–2000)" 221–40 in *Mediterranean Mosaic: Popular Music and Global Sounds*, edited by Goffredo Plastino. New York: Routledge Publishing Inc., 2003a.

———. "Lyres and the Body Politic: Studying Musical Instruments in the Cretan Musical Landscape." *Popular Music and Society* 26, no. 3 (2003b): 263–83.

———. "'Power-Geometry' in Motion: Space, Place and Gender in the *Lyra* Music of Crete." 55–65 in *Music, Space, and Place: Popular Music and Cultural Identity*, edited by Andy Bennett, Sheila Whiteley and Stan Hawkins: Ashgate 2004a.

———. "Island Musicians: Making a Living from Music in Crete." 65–75 in *Island Musics* edited by Kevin Dawe, New York: Berg Publishers, 2004b.

——— ed. *Island Musics*, New York: Berg Publishers, 2004c.

Du Boulay, Juliet. *Portrait of a Greek Mountain Village*. Oxford: Clarendon Press, 1974.

Gilmore, David. *Manhood in the Making: Cultural Concepts of Masculinity*. New Haven: Yale University Press, 1990.

Herndon, Marcia and Naomi McCleod. *The Ethnography of Musical Performance*. Norwood, Pa.: Norwood Editions, 1980.

Herzfeld, Michael. *The Poetics of Manhood: Contest and Identity in a Cretan Mountain Village*. Princeton, New Jersey: Princeton University Press, 1985.

———. "On Mediterraneanist Performances." *Journal of Mediterranean Studies* 1, no. 1 (1990): 141–47.

Kazantzakis, Nikos. *Zorba the Greek*. London: Faber, [1961] 1988.

Loizos, Peter. "A Broken Mirror: Masculine Sexuality in Greek Ethnography". 66–82 in *Dislocating Masculinity: Comparative Ethnographies*, edited by Andrea Cornwall and Nancy Lindisfarne. London: Routledge Publishing Inc., 1994.

Lortat-Jacob, Bernard. *Sardinian Chronicles*. Chicago: University of Chicago Press, 1995.

Magrini, Tullia, ed. *Music and Gender: Perspectives from the Mediterranean*. Chicago: University of Chicago Press, 2003.

Plastino, Goffredo, ed. *Mediterranean Mosaic: Popular Music and Global Sounds*. New York: Routledge Publishing Inc., 2003

Schuyler, Philip D. "Berber Professional Musicians in Performance."
    91–148 in *Performance Practice: Ethnomusicological Perspec-
    tives*, edited by Gerard Behague. Westport, Conn.: Greenwood
    Press, 1984.
Stokes, Martin. *The Arabesk Debate: Music and Musicians in Modern
    Turkey*. Oxford: Oxford University press, 1992.
Sugarman, Jane. "Making Muabet: The Social Basis of Singing Among
    Prespa Albanian Men," 1–42 in *Selected Reports in Ethnomusicol-
    ogy: Issues in the Conceptualisation of Music*, edited by J. Racy.
    Los Angeles: University of California Press, 1987.

Chapter Seven

Anda Jaleo!
Celebrating Creativity in Flamenco Song

Loren Chuse

Introduction

Flamenco music and dance, the highly expressive art form that developed in Andalusia in the mid-nineteenth century, continues to thrive in the twenty-first century, both in Spain and internationally. Emblematic of all that is considered Spanish, flamenco music has traditionally been considered a male genre, with the exception of the role of female dancers, for until quite recently, the subject of female singers has not been adequately addressed. This chapter focuses on the long-standing yet often overlooked participation of cantaoras, or women singers, in flamenco. In exploring the historical data and pursuing my ethnographic research in Spain, I discovered that women singers have played a key role in the transmission and preservation of flamenco. They continue to participate in contemporary performance as active agents of creativity and change within flamenco. In so doing, Spain's cantaoras are situated in a long-standing Mediterranean tradition of women involved in expressive vocal performance. This chapter concerns female singers, their role in traditional flamenco forms and their involvement in musical transformations taking place within the flamenco complex. My investigation, which addresses issues of music and gendered behavior, is situated in sociopolitical currents that have been reshaping Spanish society since the early twentieth century, in particular the changing conditions for women in post-Franco Spain.

Flamenco performance has been key to the creation and maintenance of Andalusian as well as national identity. In truth, flamenco is a continuum of practices, musical, physical, verbal and social, that has served as a site for the negotiation of complex, multilayered and often conflicting identities of nation, region, ethnicity and gender. It is now well established in ethnomusicology that music can serve as a site for the maintenance of tradition and the creation of both cultural and individual identity. In addition, it is well accepted that music often functions as a rich site of memory that is central to processes of self-definition both for the individual and the collective (see Cowan 1990; Loza 1993; Turino 1993; Stokes 1994 and Sugarman 1997). Flamenco is one such musical practice, for it is deeply imbued with a traditional legacy that serves as a sustaining core of identity for its performers. Much recent scholarship in the social sciences has studied flamenco from the perspective of the social construction of identity (see Ortiz Nuevo 1990; Steingress 1991; García Gomez 1993; Mitchell 1994; Cruces Roldán 1996, 1997 and Washabaugh 1996, 1998). Women act within flamenco at complex and sophisticated levels, as individual agents who both maintain tradition *and* engender transformation. While conserving tradition, flamenco cantaoras also transform and enrich the genre with their creativity and innovation, making flamenco meaningful and compelling to contemporary audiences. Women's participation in flamenco, both past and present, represents the enactment of gendered selves and articulates issues of gender as they are performed in music and dance. My study investigates the social and cultural meanings of the performance of identity in flamenco, including gender among a number of other identities. Recent scholarship in ethnomusicology and anthropology is central to my investigation, as is my own research, which includes valuable information obtained through numerous interviews with cantaoras themselves.

Changing Social Conditions for Cantaoras

Since the death of Spanish dictator Francisco Franco in 1975, Spain has undergone a phenomenal and accelerated process of social and political change. This has involved exponential economic growth, the emergence of a consumer culture in Spain and increased tourism and rapid social transformation on a number of levels. Nowhere is this change more pronounced than in the lives of women; the processes of expanded opportunities and greater choice for women that have occurred over the past forty or fifty years in other parts of the Western world have taken place in just over three decades in Spain (see Graham and Labanyi 1996). The changing perception of female performers in flamenco reflects this social revolution. For the nineteenth and the earlier part of the twentieth century, professional female flamenco singers and dancers were marginalized, and the pursuit of a performance career in flamenco carried a heavy social stigma. During these years, restrictions from both community and family prevented many talented women from entertaining the possibility of singing professionally. The early 1970s saw the first public appearances of many a skilled cantaora, such as La Perrata, the mother of singer El Lebrijano, who had been forbidden by her husband to perform in public prior to this time.

In contrast to this earlier era, subsequent generations of young flamencas have benefited from the easing of social restrictions and have pursued professional careers in flamenco more confident in the knowledge that their efforts will be supported and encouraged. I interviewed many middle-aged and young singers who grew up in post-Franco Spain, whose sense of themselves as active agents in the creation of their own careers is vastly different from that of their mothers and grandmothers. In addition, the decade of the 1990s was a period of great opportunity for many of these singers, a decade that was characterized by a number of cultural phenomena that celebrated women in flamenco. One of these, a two-volume CD entitled *La Mujer en el Cante* was released in 1996 to critical acclaim in the Spanish press from journalists and flamenco critics such as Manuel Ríos Ruiz and Angel Alvarez Caballero, both for its quality and for its acknowledgment of the contributions of women to flamenco. Renowned singer Carmen Linares recorded this compilation that includes cante (songs) performed or composed by women over the last one hundred years. Another telling event was the official recognition of legendary singer Pastora Pavón, whose achievements in flamenco and show voice were honored in the city of Sevilla with a project to collect her over 400 recordings worldwide in order to create an archive of her work. One result of this campaign of re-evaluation has been that many more cantaoras have come to the forefront of flamenco and have been able to take greater control of their careers and their recording projects.

Traditional classic, "pure" flamenco, often referred to as flamenco puro, is not popular commercial music in today's Spain. However, flamenco puro is supported by a dedicated subculture of aficionados within Spain and by an ever-growing group of foreign aficionados and continues to thrive both on the concert stage and in the recording studio. Within Spain, the fusion forms of nuevo flamenco are far more commercially viable. This new flamenco is a diverse hybrid genre that ranges far and wide, from fusions of traditional flamenco with salsa, rock, jazz, blues, rhythm and blues and rap music, to fusions or mezclas of Arabic and Indian music with flamenco. Flamenco has been a hotly contested cultural phenomenon in Spain since the mid-twentieth century and has inspired many ideological disputes over its ownership and creation. One particularly contentious debate, the extent of Gypsy as opposed to Andalusian contributions to the creation of flamenco, has raged in scholarly and flamenco circles for decades (see Leblon 1991; Alvarez Caballero 1994 and Mitchell 1994). A recent ideological dispute now centers on the legitimacy of nuevo flamenco: whether it should be considered flamenco and whether it threatens to "destroy" classic flamenco cante (see Clemente 1995 and Ortiz Nuevo 2000).

In light of the various aesthetic and cultural criteria, contemporary flamenco performance can range from the traditional to the innovative. The careers of many cantaoras represent very different approaches to the issues of preservation and innovation. I present here some important singers who range in age from their early twenties to late sixties. These singers are all Andalusians and many are gitanas (Gypsies). All grew up in an environment in which they learned flamenco within the home and the community as children and began to perform flamenco professionally at a young age. Each one has chosen a slightly different path in navigating the complexities of the contemporary flamenco world, yet each of these singers is making her own unique contribution to the genre.

Contexts for Cante

In a recent interview, singer Carmen Linares referred to cante as "La Madre del Flamenco" (the mother, or the root of flamenco song). This sentiment is shared by flamenco performers and serious aficionados. It is the cante that is considered the most important component of flamenco for it expresses the core, the essence of flamenco. Cante, whose different genres are referred to as palos, was originally performed unaccompanied, a palo seco, with palmas (handclaps) or nudillos (knuckles played on a tabletop) keeping a rhythmic accompaniment. Much cante is still performed this way, such as serious martinetes, the saetas sung during Easter holy week and festive bulerías that are sung and danced to the accompaniment of complex palmas. Guitar accompaniment became a prominent feature of the style later on, in the era of the cafés cantantes (singing cafes) and has since taken on an increasingly important role as a solo instrument in flamenco.

One of the early contexts for flamenco was the bar, while another was the professional theatrical world of the café cantantes that sprang up throughout Spain from about 1860 on. At the same time, flamenco was being performed in private festivities, such as weddings and baptisms, primarily in the homes of gitanos. Women have figured in these different flamenco contexts to varying degrees and in distinctly different ways. Their level of participation has been determined by social constraints experienced by women in what anthropologist David Gilmore has termed the "homo-social" structure of Andalusian society.[1] The public versus private dichotomy of gender-separated spheres has prevailed for centuries in southern Spain, supported by the Mediterranean "honor and shame" complex and a rigid, patriarchal religious system (see Corbin and Corbin 1987 and Press 1979). Recent anthropological work, in its recognition of the importance of the female-controlled domestic sphere of the family in Andalusia, has questioned the patriarchal assumption. Crucial kinship bonds between women, especially the powerful mother–daughter bond, are also felt to support a more matriarchal interpretation. There has been an increasing move away from essentializing analyses in order to account for the multidimensional real, lived experiences of women. That Andalusian culture has been understood in terms of both matriarchy and patriarchy suggests that a complex set of ideologies and cultural practices are being negotiated (see Abu Lughod and Lutz 1990, Abu Lughod 1993 and Kapchan 1996).

The flamenco context of the bar has not been one that has been open to most women. The presence of a woman in the male-bonding social environment of the bar was felt to be inhibiting and put into question the virtue of the woman present. Here, men gather to drink and socialize, often singing and performing for one another in a spirit of camaraderie. Also in the context of the bar the after-hours juerga took place. The juerga, a get-together of flamenco singers, guitarists and aficionados, was an informal occasion of great exuberance and intensity, usually lasting well into the morning hours, paid for by señoritos, upper-class Andalusian men, who would hire a singer, a guitarist and prostitutes for their after-hours parties. Many flamenco performers depended upon these juergas to earn a living in an earlier era of flamenco. Women's participation as performers and their attendance as observers in this context was highly problematic due to social stigma and traditional constraints on acceptable female behavior.

Cafés Cantantes

The period from about 1860 to the first several decades of the twentieth century, often referred to as the "golden age" of flamenco, was the era of the singing cafés. A café cantante is described in the *Dicciónario*

Enciclopedico Ilustrado del Flamenco (Blas Vega and Ríos Ruiz 198£ 120) as "a locale that served food and drink and that offered recitals o flamenco song, dance and guitar." These cafés were the direct descen dants of the academias de baile that had began to offer performances o regional Andalusian dances several decades earlier and were the pre cursor of the flamenco tablaos, or nightclubs, that emerged in th 1950s. The café cantantes regularly featured professional female per formers who were singers, dancers and guitarists. Indeed, the presenc of women performers in the cafés was significant. They were singer: and dancers and many were known to have accompanied themselve: (and other singers) on guitar. The gender bias in favor of solely mal guitarists does not seem to have been the case in this earlier era of fla menco. Women continued to play guitar as accompaniment to cante and baile until the first few decades of the twentieth century, at which time the virtuoso flamenco guitar performance by men only began to predominate (see Triana 1936). These singers and dancers inhabited a marginalized world that carried a stigma of disrespectability, of mal vivir (ill repute) with connotations of prostitution. Located on the margins of society, these women were often scandalous, known for their ironic performances which often mocked male attitudes of machismo. One famed performer of the era, Trinidad Huertas La Cuenca, dressed in a matador outfit and frequently danced a parody of the bullfight (see Chuse 2003). They were often known as much for their outrageous behavior, dashing style and personal exploits as for their flamenco performance. The clientele was primarily men, many of them señoritos who paid for private juergas after the show. The participation of female performers in the cafés cantantes is an important part of flamenco history. It is well known that all three elements of flamenco performance, cante, baile and toque (guitar), were all honed and developed during the era of these cafés cantantes. Thus, the café cantante period is considered crucial in flamenco, in that it encouraged the intensification of the art of flamenco among professionals and its dissemination to an ever-growing public.[2]

In contrast to the contexts of the bar and the café cantantes, the context of flamenco performance at home or in private fiestas (parties), has been less problematic for women (though not entirely free of some of the prohibitions and restrictions mentioned for public performance). Women have always been highly regarded as singers in the fiestas that took place in gitano homes. Most flamenco performers, both women and men, learned to sing through participation and attendance at these fiestas and many, such as legendary Gypsy singers Camarón (José Mongé Cruz) and El Lebrijano (Juan Peña) acknowledge having learned the cante from their mothers. Women were as important as their male counterparts in these fiestas and were accorded recognition and respect for their skill as singers.

Women often perform as saeteras (singers of the saeta, a form of flamenco sung during Semana Santa, or holy week, in Andalusia). The performance of this highly emotional, passionate cante, sung a capella, is challenging, for it requires great vocal skill and physical stamina to execute the complicated melismas characteristic of the style and a high degree of emotional and expressive capability. This form of cante was not subject to the same social restrictions as other public performances of cante. Due in part to the religious nature of the lyrics and the fact that these songs are directed at religious images, the public performance of saetas by women was not considered socially compromising for women. There have been many well-known female saeteras. Many of the cantaoras whom I interviewed regularly work as professional saeteras during Semana Santa and, in fact, some made their public debut as young girls, singing saetas from the balconies of their family homes.

The Cantaora Today

In a recent article in the Spanish newspaper *ABC,* noted flamenco critic Ríos Ruiz reviewed a concert in honor of legendary singer La Niña de los Peines that took place at the Teatro Albéniz in Madrid. In his description of the program given by cantaoras Tina Pavón, Remedios Amaya, La Negra and La Cañeta, Ríos Ruiz noted the strong presence of women throughout the history of flamenco and made the following comments about the role of women in cante flamenco:

> We are experiencing a time in which women once again have a great presence in the flamenco panorama. If, in the time of the *cafés cantantes* at the end of the nineteenth century and the beginnings of this one, there were many singers, from Maria Borrico or the Niña de los Peines, from La Trini, La Parrala, la Serrana and so many others and in the era of the so-called opera flamenca a large number of them also shone, headed by the Niña de la Puebla, women have known how, in the years of the revaluing of flamenco cante, to re-interpret the cante in a very responsible way, which is proved by just citing some names: Fernanda De Utrera, La Perla de Cádiz, La Paquera, María Vargas. . . . But it is in the 1990s that more big-time cantaoras are headlining concerts. (6 March 1996)

The observations of Ríos Ruiz, a poet, aficionado and critic who has been involved with flamenco for the past thirty years, reveal the increasing presence and centrality of women in flamenco. Cantaoras have been responsible for revitalizing and renewing flamenco at every level. Since the 1990s they have been moving into new territory as they engage in projects that range from traditional recitals to theatrical productions, to experimental collaborations with jazz, classical and rock musicians. Many of them are heading up their own original projects and producing recordings and performances that reflect their own interests and decisions. These singers range from older women like La Paquera, who made her career in the 1950s, to the generation of singers in their late forties and early fifties, such as singer Carmen Linares; to Lole Montoya (younger than Carmen and a bridge to the younger generation), to emerging younger talents like Esperanza Fernández, La Macanita, Elu de Jerez and finally to the most recent generation of singers such as Niña Pastori and Marina Heredia, whose pop flamenco has had great commercial success. The specific examples of cantaoras that follow below draw on personal interview material, video footage, concert attendance and the ongoing and often heated discourse about flamenco which I frequently encountered in the popular Spanish press.

La Paquera

Cantaora La Paquera de Jerez, born in the Gypsy barrio Santiago in 1934, reveals a case of exceptional talent and agency in the realm of flamenco. La Paquera is known for her interpretations of flamenco styles from Jerez, in particular the festive bulerías. She has been an important influence for many younger singers who acknowledge her as a primary inspiration. The recent film by Carlos Saura, *Flamenco*, which features most of the important figures in contemporary flamenco today, clearly demonstrates the central role of women singers, for it begins with a performance by La Paquera. In the bulerías she performs, she is accompanied by a group of artists from Jerez de la Frontera, acknowledged as the home of the most authentic Gypsy flamenco to be found today. Paquera comes from a large gitano family and learned to sing in the family fiestas as a child in a family ambiance in which everyone knew how to sing and dance. She began performing at fiestas in Jerez but moved to Madrid in the 1960s to work in flamenco tablaos—a necessary move for artists interested in making a professional career in flamenco. She has taken on considerable responsibility for the financial support of her large family, yet she has remained single and without children.

Paquera began her work in the Madrid tablaos in 1957, a necessary move for artists interested in making a professional career in flamenco. She was a great success, performing to packed audiences at large venues like bull rings and stadiums and appearing in all the important tablaos in Madrid and throughout Spain. She has won prizes in several important competitions: the Niña de Los Peines prize in Córdoba and the De Jerez from the Cátedra de Flamencología in the same city. She appeared in a number of popular feature films in Spain in the 1960s. La Paquera is featured in several *Rito y Geografía del Cante Flamenco* (the series of highly influential Spanish television programs on flamenco produced in the early 1970s), in which she sings a powerful saeta to a statue of the Gypsy Christ of barrio Santiago during holy week. She is represented in this and other programs as very professional and less family oriented than some of the other singers. Paquera has been a regularly featured cantaora at the Bienal de Flamenco in Sevilla and in the Festival of the Bulería, a yearly event in Jerez. Her discography is quite extensive, and she is especially known for her original and masterful interpretations of the bulerías.

That La Paquera has had such a successful career has to do with her personal choices as well as her enormous talent. While social options for women have expanded considerably in post-Franco Spain, it is significant that La Paquera pursued her career during the Franco years. These were extremely repressive years for women, an era in which women were expected to be devoutly religious wives and mothers with no public roles. Despite societal restrictions and many obstacles, La Paquera has negotiated a life characterized by independence, very much in command of her career, which has included extensive touring and many years spent in Madrid. Yet she remains strongly connected to her roots as Andalusian and gitana and prides herself in carrying on the pure styles of Jerez. I had the opportunity to speak with La Paquera and attend her performance in Granada in June 2001. At that time, I was struck by her compelling and commanding presence and her continued vocal mastery despite her advanced age.

Carmen Linares

Carmen Linares (b. 1951) has been a pioneering figure in the reemergence of women in cante flamenco. Referred to in a recent article as

"The Grande Dame of Cante" she is known to newer audiences of flamenco as well as to long-time aficionados. She has an international reputation and is particularly well known in France and other European countries where she performs regularly. Carmen, an elegant, dignified women now in her early fifties, was born in the town of Linares, in eastern Andalusia and was introduced to cante flamenco by her father, an aficionado and accomplished guitarist who took her to peñas and flamenco recitals and encouraged her interest in the cante from early on. Her father taught her songs, accompanied her on guitar and supported her aspirations to be a professional singer every step of the way. In describing her beginnings in flamenco she recounts:

> I began to sing from a young age. I had a great deal of luck in that my father was an aficionado and he always supported me in a way that was very natural. . . . I wanted to sing and my father said, "Que alegría, how wonderful, if you want to sing, then sing." I never had any problem. And then, at seventeen years old I began to sing alone, to travel, to sing with flamenco companies, to sing for dancers. I have been singing for about twenty-five years, since I began with my father.[3]

She left her native Linares to reside in Madrid beginning in 1965, for much the same reasons as La Paquera had done a few years earlier. In Madrid, she pursued her career as a professional singer, making her first recording in 1971. In 1972 she performed regularly in tablaos, alongside flamenco greats Camarón, La Perla de Cádiz and Jose Mercé. She began touring early in her career: to France, Italy and the United States and soon after to Japan. Her 1994 recording, *Canciónes Populares Antiguas,* is a flamenco version of the compilation of Spanish folksongs set for piano by García Lorca and originally sung by Antonia Mercé in a 1931 recording. Carmen Linares has reinterpreted these arrangements by Lorca in flamenco style with the addition of double bass, flute, violin and percussion. Carmen followed this experiment with her acclaimed 1996 *La Mujer en El Cante,* an anthology of cante composed or made famous by cantaoras. This two-CD recording was a first in flamenco circles, for no one before Linares had brought together the work of women in cante. In this recording she collaborates with many of the best contemporary flamenco guitarists: Moraíto Chico, Vicente Amigo, Pepe Habichuela, Tomatito, Paco and Miguel Angel Cortes. She performed a concert based on this anthology of cantaoras in the Bienal (bi-annual flamenco festival) that took place in Sevilla in September 1996.

Linares is also known for her work in theater productions. In December 1996 she starred in a flamenco drama based on the life of Dolores Parrales Moreno, La Parrala, the celebrated cantaora from the café cantante era. She was musical director of the 1997 theatrical production *Un rato, un minuto, un siglo*, a musical drama celebrating the work of García Lorca, in which she performed some of the canciónes antiguas that she had recorded earlier. This musical drama was the first in a series of works commemorating the 1998 Year of Lorca, the centenary celebration of the birth of the Andalusian poet. She continues to do recitals of classic cante, as in her February 1998 Madrid concert with guitarist Moraito. Hailed as an encyclopedic singer who performs many palos of cante well, Carmen Linares is especially known for her interpretations of the cante minero, forms which originate from Eastern Andalusia and pueblos such as Linares, Jaen and Almería. She has been hailed by some as the most complete cantaora in the history of flamenco since the legendary Niña de los Peines.

In our interview, Linares acknowledged that women have always played an important role in flamenco. She commented that the era of the cafés cantantes featured many women who sang, danced and played guitar. However, she noted that women have had a harder time of it because of social conditions in Spain. She referred to the expectation that women marry and raise children: "For this reason, it has often not been easy for a women to dedicate herself to flamenco. She needed the support of her family, her parents, her husband—support that was often nonexistent." She counts herself fortunate in having grown up in a supportive environment in which she was encouraged to pursue her musical interests. Linares feels that a professional career in flamenco is now more possible for most women and that recent social changes in Spain are responsible for the greater incorporation of women in current flamenco. She has personally experienced little in the way of discrimination as a female singer; on the contrary, she has been able to count on the support of her family and her husband Miguel Espin.

Linares described her early years in Madrid, where there was a "tremendous ambiente flamenco [flamenco environment], for all the important artists lived and worked in Madrid in the 1960s and '70s . . . I regularly heard flamenco greats perform at the peñas and tablaos: Pepe de la Matrona, Juan Varea, Rafael Romero, Pepe el Culata." Linares acknowledges having learned a great deal from these "maestros." She also owes a great debt to Pastora Pavón, who she never met personally, but whose cante she has learned and interpreted. Linares lived near Plaza Santa Ana, a center of flamenco activity during the decades of the 1960s and '70s, the "golden age" of flamenco in Madrid where she began to perform in the tablao*s*. When I asked whether she feels that women have a style that differs from male singers she responded:

> In the way of expressing oneself, yes . . . the cante is the same, but I feel that I express sentiment in a different way than a man does . . . we women have a different sensibility, less embarrassment in the moment of expressing ourselves. . . . I don't know how to explain it. If we cry, we cry like no one else can; if we get angry we get angrier than anyone. I feel that we women express in another way, not better or worse than men, but we bring a particular sensibility to cante, we have a different story to tell than men, although the cante is the same.[4]

The Younger Cantaoras

The younger generation of cantaoras has grown up in a democratic Spain, where attitudes toward women (as well as attitudes toward many social and cultural practices which involve gendered behavior) have been changing rapidly. These singers have had more opportunities and fewer restrictions on their behavior than did women of the previous generation. In general, these women are better educated, for even among gitanos, many more young people have completed at least the ninth grade in school (age fourteen).[5] Younger women in Spain have benefited from the social idealism of the post-Franco years and have not questioned their right to both family and career. Many have chosen to postpone marriage and family in order to pursue their careers (unlike previous generations), another very recent development within both the gitano and Andalusian communities. Most of the younger cantaoras I spoke to seemed to take it for granted that they would earn their own living, which represents a dramatic shift, both in attitude and in economic possibilities and social realities from the previous generations. Younger Spaniards have enjoyed greater economic prosperity, reflecting the fact that Spain has rapidly become a consumer culture on a par with the rest of Western Europe. In this process, they have become familiar with North American and European popular music and culture, which has influenced many social and cultural practices.

Lole Montoya: The Inspiration to the New Generation

Lole Montoya, the oldest singer of this group, represents the transition, the bridge of the immediate post-Franco years. She has been a model and an inspiration to young singers, many of whom told me how much they have been influenced by her. Born in the Gypsy barrio of Sevilla, Triana in 1954, she grew up as part of a family of professional flamenco artists and began dancing professionally in flamenco tablaos at age fourteen. Speaking about her beginnings in flamenco, Lole told me:

> We, the gitanos, from when we are in our mothers live with flamenco. You know, you live in the house and from early on you see the fiestas of your parents. We begin very young. I began to go to the academy to study dance at age sixteen. I already knew how to dance bulerías, but I had to learn to do a martinete, a siguiriyas, soleá, fandangos de Huelva. So I studied at the academy, but also with my father, who dances very well. My mother sings, as did all my grandparents. I went to fiestas with my mother, when she sang at the feria, [fair] all over. I began to sing at a tablao in Madrid when I was sixteen, seventeen and here in Seville.[6]

Lole's mother, whose stage name is La Negra, was born in Spanish Morocco in 1936. She was married to the dancer Juan Montoya (now deceased) and is the mother of six daughters, among them Lole Montoya, who rose to fame in the mid 1970s and Angelita, with whom La Negra currently performs. The family began to work as a company, Los Montoya, in the late 1970s, performing at important festivals in Andalusia. La Negra is both a singer and dancer and is known for her interpretations of the more festive genres, especially bulerías and tangos. La Negra has been described in the Spanish press as charismatic, possessing a magical voice with deep Arab roots. She is known for setting Arabic lyrics to flamenco genres, a conscious expression of her Spanish Moroccan roots. Her daughter Lole has carried on this legacy in her own career as a cantaora.

While her daughter grew up in this professional environment and performed as a girl with the family, Lole went on to form the duo Lole y Manuel with husband Manuel Molina in the early 1970s. Lole and Manuel were foremost exponents of what came to be known as the nuevo flamenco, or new flamenco. They wrote original lyrics or set contemporary poetry to music in flamenco style, using traditional flamenco forms while expanding them. Their release *Nuevo Dia* or (New Day), came out in 1975, just after the death of Franco and heralded a new era of freedom and possibility. As pioneers of this new genre, they inspired many of the nuevo flamenco groups that have appeared since the mid 1980s. For the past twenty years, Lole and Manuel have continued to experiment, composing new lyrics and new arrangements for flamenco. Lole also expresses an identification with her Spanish Moroccan heritage from her mother. This is reflected in her concert dedicated to the work of famed Egyptian singer Umm Kulthum, as well as her numerous recordings of flamenco styles in Arabic.

She spoke of her professional career and her marriage to Manuel and noted that, "In flamenco before Lole and Manuel, poetry and melody combined in the unique way that we did it didn't exist. We created styles of newer flamenco with new lyrics. It was not easy to do, but the public wanted to hear songs with a message." In describing the creative process involved, she said, "To do something new in flamenco, to add a chorus of voices, or a bulerías with piano, you have to have the 'feeling.' Not everyone can do it." She said that she comes from a long line of flamenco artists. Her grandparents were from Jerez and her parents, the entire Montoya family, as well as Manuel's family had been flamenco artists. According to Lole, she and Manuel always had "la mente abierta" (an open mind).

> We liked classical music and we could use it, within the flamenco. I always like to learn new things, a new interpretation, much emotion, much "feeling." [Lole attributes this capacity to express "feeling" in her music to her inheritance of flamenco artists on both sides of the family.] I want my musician and composer friends to offer me fresh material, new themes.[7]

Lole also considers the Arab musical influence an important part of her heritage. She especially likes Egyptian music and said that she would like to record the songs of Umm Kulthum that she performed years before in concert. Lole told me that she learned to sing in Arabic from her mother, who sings in the language, although she does not speak it. From age twelve on, Lole began to listen to Arab music and incorporate it in her flamenco vocal styling.

The youngest of the Montoyas, Angelita, is now coming to prominence performing with her mother. She too learned everything within the family and began performing at a young age, primarily dancing and providing percussive palmas, or rhythmic accompaniment, in the family productions. The Montoya family is typical of many flamenco professionals, in that their focus is on the family, for the continuance of the flamenco tradition within the lineage of the family is the norm. The case of the Montoyas is especially noteworthy in that it demonstrates not only how strongly the flamenco tradition is learned and passed on through generations, but in this case, through the female line, from mother to daughters. While the Montoyas represent a particularly engaging example of this, they are far from unique, for it is quite common in professional flamenco for families to perform together and for the younger members to develop their art within the confines of the family. The Montoya women, involved in both traditional and innovative styles, also represent some of the sophisticated, nuanced and multidimensional roles available for women within contemporary flamenco practice. While presenting themselves as a family and as carriers of a long-standing tradition, they have also engaged in experiments which have expanded the borders of flamenco, whether in the direction of interpretations of Arabic music or forms of hybrid nuevo flamenco.

Esperanza Fernández: New Directions in Cante

Esperanza Fernández continues in the direction set forth by Lole Montoya, as a more liberated, independent gitana who is active in flamenco musical innovation. Esperanza was very influenced by the style of Lole Montoya in the early days of her singing career. Born a decade later than Lole in 1966, she is the daughter of well-known Gypsy singer Curro Fernández and comes from a family of flamenco performers. Like Lole, she began as a dancer, studying in the Sevillan dance academies. In the traditional gitano fashion, she began singing and dancing in family parties and later participated in the closing fin de fiestas (end of the bulerías in which everyone takes a turn singing or dancing) in family performances. Esperanza spoke about how she began in flamenco and the family influence.

> Well, as you know, my father is Curro Fernández. My mother never was professional, but she comes from a family of singers. So I grew up in a flamenco household. When I finished studying at colegio (high school), I told my father that I wanted to be an artist. He said fine, that he didn't want to force me to do anything I didn't want to, but he warned me that I would have to work very hard because the life of a performer is difficult. He told me that I must be well prepared, that I must study and become a good professional. At first, I began as a dancer, but what I really loved was the cante. The problem was, at first I felt embarrassed to sing. I don't know exactly why. I spent some years dancing but then my mother encouraged me to sing. She heard me and said that I couldn't continue dancing; that my tal-

ent was for the cante, because I had a good voice and sang well in
tune.[8]

She began her career as a soloist at age thirteen in the family cuadro
(ensemble). Following the model set by the Montoya family, Los
Fernández performed in flamenco festivals and concerts throughout
Spain and abroad. Although she still works with her family on occasion, Esperanza has followed new and innovative paths in her solo career. Esperanza worked in the company of dancer Mario Maya in his
production *La hora del Amargo* (1986). Along with Enrique Morente
she premiered *A Oscuras* by Jose Miguel Evora, a piece based on texts
of Latin American women poets, in the Bienal Festival of Flamenco in
1994. Esperanza described the projects she has been involved in over
the past four years:

> I was in the Bienal of Flamenco two years ago [1994] and it was a
> big breakthrough for me. I've been in flamenco for years, since
> childhood, but you always need a lucky opportunity to really "make
> it." This happened for me two years ago with *A Oscuras.* I worked
> with Enrique Morente on this work by Isidro Munoz and José Miguel
> Evora, brothers of Manolo San Lucar.

Esperanza currently has two recordings: a performance of *El Amor
Brujo*, by Manuel de Falla, and a recent solo CD simply titled
Esperanza Fernández. This recording, the realization of a long-awaited
dream, is, in her own words:

> A mix of things, because flamenco has evolved a lot. I am young, but
> I never abandon my roots, because that is where we learn. It is im-
> possible to leave your roots entirely, because when you start out, you
> listen to all the old recordings to learn what a soléa is. First you listen
> to the older singers to learn, then you can create your own style, with
> your own personality. But the roots, these you can never lose. Since I
> was a little girl, we always listened to older singers. I perform inno-
> vative pieces, without ever leaving behind the roots. For example, I
> may sing a soleá or an alegrías with some modern variations, but it is
> still a soleá or an alegrías. They are modern versions, like the fan-
> dango we did at the show *Estrellas de la Bienal*, the fandangos with
> piano. It was beautiful and it is very flamenco, although it is some-
> thing new with piano. There are people who like this and others who
> don't. Normally, in my shows, I do the first part with more traditional
> flamenco and then in the second part, I do innovations, like using the
> piano. But I never leave behind my roots in cante—they are always
> with me.[9]

Negotiating Power Relations in Andalusian and Gitano/a Flamenco Performance

I have presented some examples of the ways in which issues of multi-faceted identities are enacted by female singers within the artistic/aesthetic world of flamenco. Cantaoras from the older generation obviously had a very different set of circumstances to deal with than today's singers. La Paquera, the compelling singer from Jerez, has been a highly successful cantaora, despite the fact that she pursued her career during the Franco years, in an extremely repressive atmosphere for women, in which women were expected to have no public roles. While an exponent of the traditional cante, at the same time she is a thoroughly professional singer who performs elegantly dressed, with no apparent Andalusian clichés in her clothing, such as the fan or mantón de manilla (fringed shawl), nor in her stage sets. This is in contrast to a great many flamenco performances in which scenery and props depicting stereotypical Andalusian symbols are common. La Paquera consistently negotiates a sense of herself that is modern and sophisticated, yet remains strongly connected to her roots as Andalusian and gitana who prides herself in carrying on the pure styles of Jerez.

Cantaoras from the middle generation have had greater freedom in which to develop and have had fewer restrictions than the older singers, as most of their careers began toward the end of the Franco regime. The world that they have inhabited as performers and women has become more complex, more confusing in its heterogeneity and at the same time more liberating in terms of social and creative options. Carmen Linares went to Madrid in her teens and got her start in singing cante for dancers in the tablaos. Though originally from eastern Andalusia and known for her specialization in cante minero, one of the main forms of cante from the region, she has remained in Madrid. She is internationally known, particularly in France where she has toured and recorded extensively. A sophisticated, elegant, very cosmopolitan woman, she is also a wife and mother. She is seen as the successor to La Niña de Los Peines for her encyclopedic knowledge of all the palos of cante. Notwithstanding her innovative recordings and projects, she considers herself a singer of the older cante, a classic singer and yet one who "lives in her time" (*El Giraldillo* [September 1996]).

The younger cantaoras have grown up in a democratic Spain. While they have put a great deal of the tradition behind them, at the same time, they consciously and very proudly continue these traditions. The cante they perform reflects recent influences and old roots simultaneously. Lole Montoya, from the pioneering duo Lole and Manuel, was instrumental in changing the face of flamenco for younger generations. Both the lyrics and the music done by Lole and Manuel were new and experimental and have reached a wide and diverse audience of younger people. In fact, many of the younger generation were introduced to flamenco through their recordings. Lole made it clear in our interview that their choice of lyrics, both in theme and in poetic structure, was quite intentional. They wanted to say something new with the cante, to represent their gitano heritage in a new and more positive way and to express idealism and hope. Yet these new themes and forms are set in a very traditional flamenco idiom, both musically and vocally. In taking a major role in the creation and the definition of nuevo flamenco, Lole and Manuel broke new ground. But they did so very consciously as gitanos from Seville, always presenting themselves and their music as firmly rooted in this celebrated heritage.

Another heritage they celebrated, the legacy of Al-Andalus, is that of Lole's mother, La Negra, from Spanish Morocco. Following in her mother's footsteps, Lole learned to sing in Arabic, listening to the many recordings of Arab music that they had at home. La Negra is known for performing cante, in particular the tangos, to Arabic lyrics. Lole and Manuel have recorded songs that feature Arabic vocals and Lole has also performed the songs of Egyptian diva Umm Kulthum. Connections with the Moorish past are yet another facet of identity that is often expressed in flamenco performance.[10] In Lole's case that heritage comes directly from her own family. In the case of other flamenco singers, the celebration of the Moorish roots and the long-standing cultural connection with North Africa are not so much personal as consciously Andalusian, an expression of the Andalucismo, specifically the history of Al-Andalus and its continued relevance and meaning in modern Spain.

Esperanza Fernández is another very forward-looking singer who has been involved in a number of innovative versions of cante. Her background is very traditional and like Lole, she performed in the family flamenco company in her early years. But Esperanza identifies with present experimentation in flamenco and has done her part to contribute to them. She has sung cante based on Spanish women poets to jazz-inspired piano accompaniment. She has performed with symphony orchestras and with experimental ensembles of guitar and cello. Her familial ties, her roots in Seville and in the gitano and flamenco communities are strong, but they do not confine her. In addition, she is of the new breed of gitanas who postponed marriage and family in order to begin a professional career. At present, she is skillfully combining her performance career with marriage and motherhood with a freedom and flexibility not possible in previous generations. This change in attitude is very recent in the social value system of the more traditional gitano community. It has taken place just in the last generation and is in marked contrast to previous perceptions of acceptable roles for gitanas.

Conclusion

Women flamenco performers have been juggling opposing forces and negotiating social and cultural contradictions since flamenco began. Many are closely associated with very traditional, classic forms and are considered transmitters of cante, the very matriarchs of flamenco song, just as many are deeply involved in the wide range of innovations taking place today. They will continue to move flamenco in new directions while they carry on its legacy and honor the flamenco heritage. Over the past several decades, they have taken an increasingly prominent role in the articulation of cante flamenco, just as they have in flamenco dance. Their active mediation in the evolution of flamenco performance has been paralleled by their central participation in the re-negotiation of flamenco identities. As they reinterpret traditional regional, ethnic, gender and class identities, cantaoras re-create flamenco. The twenty-first century will surely see an acceleration in this process, as women move into ever new terrain in flamenco, more active and experimental than ever as innovators of cante, as producers, directors, composers and no doubt before too long, as professional guitarists. The gender bias in favor of male guitarists (which began in the early twentieth century, when the guitar began to be highlighted as a solo virtuoso instrument) continues to prevail in flamenco. Social values of gender separation continue to restrict the possibilities for women flamenco guitarists. While discrimination against women guitarists persists, it is (in the opinion of some cantaoras such as Carmen Linares and Lole Montoya) only a matter of time until the efforts of a younger generation of women break this barrier down, and women will take their place as respected flamenco guitarists alongside their male counterparts.[11]

   The cantaoras who make up today's talented, creative group are following in the footsteps of the many remarkable nineteenth-century singers. Like their predecessors from the era of the cafés cantantes, they transmit and preserve flamenco song as they continue to cross barriers and overcome obstacles. They acknowledge the legacy that they have inherited from their predecessors, while at the same time they are breaking new ground in the constantly evolving, dynamic tradition of cante flamenco.

In this chapter I have touched upon some of the important social and cultural transformations that have enabled women to transcend the social stigma and behavioral restrictions of the past and take a prominent role in the direction of flamenco today. I have examined the contributions of certain cantaoras who represent different generations of women, involved in ongoing negotiations that strive to balance the tensions between processes of preservation and those of innovation. These singers honor the past and at the same time embrace the future. Through their individual styles and repertories and creative choices, these singers create a bridge between tradition and innovation in flamenco practice. Involved in a creative dialogue with a deeply symbolic inherited legacy, these and other women flamenco singers reveal how music can be simultaneously a rich site of memory, that is, a valued and collectively shared heritage and a site for creativity and experimentation. This multifaceted sense of identity actively engages issues in the expanded framework of the Spanish cultural landscape as the twenty-first century begins. Like their predecessors, contemporary cantaoras, both young and old, explore, articulate and ultimately celebrate what it means to be Spanish Andalusian, gitana and above all, flamenca.

Notes

1. This term refers to traditional Mediterranean social practices of gender separation and references the public/private dichotomy noted by many researchers (Gilmore, Corbin and Corbin, Peristany and Press) among others. In Andalusia the public space of the bar or tavern belongs to men, while the domestic space is traditionally the domain of women. As a result, social situations which are separated by gender have been the norm and have given rise to the term *homo-social* in the Mediterranean and more specifically Andalusian, context (see Gilmore 1987, 1990).

2. Blas Vega provides an interesting account of the era in his detailed study *Los Cafés Cantantes de Sevilla* (1980), in which he cites numerous press releases and concert reviews of the era.

3. Personal interview with author. Madrid: December, 1996.

4. Personal interview with author. Madrid: December, 1996.

5. This is in marked contrast to previous generations when the rate of illiteracy among gitanos and other Andalusians was very high.

6. Personal interview with author. Sevilla: October 1996.
7. Personal interview with author. Sevilla: October 1996.
8. Personal interview with author. Sevilla: October 1996.
9. Personal interview with author. Sevilla: December 2001.
10. Other recordings with Arabic and North African influences in flamenco have been done by singer El Lebrijano in his Encuentros, by Cantaora Enrique Morente and most recently by nuevo flamenco group Radio Tarifa.
11. I met only one professional female guitarist in all my fieldwork in Spain, María Albarrán. See Chuse (2003: 207–16) for a revealing interview in which she speaks of the many challenges she faces as a flamenco guitarist and the musical director of her family flamenco troupe in Madrid.

Bibliography

Abu Lughod, Lila. *Writing Women's Worlds: Bedouin Stories.* Berkeley: University of California Press, 1993.

Abu Lughod, Lila, and Catherine Lutz, eds. *Language and the Politics of Emotion.* New York: Cambridge University Press, 1990.

Alvarez Caballero, A. *El Cante Flamenco.* Madrid: Editorial Alianza, 1994.

Blas Vega, José. *Los Cafés Cantantes de Sevilla.* Madrid: Editorial Cinterco, 1980.

Blas Vega, Jose, and Manuel Ríos Ruiz. *Diccionario Enciclopedico Ilustrado del Flamenco.* 2 volumes. Madrid: Editorial Cinterco, 1988.

Chuse, Loren. *The Cantaoras: Music, Gender and Identity in Flamenco Song.* New York: Routledge Press, 2003.

Clemente, Luis. *Filigranas: Una Historia de Fusiones Flamencas.* Valencia: Editorial la Máscara, 1995.

Corbin, J. R., and M. P. Corbin. *Urbane Thought: Culture and Class in an Andalusian City.* Aldershot U.K.: Gower, 1987.

Cowan, Jane. *Dance and the Body Politic in Northern Greece.* Princeton, New Jersey: Princeton University Press, 1990.

Cruces Roldán, Cristina. "La Dimension Socio-politico en las letras Flamencas." in *Historia del Flamenco* V, edited by José Luis Navarro García and Miguel Poero Nuñez de Tejada. Sevilla: Ediciones Tartessos, 1997

———, ed. *El Flamenco: Identidades Sociales, Ritual y Patrimonio*

Cultural. Jerez de la Frontera: Centro Andaluz de Flamenco, 1996.

El Giraldillo (September 1996).

García Gomez, Genesis. *Cante Flamenco, Cante Minero.* Barcelona: Editorial Anthropos, 1993.

Gilmore, David. *Honor and Shame and the Unity of the Mediterranean.* Washington: American Anthropological Association, 1987.

———. "Men and Women in Southern Spain: 'Domestic Power' Revisited." *American Antropologist* 92, no. 1 (1990).

Graham, Helen, and Jo Labanyi, eds. *Spanish Cultural Studies.* Oxford, New York: Oxford University Press, 1996.

Kapchan, Deborah. *Gender on the Market: Moroccan Women and the Revoicing of Tradition.* Philadelphia: University of Pennsylvania Press, 1996.

Leblon, Bernard. *El Cante Flamenco: Entre las músicas Gitanas y las tradiciones Andaluzas.* Madrid: Editorial Conterco, 1991.

Loza, Steve. *Barrio Rhythm: Mexican American Music in Los Angeles.* Urbana: University of Illinois Press, 1993.

Mitchell, Timothy. *Flamenco Deep Song.* New Haven: Yale University Press, 1994.

Ortiz Nuevo, Jose Luis. *Se Sabe Algo? Viaje al conocimiento del Arte Flamenco en la prensa sevillana del XIX.* Sevilla: Ediciones El Carro de la Nieve, 1990.

———. *Alegato Contra la Pureza.* Madrid: Editorial Démofilo, 2000.

Press, Irwin. *The City as Context: Urbanism and Behavioral Constraints in Seville.* Urbana: University of Illinois Press, 1979.

Steingress, Gerhard. *Sociología del Cante Flamenco.* Jerez de la Frontera: Centro Andaluz de Flamenco, 1991.

Stokes, Martin. *Ethnicity, Music and Place.* Oxford: Oxford University Press, 1994.

Sugarman, Jane. *Engendering Song: Singing and the Social Order at Prespa Albanian Weddings.* Chicago: University of Chicago Press, 1997.

Triana, Fernando el de. *Arte y Aristas Flamencos.* Madrid: Imprenta Helénica, 1936.

Turino, Thomas. *Moving Away from Silence.* Chicago: University of Chicago Press, 1993.

Washabaugh, William. *Flamenco: Passion, Politics and Popular Culture.* Oxford: Berg, 1996.

———, ed. *The Passion of Music and Dance: Body, Gender and Sexuality.* Oxford: Berg, 1998.

Part 4
"Mediterranean Music"

Chapter Eight

Anchors and Sails: Music and Culture Contact in Corsica

Caroline Bithell

Introduction

The unique situation of the Mediterranean as a culture area that impinges on three continents—Southern Europe, North Africa and Asia Minor—and whose central mass is defined by water rather than land has historically allowed ample scope for contacts and exchanges between the different cultures that flourished on the shores of the "great sea" and on her numerous islands. In the case of Corsica, references can be found both in the literature and in accounts given by contemporary musicians to one or another feature of the island's musical heritage having its roots in other times and places—a notion that has in some ways served to add a somewhat romantic or refined patina to the island's complex and frequently troubled past. In the first part of the present discussion I offer a brief examination of the types of influences and affinities that have been postulated for Corsica's musical evolution. It is only in the island's more recent history, however, that it is possible to document with a surer confidence instances of direct intercultural contact on a specifically musical plane and it is to an exploration of some of the most recent cases that I turn my attention in the second half of this chapter. In the course of this discussion with its more "global" frame of reference, I aim to offer an insight into the motivations behind contacts that have been actively courted and the implications of both literal contacts and perceived affinities at both a practical and a politico-philosophical level. Finally I refocus on the question of "Mediterranean" music as I examine the impulse on the part of contemporary Corsican musicians to explore the specifically Mediterranean roots of their island's music and, in some cases, to forge links with musics and musicians from other Mediterranean traditions based on a perception of shared heritage.

The Historical Jigsaw

The main aim of the present discussion is neither to attempt a reconstruction of the island's musical development based on verifiable historical "fact" nor to seek to prove the legitimacy or otherwise of the various claims that have been made regarding origins and influences from across the sea. I begin, nonetheless, with a brief foray into Corsica's tangled history and, more specifically, the types of observations and speculations that have been generated regarding the island's musical evolution.

Corsica at the Crossroads of the Mediterranean

As a result of its strategic position in the western Mediterranean basin, Corsica has always been caught in the crosscurrent of peoples and powers that have conducted their business, legitimate or otherwise, by means of the Mediterranean. Over the centuries, the island has been occupied in turn by Greeks, Etruscans, Carthaginians, Romans, Vandals, Byzantines, Ostrogoths, Lombards and Saracens, subsequently coming under the control of Pisa, Genoa and Aragon, before finally being ceded to France in the Treaty of Versailles (1768). The fact that the island might now count for many as "French" should not therefore be allowed to obscure the fact that the sphere of influence in which Corsica existed in past times owed as much to cultures emanating from, or passing through, North Africa and the Near East as it did to continental Europe. The island has its own language, Corsican (Corse), which is still in use today despite having suffered serious displacement in favor of the official French language and many aspects of the traditional culture and lifestyle continue to relate closely to those of the neighboring island of Sardinia, now part of Italy.

Roots and Relations

Sporadic, largely unsubstantiated but much-quoted references to the supposed origins of some part of the Corsican musical canon in other lands in or bordering on the Mediterranean can be found in the semi-scholarly literature as penned by folklorists, amateur cultural commentators and others in the nineteenth and twentieth centuries. Mathieu

Ambrosi, for example, was able to write in 1938 (27) that "Corsican song is an African song,"[1] while the disc notes to Maurice Bitter's collection *Musique Folklorique du Monde: Corsica* (n.d.) state, with reference to a paghjella (a polyphonic song for three voices) from the village of Isulacciu, that: "The paghjella plunges its roots into the most distant past. A Spanish past moreover and more specifically, it is said, a Majorcan one," while a second paghjella from Castirla is referred to as "this paghjella which our ancestors brought from Kabyle." The reference to Majorca echoes a similar reference in a footnote in Austin de Croze's *La Chanson Populaire de L'Ile de Corse* of 1911 (6), although here—confusingly—it is appended to a description of the paghjella as monodic song, occurring in the context of a discussion of serenades, election songs and laments. The description given appears to be simply that of the old indigenous style of singing—incantatory, long, drawn out and often highly melismatic, with frequent use of quartertones and other reduced intervals, extended finals and a tendency towards nasalization (sometimes with an element of glottal constriction)—a style that has traditionally been used for original compositions and improvisations as well as characterizing the upper voices in polyphonic singing.[2] This style certainly resembles singing styles found in other parts of the Mediterranean: similarities with flamenco, for example—chiefly with respect to voice placement, timbre and vocal impulse—have frequently been noted. It is also this style that is often popularly perceived as having "Arabic" overtones, an association that is not restricted to Corsica alone. Sorce Keller, for example, comments that "by the time Sicily is reached the embellished character of the melodies and the nasal quality of voice production are strongly reminiscent of Arabic music" (1994: 44–45), going on to propose that "this is not surprising, since southern Italy was once ruled by Spain (which has had close contact with the Middle East) and Sicily, in particular, was once ruled by the Arabs (ninth and tenth centuries A.D.)" (44–45). This leads him to portray the Italian peninsula as "a bridge between the European mainland and the Middle East." Meanwhile, parallels in terms of the characteristic posture adopted by the singer whereby one hand is raised to the ear have also been widely noted, as has the antiquity of the gesture as evidenced by iconographical representations dating from ancient Egypt.

Allusions such as those found in Ambrosi and de Croze might be tantalizing but they are disappointingly imprecise and remain unsupported by any hard evidence or detailed comparison. Laade (1981, vol. 1: 137) reports that, despite the regularity with which the claim that the paghjella originated in the Balearics is reiterated throughout the literature, his own investigations revealed no obvious parallels. He also makes the observation (133–34) that, in the case of writers such as these whose musical perception as well as direct acquaintance with many of the traditions they invoke was often limited, any music that was unfamiliar would automatically have been seen as "archaic" and, as such, assigned uncritically to the same box as "Oriental" and other supposedly "primitive" musics. In a similar spirit, the "archaic" modalities of old folk melodies would immediately have suggested an association with Gregorian chant—hence the equally frequent proposals that Corsican melodies are derived from, or at least have been substantially influenced by, Gregorian chant.[3]

Nonetheless, in view of the island's location and history and the relative ease of mobility in the Mediterranean region as a whole, it should not seem unlikely that we should find echoes of, if not direct borrowings from, the musical cultures of some of Corsica's Mediterranean neighbors. Many of the island's former occupiers have conspicuously left their mark on the landscape in the form of megaliths and stone statues, other prehistoric stoneworks offering links with Sardinia, Malta and the Balearics, Greek and Roman remains, Pisan churches, Genoese watchtowers and bridges and the great citadels of Bastia, Calvi and Bonifacio. Place names such as Morosaglia, Campu Moru and Muratu offer continuing testimony to the Moorish presence of the ninth to eleventh centuries. To assume that some, at least, of these peoples would also have left traces of their musical practices would not seem unreasonable, although the extent to which occupying forces would have penetrated the more isolated and inaccessible interior regions of the island has also been questioned.[4]

Reflections on the Archaeology of Music

All that we can perhaps say with complete impunity is that the types of resemblances that have been noted do point to what we might conceive of as a shared portfolio of cultural practices and a wide diffusion of stylistic traits across the Mediterranean region as a whole. Such resemblances do not of themselves, however, justify seeing the paghjella or any other manifestation of Corsican song as being specifically *derived from* another similar style. In particular, I would argue that we should remain wary of the ease with which the older singing style has often been so readily identified simply as "Arabic." One must, moreover, treat with due circumspection any approach that appears to view "Corsican music" as a unified entity that can be conclusively defined.

Clearly there are different layers to any culture, both vertical and horizontal, across time and space and across professions and social classes, which, where music is concerned, will point towards different lines of kinship for different genres.

Temporal Stratification

Within the Corsican musical canon as represented by the field recording collections made by Félix Quilici and Wolfgang Laade between 1948 and 1973 (some genres having since fallen into disuse), a number of different styles can be identified that clearly relate to different historical layers. (For a broadly chronological overview of the most important genres, see Laade 1981, vol. 1: 41.) In terms of shared Mediterranean roots, it is the oldest layer that is potentially of the greatest interest. Given that most forms of musical expression have specific functional determinants or ritualistic associations, however, stylistic resemblances may be accounted for by the fact that they are to some extent determined by the situation itself and by the emotions that give impulse to the "performance." At a broader level, what might strike the observer primarily is the similarity of the situation as a whole, including the ritualistic use of music and aspects of performance practice, rather than a more specific similarity at the level of melody and other strictly musical components.

Perhaps the most obvious case in point is that of laments, which occupy a position of prime significance in many Mediterranean societies. The extemporized laments for the dead (voceri, sing. voceru), which belong to the oldest extant layers of Corsican song and continued to be "performed" into the middle decades of the twentieth century, have clear parallels in the Sardinian attitu as well as further afield in the Greek lament tradition. (It is relevant to note here that Sorce Keller [1994: 43], citing de Martino [1908], sees the funeral lamentations as still practiced in the south of Italy as offering tangible proof of the fact that, in antiquity, "Southern Italy was an integral part of the Greek world . . . indeed . . . in all respects part of Greece.") This is not to say that the laments "sound the same"—even if Iannis Xenakis, listening to recorded musical examples while writing the preface to the first volume of the *Antulugia di u Cantu Nustrale* (de Zerbi and Raffaelli 1993), did claim to detect specifically musical resemblances between a melody used for *A nanna di u Cuscionu* (The lullaby of the Cuscionu) and recently deciphered ancient Greek melodies—but rather that they are performed in consonant circumstances and share many similarities in terms of function and motivation, particularly when they are associated with deaths resulting from the vendetta,[5] and that this in turn accounts for certain resemblances in aspects of vocal production and the patterning of the vocal line.

The sung improvised debate known as chjam' è rispondi, which is still practiced in Corsica today, similarly has parallels in the Sardinian gara poetica, the ottava rima found in mainland Italy and the Maltese spirtu pront.[6] While these forms diverge in terms of musical detail—the melodies themselves are in each case quite distinctive, often relating to other genres in the same culture and while the chjam' è rispondi is unaccompanied, the singers' stanzas in a gara poetica are punctuated by a small polyphonic ensemble and the spirtu pront singers are usually accompanied by guitars—the different manifestations share certain paramusical traits that can in some cases be linked to the circumstances of performance, as well as undeniable commonalities in terms of function.

Genres belonging to later strata reveal quite different lines of kinship. As Corsica has been increasingly assimilated into the modern western European world, the effects of contact with the Western musical system and aesthetic have inevitably been felt, the strongest pull being exerted by the equal-tempered scale, functional harmony and rhythmic regularity. Even before widespread diffusion of "Western" styles via the media, the introduction of the guitar and mandolin as accompanying instruments had heralded significant changes at the level of modality and rhythm. It is, perhaps, not surprising that the barcaroles and accompanied serenades that became popular from the eighteenth century betray Italianate influence. Moreover, these songs were associated primarily with the culture of the larger towns and coastal ports, pointing also to the geographical and social stratifications to which I will return below. Songs from this layer, together with a number of dance tunes, have been preserved in the repertories of the folkloric ensembles that are still active in the main towns of Bastia in the north and Ajaccio in the south.

Clearly, the styles involved in the different genres alluded to thus far are widely divergent, yet they are all seen as part of Corsica's musical heritage. It is also the case that the different temporal strata referred to do not equate only to different genres. Within the polyphonic paghjella in the form in which it exists today, for example, there are clearly different layers, with what might be assumed to be the latest accretion being the addition or modification of a bass line (bassu) operating along functional principles and offering harmonic support to the more tightly fused pair of the two upper voices (secunda and terza) with their vibrant timbres, narrow range and intersecting melismatic figures. In the case of the terza, the now distinctive tierce de Picardie–type final cadence would likewise appear to be a feature acquired at a relatively late stage, the overall character of the voice with its extremely restricted range, incantatory quality, ringing timbre and role of assuring continuity of sound pointing to more archaic roots. The prototypical melody underlying many variants of the secunda line, meanwhile, bears an uncanny resemblance to what would appear to be the oldest type of lament melody. Meanwhile, the two other types of polyphonic song found in the secular tradition, the terzetti and madrigale, have much in common in terms of musical style with the paghjella but at the level of the textual format and language they betray a more literary influence. The terzetti's stanzaic format of three lines of (nominally) eleven syllables is usually identified in the literature as being based on a form found in classical Tuscan poetry of the fourteenth century onwards, as represented by Dante, Tasso and Arioste,[7] while the language used for the texts of the small body of pieces commonly referred to as madrigali has been designated "u cruscu," a Corsicanized form of Tuscan (the latter having functioned as the island's official language during five centuries of Genoese control).

Geographical and Social Stratification

The long-standing division of the island into two quite distinct halves (essentially north and south) must also account in part for the different lines of musical development. From the end of the thirteenth century until the middle of the fifteenth, Corsica was in dispute between Genoa and Aragon, and at this time the natural division of the island into north—referred to by the Genoese as di qua da i monti (this side of the mountains)—and south—di là da i monti (the other side of the mountains)—was reinforced by a divergence in their political orientations, with the village communities who controlled the ancestral lands in the north enjoying the protection of the Genoese while the south remained in the power of the feudal lords who relied for their support on Aragon.[8] In this context it is interesting to note that, while the historical record is by no means complete, polyphonic singing has been attested mainly in the central and northern parts of the island, the south showing a greater predilection for monodic song and solo improvisation.

In Corsica's more recent history, musical practices in the coastal towns—with their growing concentration of professional and commercial activity and their greater openness to outside influences and changing fashions—have inevitably developed along very different lines to those of village and mountain populations who have continued to pursue more traditional pastoral lifestyles and retain more of the old "folk" rituals. Musical styles relating to a more refined "art" tradition were favored by the quasi-urbanized educated classes whose offspring would often be sent to complete their education in Italy.

In the early decades of the twentieth century a significant influence in terms of vocal style was exerted by opera singers whose performances could be heard at Ajaccio's San Gabriel—considered to have one of the best acoustics in Europe prior to its destruction by fire in 1927—and whose voices found their way even to the more remote villages via the gramophone. A new, continentally inspired lyrical style was epitomized in the singing of Ajaccio-born star Tino Rossi (1907–83), king of the so-called chanteurs de charme and the new romantic idol of the French entertainment industry in the 1930s, who in addition to recording over a thousand songs also starred in twenty-four films and four operettas. In the postwar years, broader contact with a more modern, urbanized and supposedly civilized European culture was to account in large part for the rejection of traditional singing styles and in particular those traits that were seen as "Arabic," as is made explicit in the types of responses that greeted radio broadcasts of field recordings made by Félix Quilici in the late 1940s—epitomized in the wail "whatever will the Continentals think of us?"[9]

Culture Contact in the Postmodern Era

I turn now to a consideration of the musical world occupied by those of my own generation in Corsica and of the more conscious choices that have been made with regard to the directions taken by their music. In many senses, the gulf between the world of today's musicians and their audiences and that of the previous generation is wider than it has ever been. That the mobility of musics and musicians at a global level has brought profound changes not only in terms of the available musical palate but also with respect to musical behavior hardly needs restating. A striking feature of the music scene in Corsica since the 1970s has been the number of young people who have constituted themselves into formalized "groups" against the backdrop of the cultural renaissance that has gathered pace over the past three decades. For many of these groups now operating at a professional and semiprofessional level, international mobility has become part and parcel of the lifestyle. Those who helped pave the way in the late 1980s and early 1990s included the group Les Nouvelles Polyphonies Corses whose early career was given a kick-start when, on the strength of their first disc (*Les Nouvelles Polyphonies Corses*, 1991), they were chosen to perform at the opening ceremony of the Winter Olympics at Albertville in 1992. More recently, a number of Corsican groups have been engaged to lend their distinctive vocal style to film soundtracks. Recent successes include A Filetta's performance in several of Bruno Coulais's film scores, including *Don Juan* and *Himalaya*. I Chjami Aghjalesi added to their portfolio a performance in the soundtrack for *La Reine Margot*, while I Surghjenti featured in the soundtrack of José Giovanni's *Mon Père*. As a result of the experience and discipline of working with continental composers and directors, some have now learned to read music while also adding a greater degree of sophistication to their own composing skills. One of the undisputed masters in this respect is Jean-Claude Acquaviva of the group A Filetta who, by his own admission, has found himself moving in a more "classical" direction (*Corse-Matin*, 21 August 2001). Many groups now have continental agents and have notched up a steady stream of successes with tours and festival appearances all over the world. I Chjami Aghjalesi, for example, have recently toured South America, while Jean-Paul Poletti and his male voice choir from Sartène have performed in countries as diverse and far-flung as Hong Kong, Iran and Mexico.

Physical appearances by the various groups outside the island have played an important part in introducing Corsican music, together with the language and aspects of the island's political concerns, to a wider audience. At the same time, they have served to bring Corsican musicians into direct contact with fellow musicians from other cultures, allowing them to undertake what one group member referred to as "un collectage à l'extérieure" (the opportunity to "collect" music outside the island), from which they can then draw additional inspiration for their own arrangements and compositions.

Musical Meetings and Political Affinities

One of the most interesting stories of recent times is undoubtedly that of the musical encounters that occurred in the 1970s, primarily as a result of political affinities. This decade—which provided the main impetus for the cultural revival or riacquistu—was one of particular turbulence in Corsica as a new surge of nationalist activity inspired by the reinvigoration of the movement for autonomy met with increasingly heavy-handed suppression by the French state.[10] At a time when events in the Pays Basque, Northern Ireland and Chile were making international headlines, the young Corsican militants were to draw ideological as well as moral support from the struggles of other minorities and, where politics led, music was often not far behind. Corsican singers had already begun to form themselves into groups, motivated by an urge to safeguard the island's cultural heritage and to breathe new life into the musical traditions of the older generation, which were perceived to be in danger of dying out. The seminal groupe engagé of this period, Canta u Populu Corsu, is still active at the time of this writing after a break in its activities from 1984 to 1994. A number of groups were to follow the lead of Canta in aligning themselves with the aims and ethos of the autonomist movement and adding to the growing body of newly composed chansons engagées—referred to in Corsican as cantu indiatù—that commented on and responded to political events of the time.

One of the most significant and more lasting influences was that exerted by the nueva canción (new song) movement that had evolved in Latin America as part of the resistance to the corrupt and oppressive totalitarian regimes of countries such as Chile and Argentina, where a parallel resistance to U.S. hegemony had led to the adoption of indigenous musical styles and genres—embraced as authentic forms of expression of the "folk"—as vehicles for the call for justice and democracy. Canta and others drew inspiration in particular from the Chilean group Quilapayún who, at the time of the military coup that prematurely ended Salvador Allende's rule in 1973 and heralded a period of unprecedented terror under Pinochet, were on tour in Europe where they then remained in exile. From their base in Paris, they performed thousands of concerts all over Europe—including Corsica—as a means of mustering support for human rights in Chile. It was largely the example of the nueva canción artists with their notion of the song as bullet and the guitar as gun that brought Corsican militants to the realization that songs could be used to spread a political message and musical performance could be embraced as an extension of militant activity. Following in the mold of nueva canción, Canta's early "creations" featured new topical texts set to melodies that resembled those of traditional songs of the oral tradition. At the level of the musical fabric itself, the South American influence was to find joyous expression in Natale Luciani's song *Compañero* (featured on the disc *Ci hè dinù*, 1982), where the distinctly Andean rhythmic coloration is reinforced by the use of charango and panpipes—instruments that reappear today in the lineup of the young group Vaghjime, whose members met at

Luciani's scola di cantu in Ajaccio.[11] Meanwhile, as recently as August 2002, Canta and Quilapayún once again shared the stage for a concert in Ajaccio, a testimony to the strength and depth of their affinity.

Elements from other song traditions were appropriated for purely aesthetic reasons as part of a conscious attempt to make Corsican music more comprehensible and palatable to a wider audience. As Corsican groups were increasingly invited to perform outside the island, they realized that the way in which they were received by their new audiences would, in the absence of an understanding of the song text which hitherto had been privileged in the urgency to "pass on the message," be dependent on the musical element alone. A number of musicians have commented on their intimation that the musical component in isolation was not overly stimulating and ran the risk of becoming monotonous or soporific: one musician characterized the typical Corsican song as "sad and heavy." In particular, the rhythmic aspect was not high on the agenda where most traditional Corsican genres were concerned; indeed, the majority of traditional songs were unaccompanied. This led to a deliberate "borrowing" of rhythms and of instrumental accompaniment in general from other Mediterranean traditions of popular song: Portuguese fado and Greek rembetika have both been cited as examples. These various influences combined to form a new style of chanson that continues to thrive and that is now seen by many of the younger generation as "traditional."[12]

Encounters Performed: Polyphony, World Music and Fusion Projects

An event that proved decisive in terms of the directions taken by Corsican music in the 1990s—with respect to both performance and composition—was a visit by the so-called Bulgarian Voices (as featured on Cellier's discs issued as *Le Mystère des Voix Bulgares*, 1988, 1989 and 1990). I have discussed elsewhere (Bithell 2003a) the way in which the Bulgarian phenomenon offered some of the inspiration for the internationally successful career of the group Les Nouvelles Polyphonies Corses (formed in 1989) and its importance in fueling the more progressive stage of Corsica's polyphonic revival. The Bulgarian encounter and the whole "world music" wave of which it was a part also stimulated a more intense interest in other polyphonic traditions: just as the cultural militants of the 1970s had established contacts with musicians from other parts of the world who shared a similar political history, so those of the 1990s were to seek out singers from other cultures with whom they had the phenomenon of polyphony in common. The annual Rencontres Polyphoniques that takes place in Calvi in the Balagne serves as a meeting point for diverse polyphonic traditions, invitations being extended each year to a number of ensembles from various parts of Europe and beyond, but with Sardinia, Bulgaria, Albania and Georgia featuring on a regular basis.[13] Corsican groups in their turn receive regular invitations to appear at similar festivals overseas. Such encounters and exchanges, together with the relatively easy availability of recordings of other musical traditions via world music distribution networks, have again led directly to musical influences. Some groups happily acknowledge that one or another of their new compositions has been inspired by, or consciously incorporates elements from, other polyphonic styles: Cinqui Sò's song *Com'a Acqua Linda* on the disc *Chants Polyphoniques Corses* (1992), for example, is listed as "inspired by a traditional Albanian song." Others import songs from other traditions directly into their own repertoire. Members of the group A Filetta have, over the years, developed a particularly close association with Georgia and regularly include one or more Georgian songs in their concerts. The ensemble Soledonna (a latter-day incarnation of Les Nouvelles Polyphonies Corses) has similarly developed contacts with Georgian singers and musicians, several of whom feature on their 2001 disc *Isulanima*; the disc itself was recorded in Tbilisi.

Perhaps the most literal form of culture contact in the present age, sometimes appearing as a natural extension of the festival ethos, is the semi-composed, semi-improvised fusion project, which offers a literal reenactment of a meeting between two or more quite distinct musical cultures ("ethnic" or otherwise). The 1995 Calvi Jazz Festival, for example, ended with a performance appositely entitled *Encontra*, which featured the Corsican female ensemble Donnisulana, who had risen to fame with their a cappella renditions of Corsican polyphonic songs, together with Andy Emler's jazz ensemble.[14] The performance was based on a score by Emler himself who, in an article in *Corse-Matin* (1 July 1995), defined "the unexpected mix jazz/polyphonies" as "a living European music of the end of the century." This was, however, not the first meeting between Corsican polyphony and jazz. Tavagna's 1983 disc, with the similar title *Incontru*, was a collaboration with the André Jaume Quartet that grew out of the meeting of the two ensembles the previous year when they had shared a stage at Seyne-sur-Mer. Subsequent discs that have resulted from performance projects inspired by a similar ethos, exploring traditional songs in an experimental manner with input from musicians from outside the island, include *Trà Ochju É*

Mare (1991). Conceived and directed by Mighele Raffaelli with arrangements by David Rueff, the disc features a selection of traditional monodic songs, including several laments, a lullaby and a threshing song, overlaid with instrumental lines played on saxophones, trombone, berimbau and synthesizer. Other groups such as Les Nouvelles Polyphonies Corses and I Muvrini have used synthesized and electroacoustic input to situate their product more firmly in a "world music" framework.

I have commented elsewhere (Bithell 2003b) on the way in which this fashion for crosscultural fusion and collage can be understood in part as belonging to a new climate of supposedly global dialogue. Indeed, the symbolic link between crosscultural musical fusion and a postmodern ethic of intercultural understanding was explicitly encapsulated in Michel Codaccioni's portrayal of Patrizia Poli (who, together with Patrizia Gattaceca, is the inspirational mainstay of Les Nouvelles Polyphonies Corses) in a brief profile in *Kyrn* magazine (no. 396, January 1993) as "the magnificent prowhead of a Corsican culture nourished by modernity, by crossbreeding, by questioning, by respect for the other, by exigency and by self-confidence." In the case of I Muvrini, a similar sentiment of "opening up" to the rest of the world is reflected tangibly in the group's instrumental lineup, which now typically includes hurdy-gurdy, bagpipes and a variety of percussion, including African drums, while lead singer Jean-François Bernardini has described the group's concerts as "places of meeting and dialogue" (*Corse-Matin*, 30 May 1994). In a similar vein, a more recent Canta concert (Ajaccio, August 2001), which included three songs performed by a trio of young Basque women, was commented upon in the press the following day in these now familiar terms: "It's also that, Canta u Populu Corsu: openness to others and a sharing of the heart" (*Corse-Matin*, 20 Aug. 2001). Meanwhile, an enduring connection with other oppressed minorities that is expressed both literally through the song lyrics and metaphorically through musical references is made explicit in a press report on a performance by the group L'Arcusgiu, which states that "L'Arcusgiu sings the struggle of the Corsican people but also that of all oppressed peoples," going on to note that the group's latest album, *Testimone a Veternu*, "crosses the musicality of other cultures" (*Corse-Matin*, 22 Aug. 2001).

Returning to the Mediterranean Source

A renewed interest in exploring ways in which traditional Corsican music might be directly related to the musics of other cultures (as opposed to lending itself to a more or less comfortable alliance with an apparently unrelated idiom) has equally been facilitated by the ease of dissemination and mobility in the postmodern era. The surge of interest in polyphonic singing traditions has already been noted. Of central interest in the context of this chapter is the way in which a number of musicians in Corsica itself have, in recent years, begun to turn their attention to exploring the specifically Mediterranean roots of their music.

Mediterranean Identity and Oriental Overtones

Quite apart from the nationalist impulse which, as we have seen, has played a significant role in the renaissance of interest in traditional musical styles in Corsica in recent decades, increased contact with—some might say invasion by—the musical products of an ever more homogenized global culture has in its turn served to refocus attention on older indigenous styles and has even resulted in a conscious resistance on the part of some musicians to what was commonly referred to in the 1990s as the "colonization of the ear." While this culture clash is by no means unique to Corsica, it has been thrown into particularly sharp relief by the island's ongoing problems with its French surrogate parent. The rejection of a French identity and the need to establish a clear difference between Corsican and French culture has forced a certain amount of musical reflection that has resulted in a rudimentary system for defining difference via a set of oppositions such as tempered/nontempered, regular/irregular, syllabic/melismatic, tonality/modality and harmony/polyphony.[15] At the same time, it has added further fuel to a specific interest in exploring the premodern and non-Western roots of Corsica's musical heritage. Among those most dedicated to this line of enquiry is the musician, composer and director Mighele Raffaelli. The disc *U Cantu Prufondu*, conceived and directed by Raffaelli, is subtitled *Presence of the Middle East, the Middle Ages and the Renaissance in Corsican Traditional Music* (Mighela and Raffaelli 1993). The disc features a range of traditional monodic songs performed by the singer Mighela Cesari, accompanied on a variety of instruments by Raffaelli himself and sets out to explore and demonstrate possible ways in which the material might have been performed in the past with respect to the style of instrumental accompaniment and at the same time to highlight features that are suggestive of Oriental, Medieval and Renaissance traditions.

In particular, Raffaelli has been keen to site Corsican music within a Mediterranean as opposed to a western European lineage, with the Mediterranean itself occupying that privileged, pivotal, intercontinental position on account of which its islands have long been viewed as such desirable vantage points. In the disc notes to *Di li Venti, a Rosula* (Cesari and Raffaelli 1997), the island is imagined as being located at a cultural crossroads with the winds that have fertilized its music blowing over it "from the four points of the compass." Embracing a specifically "Mediterranean" identity allows today's musicians to exist in the tension between—or simply the meeting place of—east and west. Explicit reference to this liminal position is, in fact, found in many of the groups' edicts and reproduced in disc notes and press reports. A recent report on the ensemble Soledonna, for example, speaks of the group's music being an expression of "the Latin and Oriental Mediterranean" (*Corse-Matin*, 10 August 2001).

Mediterranean Past and Future

This interest in Mediterranean affinities is not solely backward looking, it encompasses an intention not only to reconstruct the routes of the past but also to forge new pathways for the future. The song *Rosula d'Orienti* from Les Nouvelles Polyphonies Corses' first (eponymous) disc of 1991, for example, is described in the disc notes as "a song which uncovers and projects connections past and to be tied by the roots of the Mediterranean." A similar search for connections both past and future throughout the Mediterranean basin is intrinsic to the identity of the group Cinqui Sò. The disc notes to their 1994 disc, *Com' Acqua Linda*, state that: "Since its creation, the group Cinqui Sò, taking as its starting point traditional Corsican music, has tried to integrate into its musical research the traditions of other Mediterranean peoples, while not being content to reproduce but adding a sensitivity which is its own." When asked to comment specifically on the features that they saw as being common to different Mediterranean musics, group member Ghjuvan Petru Godinat referred to resemblances "at the level of the instruments, at the level of the voices, . . . at the level of the rivucate (melismas), at the level of the intervals between the voices" (personal interview 1995). In particular, the group's adoption of the darabuka lends many of their songs a quasi-Arabic coloration (see, for example, the group's arrangement of the *Lamentu di Tramoni*, a traditional bandit's lament, on *Com' Acqua Linda)*, at the same time as shifting the music towards a more rhythmic, upbeat style (recalling the earlier "borrowing" of Portuguese and Greek rhythms for similar ends). Cinqui Sò's next disc, tellingly entitled *Tarraniu* ("Mediterranean," 1996), featured the Sardinian singer Elena Leda, the Occitan singer Miquèla Bramerie and the Catalan musician Pedro Aledo, with the disc notes stating that "with *Tarraniu*, Cinqui Sò strives to envelop the plurality of identities defined by the Mediterranean."[16]

Conclusions

Though ideas about the way in which Corsican music may have been influenced in the early stages of its evolution by styles from other parts of the Mediterranean may be based more on conjecture than on demonstrable fact and, in particular, attempts to find the "origins" of a specific genre outside the island may be misguided, suggestions of lines of kinship with other musical traditions from across the sea continue to fire the Corsican imagination. Perhaps more than ever before, we have the opportunity today to witness links being forged in the present and to observe the effect not only of literal contact but also of ideas about musical kinship and commonalities on evolving musical practice. In the case of Corsica, we have seen how some groups have deliberately looked to North Africa, the Levant and other parts of the Mediterranean, both in an attempt to rediscover musical affinities and in their search for artistic inspiration. What is most interesting about this trend, I propose, is the power of suggestion, particularly when this has very tangible results in terms of the way in which it colors both the interpretation of traditional material and the style of new compositions.

Whereas in the past culture contact might have been seen as either accidental or naturally occurring (or, in some cases, imposed from the outside), in Corsica today a more conscious process of selection would appear to be at work—at least on the part of professional and semiprofessional musicians—with some forms of contact and opportunities for cross-fertilization being actively courted. In the foregoing discussion I have alluded to the different motivations and rationalizations behind different attempts to draw attention to cultural similarities or differences. In some cases, as we have seen, this impulse is part of a broader political agenda—whether this be in terms of expressing solidarity with other oppressed minorities, paying homage to a putative universal brotherhood or simply drawing attention to the complex of roots that lie outside the western European frame of reference.

Of particular interest in the context of the embracing of a Mediterranean identity has been the changing attitude towards the perceived presence of Arabic overtones in Corsican music. In the period immediately following World War II with its modernizing, urbanizing ethos, supposedly Arabic overtones in the "old" style of singing were seen by the upwardly mobile sectors of Corsican society as an embarrassment, a kind of blot on the copybook that betrayed Corsica's distance from the more civilized culture of the continent to which many people now aspired. We have seen how in latter years, however, the impulse to establish Corsica's difference from French/continental culture has combined with a more academic line of enquiry to fuel exploration of the Oriental side of the island's heritage and this has led some musicians to place particular emphasis on those features of the music that are identified as being resonant of Arabic music and, in some cases, to reinforce the Arabic coloration through the use of instruments such as the darabuka, the 'ud and the ney. From the point of view of insular audiences, a new appreciation of Arabic resonances has no doubt been aided by broader exposure to the realities of music from Arab countries and in particular to the relative sophistication of the more classical traditions.

At a broader level, it has been interesting to observe, over the past twenty to thirty years, the shifts in attitude on the part of Corsican critics towards the adoption of "foreign" musical elements. In the early years of the riacquistu, culture contact was often seen in terms of contamination. A review of L'Albinu's first disc in *Kyrn* magazine (no. 167: 39, January 1986) repeats doubts expressed in several previous reviews with respect to "the difficulties presented by the evolution of the Corsican chanson" and in particular by the "integration of melodic, rhythmic and harmonic elements that come from other sources." By the late 1990s, such integration was being positively celebrated in the daily press (*Corse-Matin* and *La Corse*) as a manifestation of Corsica's engagement both with world music as the new genre and with the much-vaunted age of so-called global dialogue that appeared to be the next step for a post-nationalist Corsica. This is not to say that any sense of caution has been thrown to the wind. Outside the culture of promotion of which the press is very much a part, some continue to voice their unease at the precipitous rate of acculturation in modern times (see, for example, Salini 1996). Older people in particular tend to be skeptical about the current vogue for "fusion" on the grounds that the distinctive character of the indigenous tradition is in danger of being swamped. A decade ago, Ghjacumu Fusina countered similar criticisms with the argument that: "The exchanges allowed by modern means of communication impose a permanent mixing of ideas and of signs that no-one can now claim to avoid, whether he wants to or not. . . . What counts is not the source, but rather what one is capable of creating on the basis of that source!" (1993: 184). It is certainly the case that, as individual musicians become more competent as practitioners and become conversant with a more professional mode of operation, they enter into what is perhaps a natural process of evolution whereby they develop into more sophisticated performers and composers with the urge to experiment and to explore their own creativity as they fine-tune the tools of their trade in terms of both practical agility and theoretical understanding—a development that is as much a result of the increased time and focus invested in their musical activities as it is a corollary of some all-embracing notion of "Westernization." It would, however, be misleading to suggest that the groups themselves have simply traded the Corsican elements of their music; on the contrary, a concern that their music should "sound Corsican" is as strong as ever and in many cases a group's style is composed of a judicious and conscious mix of both local and imported ingredients.[17]

The recent and contemporary developments that I have described in this chapter do, it must be stressed, relate primarily to the culture of the "groups" and other professional or semiprofessional musicians and as such they are, perhaps, of a different order to questions of culture contact at a more comprehensive level in former times. That said, the new hybrid styles that have evolved have inevitably been assimilated more broadly into Corsican society to the extent that the songs of the current groups can be heard emanating from sound systems on almost every corner (at least in the towns)—they constitute the music of choice in many bars, supermarkets, open-air markets and fairs and hits both new and old are played on the radio on a daily basis. Every year, a new crop of amateur groups appears on the scene, typically beginning by performing covers of the songs of their favorite groups before graduating to their first attempts at composing songs in a similar style. At the same time, however, traditional rural genres such as the paghjella and the chjam' è rispondi continue to be sung by ordinary people in their natural settings, apparently in much the same way as they have been for generations. And while they might resemble, at one level or another, similar genres found in neighboring parts of the Mediterranean, they retain their own distinctive sound that is, in the soundscape of today's world music, indisputably and intrinsically Corsican. As far as contemporary styles are concerned, many of the practitioners themselves are of the view that creative experimentation is not in danger of provoking irrevocable change or lasting damage to the culture as a whole: in the longer term, they propose, it is only the more logical developments that will be acceptable and thereby prove tenacious. As Mighela Cesari and Mighele Raffaelli express in their introduction to their 1997 disc, *Di li Venti, a Rosula*, "time will tell whether or not the compass has indicated the right direction."

Notes

1. For a fuller discussion of Ambrosi's proposals regarding the history of Corsican music, see Laade 1981, vol. 1: 105. It is interesting to note that Ambrosi treats musical evolution as being inseparable from the evolution of the language, with the implication that evidence that points to, for example, a strong Berber element in the language at a particular point in time would suggest that there might have been a similarly significant influence on the music. This perspective is also informed by the notion that the melodic line would be shaped by the rhythms and stresses of the language.

2. Numerous examples can be found in the field recordings of Quilici and Laade, copies of which are available for consultation at the Phonothèque of the Musée de la Corse in Corte. A well-known and particularly florid example is the *Lamentu di Filiccone*, a lament for a hunting dog composed by the dog's master, Pepedru u Barbutu, in the 1920s; a rendition by the composer's son, recorded by Quilici in the early 1960s, can be found in the collection *Musique Corse de Tradition Orale* (1982).

3. Laade notes elsewhere (1990: 4) that: "The very active amateur folklorists of the late 19th and early 20th century saw the roots of Corsican song and poetry in the ancient Greek and Roman cultures, while the singing style was supposed to be distinctly Arabic. None of this is acceptable." He goes on to dismiss their proposals regarding the origins and history of Corsican folksong as "pure speculation and romantic mystification."

4. Since the sixteenth century, immigration has also been a significant factor as Corsica has offered refuge to political refugees and has imported workforces, mainly from the North African countries and mainland Italy. While these incomers, too, would presumably have

brought their own musical repertoires with them, little study has been done concerning their possible interaction with indigenous styles.

5. For a more detailed discussion of the *voceru* and its connection with the vendetta in Corsica, see Bithell 2003a.

6. It should be noted that similar traditions of improvised debate are also found in more distant parts of the world.

7. The disc *Polyphonies Corses* by Jean-Paul Poletti and Le Choeur d'Hommes de Sartène does in fact contain stanzas from Dante's *Divine Comedy* sung as terzetti (U Purgatoriu). The disc notes comment: "In this form, Dante's *Divine Comedy* has been peddled from mountain to mountain by Corsican shepherds during their peregrinations. It is remarkable that a corporation should thus pass on one of the major works of Italian literature in the form of a very ancient three-part polyphonic song."

8. The present-day partition into the two départements of Haute Corse and Corse du Sud respects roughly the same boundary.

9. For further examples see Musée de la Corse 1997, 68–73. For further discussion of changing perceptions, values and motivations at both an aesthetic and a political level, see Bithell 2003b.

10. The establishment of the Front Régionaliste Corse and the Action Régionaliste Corse, in 1966 and 1967, was followed by the Front Populaire Corse de Libération in 1973 and the Front de Libération Nationale de la Corse in 1976.

11. A number of *scole di canta* (singing schools) were established by members of Canta and other groups from the 1970s onwards as a vehicle for transmitting musical repertoire and technique to other young singers, particularly those who were growing up in the towns and so did not have direct contact with, or experience of, traditional practices. A number of these schools—which usually take the form of a weekly or biweekly class or rehearsal, using a church, schoolroom or other community venue as a base—continue to flourish.

12. Meanwhile, the inclusion in *Ci hè Dinù* of a Basque song (Haika Mutil), a Catalan song (Rossignyol) and an adaptation of Paco Ibanez's *A Galoppar*, as well as a Sardinian *Dio ti salve Maria* and an adaptation of a George Brassens song, bears witness to the widening of Canta's contacts and the way in which this led not only to stylistic influences but also to direct exchanges of songs.

13. The *Rencontres Polyphoniques* are hosted by the cultural association U Svegliu Calvese, together with locally based group A Filetta and take place each September. Other established festivals that feature ensembles from overseas, in addition to a number of insular artists, are Festivoce, a festival of the performing arts held in July of each year

under the auspices of the association Festivoce (part of the federation E
Voce di U Cumune, based in the village of Pigna in the Balagne) and
Settembrinu in Tavagna (September in Tavagna, the Tavagna being a
region on the edge of the Castagniccia near the island's east coast), a
festival that is deliberately held slightly after the main summer tourist
season as part of a politic that involves bringing cultural animation to
regions of the island's interior for the benefit of the inhabitants themselves.

14. Donnisulana, under the direction of Mighele Raffaelli, was first
given exposure to noninsular audiences via their appearance at the 1989
Festival de Musique Contemporaine at Lille, which in turn led to their
being chosen by Xenakis to perform in his production of *Hélène* at the
Opéra Bastille.

15. For a more detailed exploration of the import of such oppositions, see Bithell 2003b.

16. The explicit situating of the disc in a Mediterranean as opposed
to a specifically Corsican frame of reference via the album title recurs
in Giramondu's 1999 disc, *Mediterraniu.*

17. For an analysis of the way in which Corsican groups today
combine traditional and contemporary elements in their own compositions, together with a discussion of the way in which they articulate
their relationship to the tradition, see Bithell 2001. For a discussion of
the way in which traditional material has evolved in their arrangements,
see Bithell 1996.

Bibliography

Ambrosi, Mathieu. *Le Chant Corse.* Nice: 1938.
Bithell, Caroline. "Polyphonic Voices: National Identity, World Music
    and the Recording of Traditional Music in Corsica." *British Jour-
    nal of Ethnomusicology* 5 (1996): 39–66.
———. "Telling a Tree by its Blossom: Aspects of the Evolution of
    Musical Activity in Corsica and the Notion of a Traditional Music
    of the 21st Century." *Music and Anthropology* 6 (2001).
    www.muspe.unibo.it/period/MA/
———. "A Man's Game? Engendered Song and the Changing Dynam-
    ics of Women's Musical Activity in Corsica." 33–66 in *Music and
    Gender: Perspectives from the Mediterranean*, edited by Tullia
    Magrini. Chicago: University of Chicago Press, 2003a.
———. "Shared Imaginations: Celtic and Corsican Encounters in the

Soundscape of the Soul." 27–72 in *Celtic Modern: Music at the Global Fringe*, edited by Philip V. Bohlman and Martin Stokes. Lanham, Md.: Scarecrow Press, 2003b.

Corse-Matin (30 May 1994).

——, (1 July 1995).

——, (10 August 2001).

——, (20 August 2001).

——, (21 August 2001).

——, (22 August 2001).

de Croze, Austin. *La Chanson Populaire de L'Ile de Corse*. Paris: Librairie Honoré Champion, 1911.

de Martino, Ernesto. *Morte e Pianto Rituale*. Turin: Boringhieri, 1958.

de Zerbi, Ghjermana and Mighele Raffaelli. *Antulugia di u Cantu Nustrale*. Vol. 1. Ajaccio: La Marge, 1993.

Fusina, Ghjacumu. "C'hè Dinù." 178–86 in *Canta u Populu Corsu*, Ghjermana de Zerbi et al. Levie: Editions Albiana, 1993.

Kryn, no. 167 (January 1986).

——, no. 396 (January 1993).

Laade, Wolfgang. *Das korsische Volkslied: Ethnographie und Geschichte, Gattungen und Stil*. 3 vols. Wiesbaden: Franz Steiner Verlag, 1981.

——. Disc notes for *Corsica: Traditional Songs and Music*. Jecklin-Disco, 1990.

Musée de la Corse. *Cahier d'Anthropologie no. 4: 100 ans de collecte en Corse*. Corte: Musée de la Corse, 1997.

Salini, Dominique. *Musiques Traditionnelles de Corse*. Ajaccio: A Messagera/Squadra di u Finusellu, 1996.

Sorce Keller, Marcello. "Reflections of Continental and Mediterranean Traditions in Italian Folk Music." 40–47 in *Music-Cultures in Contact: Convergences and Collisions,* edited by Margaret J. Kartomi and Stephen Blum. Basel: Gordon and Breach, 1994.

Discography

L'Albinu. *Albinu versu tè*. Kallisté KA JC 35, 1985.

Bitter, Maurice. *Musique Folklorique du Monde: Corsica*. Musidisc 30CV 1385, n.d. Recordings collected by Bitter.

Canta u Populu Corsu. *Ci hè dinù*. Ricordu CDR 037, 1982.

Cesari, Mighela, and Mighele Raffaelli. *U Cantu Prufondu*. Ricordu CDR 088, 1993.

Cinqui Sò. *Chants Polyphoniques Corses.* 7 Productions WMD 242 040, 1992.

———. *Com' Acqua Linda.* Ricordu-Planett 242069, 1994.

———. *Tarraniu.* Albiana CDAL 003, 1996.

Coulais, Bruno/A Filetta. *Original Motion Picture Soundtrack Don Juan.* Naïve K 1610, 2002.

Donnisulana. *Per Agata: Polyphonies Corses.* Silex Y425019, 1992

Giramondu. *Mediterraniu.* Altugiru/Warner Music France (no ref.), 1999.

Laade, Wolfgang. *Corsica: Traditional Songs and Music.* Jecklin-Disco JD 650-2, 1990. Field recordings, 1958 and 1973.

Le Mystère des Voix Bulgares Vol. 1. Nonesuch 79165, 1987.

———. Vol. 2. Nonesuch 79201, 1988.

———. Vol. 3. Polygram/Fortuna 846626, 1990.

Les Nouvelles Polyphonies Corses. *Les Nouvelles Polyphonies Corses.* Philips 848515-2, 1991.

Les Nouvelles Polyphonies Corses/Trio Soledonna. *Isulanima.* Philips 014 791-2, 2001.

———. *Di li Venti, a Rosula.* Auvidis Chorus AC 6458, 1997.

Poletti, Jean-Paul/Le Choeur d'Hommes de Sartène. *Polyphonies Corses.* Auvidis Ethnic B 6841, 1996.

Quilici, Félix. *Musique Corse de Tradition Orale.* Archives Sonores de la Phonothèque Nationale, Paris APN82-1/3, 1982. Field recordings, 1961–63.

Raffaelli, Mighele. *Trà Ochju é Mare.* Silex Y425004, 1991. Conception and direction by Mighele Raffaelli.

Tavagna. *Incontru.* Nato 194, 1983.

Chapter Nine

Open Textures: On Mediterranean Music

Goffredo Plastino

A New World

"We sing a certain idea of Mediterranean-ness, mostly in Arabic, but Arabs are only half of the Mediterranean." These are the opening words of the liner notes of *New World* by Dounia.[1] The band is composed of Palestinian singer Faisal Taher (from Jenin) and three Sicilian musicians: Giovanni Arena (double bass, bass guitar, vocal), Vincenzo Gangi (guitars, vocal) and Riccardo Gerbino (percussion, vocal). On the album cover Africa and the Mediterranean are depicted as the center of a new world, with an irregular border: an image suggesting a new and different centrality for the Mediterranean as a connecting area, a cultural and musical untangling. On its website Dounia describes itself this way:

> Four musicians from various artistic backgrounds came together in 1996 and formed Dounia. The desire to explore more profoundly the panorama of the World Music began to evolve from their live appearances. Considering the backgrounds and the ideals of the members, Dounia center their musical project on a predominant acoustic base, giving each individual instrument the privilege to express, through its own timbre, the fascination and suggestion which are part of the world, its traditions and the evolution of all of the musicians who are part of it. Dounia blends the peculiar middle-oriental voice of Faisal Taher with a special amalgam of melodies, harmonies and rhythms from all over the world.
>
> The result exceeds any form of contamination creating Dounia's little world, where each sound is given importance, even a meager chord. Thus causing a surge of emotion for the listener, letting them feel free in this open and interactive listening space: imagination.
>
> They are a determined group with a clear vision, that is to produce music which reaches every single member of their audience. In concert, music is taken from *New World* and from traditional middle oriental music but interpreted by the unique sound of Dounia. (http://www.dounia.it/english/bio.php)

The texts of Dounia's songs describe, often elliptically, the conditions of the contemporary Mediterranean. For example, *Gheru* highlights the drama of illegal immigration, in lines that contrast the bitterness of a sea voyage with the concept of the Mediterranean as a place of vacation and relaxation: "I am only another one, cargo stowed in your memory, jumbled between an appendectomy and a summer trip to the seaside."[2]

The issue of the plight of the immigrant is also raised in *Ghourba*: here a dialog between a mother and son serves to exemplify the bitterness of living as a foreigner that modifies behavior and induces sadness and yet also gives rise to altered ways of thinking and possibilities for new opportunities (and not necessarily only economic ones):

> How bitter, mother, to live as a stranger, as bitter as changing one's way of looking and of singing.
>   My son, why are you so changed? / What has happened to you? / What has changed you? /
>   Living as a stranger, mother, offers opportunities but makes you miss others. Living as a stranger is bitter, mother, / it makes you taste different flavors and mature new experiences. / There is sorrow in my heart and the consciousness of acquiring so many other things."[3]

What predominates in the music of Dounia is dislocation. None of their songs can be referenced to a particular Mediterranean musical culture, but all sound in many ways Mediterranean. There are no citations (at least on the surface of their musical discourse) and, since Dounia is, by choice, a strictly acoustic band, the processes of recomposition of musical fragments through sampling is precluded. Repeated listening to *New World* gives a sensation of closeness to a Mediterranean that seems neither actually present nor even evoked (even Taher's voice has this effect). This sense of dislocation is consciously sought by Dounia. Roberto Catalano notes (while the disc was in preparation) what could be the meaning of *New World*: calling it "an unconscious matter to go beyond borders . . . into non-existing lands more than anything" (Catalano 1999: 93). Dounia does not operate by mixing elements of different Mediterranean musical traditions, rather they wish to "contaminate without predetermination" (93), avoiding explicit references to the musical cultures to which each member of the band belongs. Without using samples and techniques of quotation, the members of Dounia wish to depict a new world of music and song, while still transmitting a certain idea of "Mediterraneanness".

Mediterranean Music?

According to Bernard Lortat-Jacob, an ethnomusicology of the Mediterranean does not exist, although, he adds, there exist numerous ethnological studies of the Mediterranean and the concept of "Mediterranean music" is not completely meaningless. For Lortat-Jacob, attempts to define and analyze Mediterranean music notwithstanding,[4] a "Mediterranean" ethnomusicology cannot be established, because the existing idea of Mediterranean music is not what ethnomusicologists ought to be interested in. "Mediterranean music" is a concept for advertising and travel agents: a repertoire or performance category aimed above all at tourists. It is a marketing concept that offers "an illusion of coherence" and is mostly useful for raising public funds for music festivals (2001: 539).

Yet, although he is skeptical about ethnomusicology's ability to consider Mediterranean music as an object of study, Lortat-Jacob, together with Gilles Léothaud, propose a unified analysis, albeit a problematic one, of Mediterranean vocality (Léothaud and Lortat-Jacob 2002). According to them, the peoples and languages of the Mediterranean do not have unifying characteristics. Their relationships are organized along two geographic and cultural axes: the North–South axis, characterized by a clear opposition; and the East–West axis, which exhibits a greater, obvious fluidity (even in musical forms). Specifying that comparisons of musical phenomena can only be achieved within their own functional categories, Lortat-Jacob and Léothaud define the pertinent traits of an identifiable Mediterranean vocal style, first clarifying that it is easily perceptible, at first hearing, but going on to say that it is equally hard to explain and that, in any case, its constituent traits have no functional autonomy (2002: 9–10). Excluding from analysis traits that are strictly musical and making reference to a "Mediterranean" region (which includes North–South and East–West axes), Lortat-Jacob and Léothaud identify four fundamental characteristics of Mediterranean vocality: the voice strongly projected outward; a nasal timbre and the "voix granuleuse"; melismatic ornamentations of the entire melodic phrase; and a narrow upper range (11). But not all these Mediterranean vocal practices are consistent with this trait list (which in many respects resembles that already proposed by Alan Lomax in *Cantometrics* 1976: 45–46): there are also ways of employing the voice in the Mediterranean that are derived from the influence of another musical conception of vocality, developed in cultivated, urban environments. This other vocal "pole," when it came into contact with the preceding, produced forms of musical acculturation—a process that Lortat-Jacob and Léothaud view positively when it successfully assimilated and results in the creative enrichment of the "initial musical material" (14). According to them, this process of enrichment of the Mediterranean ambit is distinguished from more recent acculturation, which introduces "international" musical forms through the mass media and results in a growing marginalization and even negation of local musical traditions: "this type of acculturation . . . *ultimately* risks the death of the most beautiful musics of Mediterranean oral tradition" (2002: 14).

Thus, both so-called Mediterranean music and the modern repertoires performed in the Mediterranean ought to be off limits to ethnomusicologists, since their very presence and diffusion are the main dangers to the musical forms that are their legitimate objects of study.

Tullia Magrini proposes yet another possibility of reading "Mediterranean music." Considering the processes of musical syncretism in the Mediterranean, Magrini holds that, strictly speaking, the term "Mediterranean music" ought to be used only for those musical phenomena that, originating from different geographical areas of the Mediterranean, demonstrate that they are rooted in practices of cultural contact and historically and genetically verifiable influences. She writes, "we would use the term ["Mediterranean music"] for those musical phenomena which cross the sea, which have in their DNA a genetic patrimony that unites elements of different cultures." (1999: 175–76).

According to Magrini, this perspective and this terminology are valuable insofar as they can be used to consider the Mediterranean as a region of musical interactions in the past and, "on the level of popular music," as a region that is currently undergoing tendencies toward "contamination," like those apparent throughout the world (2003: 20).

In the light of these works, an ethnomusicological consideration of Dounia might not seem pertinent or necessary. In Lortat-Jacob and Léothaud (2002), resistance to consideration of the Mediterranean as musically homogenous is accompanied by an affirmation of the existence of a problematic Mediterranean vocality, verifiable in a rather hazily defined "Mediterranean area." Moreover, their analyses are interwoven with a kind of discourse that is currently common in discussions of world music (Brusila 2003: 11–88), that considers diffusion of new musical forms the product of hybridization or "contamination," by means of a "homogenization and a compromising of indigenous cultures in an era of global industrial practices" (15). Dounia (a post–world-music band?), that blends the voice of Faisal Taher with "melodies, harmonies and rhythms from all over the world," therefore belongs at least partly to a sphere of music that is fine for tourists and travel agencies but whose very presence threatens to compromise the survival of the local musics of the Mediterranean.

On the other hand, Magrini's theoretical perspective also seems to nudge the music of the Palestinian-Sicilian band in the direction of irrelevance. Apart from remarking on some elements of a "genetic-musical patrimony" that unites Palestine and Sicily in past and present in Douina's songs, the group's declaration of "Mediterraneanness" should be considered neither pertinent nor verifiable: although one might consider their repertoire as a new kind of Mediterranean "world music," that is, a mere local variant of global musical hybridizations.

Glimpses of the Mediterranean

Dounia has also produced and arranged *Far lunari* (2003), the last CD of Sicilian singer Cecilia Pitino, in which they perform in all tracks (singer Faisal Taher is heard only on some of them). Compared to her earlier disc, *Spunta 'na rosa* (1998), *Far lunari* is a new departure for Pitino, a singer, actress and dancer, born in Modica (Ragusa). Her website states that:

> The project *Far lunari* was born from the deeply-felt artistic collaboration of Cecilia Pitino with Dounia. . . . Dounia were responsible for the artistic production of *Far lunari* and the writer Sal Costa composed the lyrics of the new pieces. . . . *Far lunari*, according to Sal Costa, is worn by her like a garment. And if the poetical themes have not changed since *Spunta 'na rosa*, if the passion and the suffering of man are still at the centre of the scene, the musical dress is scantier, slighter and every sound, even the smallest, acquires a fundamental value. (http://www.ceciliapitino.it/english/discografia.htm)

Far lunari was also distributed in Italy as a companion CD to *World Music* (the main Italian magazine dedicated exclusively to this musical "genre"), which helped place Pitino's disc under the rubric of "world music," one that she, like the members of Dounia, accepts and uses. She specifies how Mediterraneanness is an important element of her latest work:

> *Far lunari* is simply contemporary Sicilian music, a meeting-place for the perfumes, the passions and the hopes of Sicily and glimpses of the Mediterranean of which the island has always represented the geographical center and the principal cultural work-shop. Seven new

pieces and three remakes of classics show that globalization does not necessarily pervert individual cultures; rather, it enriches them.

In fact, what is most striking and astonishing about this work is the singular naturalness with which, in *Far lunari*, the languages, sonorities and traditions of the Mediterranean mingle with and are infected by the rhythms of our time, without sacrificing any of the crude and authentic "Sicilianness," which is untainted by the stereotypes that have too often confined it in the realms of folklore. (http://www.ceciliapitino.it/english/discografia.htm)

The musical project that led to the creation of *New World* is reprised and has been modified in *Far lunari*. The focus seems to have shifted to Sicily, but only apparently. The traditional Sicilian songs ("classics," as Cecilia Pitino calls them) performed on the album do not actually "sound" Sicilian. Again, the usual and predictable sound horizons are blurred and out-of-focus (and the album cover reinforces this sensation). The Sicilianness of *Far lunari* is elusive and seems to reside above all in Pitino's vocal style, which conveys other vocal possibilities, evoked and real (as when Faisal Taher performs with her). Pitino's voice does not always project outwards, its timbre is not always nasal, her vocal range is not narrow and she doesn't always sing in the upper register; even her use of melisma is discrete. Her voice seems to want to reconfigure the possibility of being perceived as "Sicilian" but in the context of musical practices that put Sicily in parentheses. In *Far lunari*, Sicily is another element of that "new world" of music performed by Dounia, another place on the map of an imaginary Mediterranean, an imagined Mediterranean. The images and the sound of the sea are used to broach the possibility of new relations between this kind of Sicily (Cecilia Pitino's voice) and a not-completely defined Mediterranean elsewhere. The encounter is desired and real; for example, in the track *Cutieddu e mola* the voices of Pitino and Taher alternate in the midst of the same musical discourse and the text speaks to us of encounters by and across the sea:

> Stiennilu 'u linzuolu stiennilu / c'è suli e un vientu veni ro mari / sientilu 'stu cori sientilu / paroli i zzuccuru voli ciatari / trova na scusa e vola / fammi cuntenta 'na vota sula / e posala 'sta manu posala / 'mpiettu a 'sta fimmina c'aspetta e mori / basula cori di basula / pigghila e vasala 'sta vucca ardenti / ora ca sugnu sula / tu si cutieddu e iu la mola / mari vicinu o mari / mi vuogghiu curcari / stisa comu la rina / aspiettu l'unna ca veni / e va, mi tira o funnu / m'avvilisci e m'acquieta / sientu 'ni li me visciri / cutieddu e mola

Spread the sheet, spread it / there's the sun and the wind from the sea
/ listen to this heart, listen to it / it wants to breathe sugared words /
find an excuse and fly / make me happy just this once, this once / and
rest this hand, rest it / on the breast of this girl who waits and dies /
heart of stone, of stone / take it and kiss my burning mouth / now that
I am alone / you are the knife and I am the grindstone / near the sea—
the sea / I want to lie / just like the sands / I await the breaking wave
that comes / and goes, pulls me under / that humiliates me and calms
me / I feel in my vitals / knife and grindstone.

A Dialogic Space

It is probably necessary, as Michael Herzfeld suggests, "to shift our
attention from essentialist questions about "what the Mediterranean is,"
to move the discussion of the geographical focus from increasingly arid
debates about its ontological status to a more process-oriented understanding of the politics of cultural identity, in a region where indeed
some people, some of the time, do find it useful to emphasize their
identity as 'Mediterranean'" (2001: 663). From the standpoint of this
theoretical perspective, contemporary anthropology is already turning
away from such unifying themes as honor and shame, hospitality,
friendship, patronage and so forth, which have been at the center of
anthropological studies of the Mediterranean since the 1960s and which
have lately become somewhat stale and even counterproductive. Such
trait lists, old and new, are becoming heuristically irrelevant, though
they still sometimes appear in spectral form (Albera and Blok 2001:
18). The Mediterranean, de-essentialized and not reified, is no longer
an object of study, but rather a field of study: "We are not referring to
an object to be defined, but to a wider and significant context" (23).

The Mediterranean then, as a liminal region, an area in which the
customary dichotomies between here and there, between the West and
the Other, between near and far (Bromberger and Durand 2001: 738)
are continually put up for discussion. According to these new anthropological perspectives, the Mediterranean represents an intermediate zone
between us and non-us and constitutes a paradigmatic example of the
crumbling of clear distinctions between "us" and "them." (Albera and
Blok 2001: 26). The Mediterranean is understood as a "dialogic space,
in which the identities of one and other are defined in a game of mir-
rors" (Bromberger and Durand 2001: 746)—to the point of prompting a
rethinking of anthropological approaches to the theme of identity
(Herzfeld 2001: 675):

It is surely the play of similarity and difference that makes the lability of Mediterranean identity so interesting. . . . It is also helpful to recognize that a local sense of regional identity constitutes an important topic of study in its own right. In particular, it provides a basis on which to measure how far the seemingly stable system of classification created by state and international bureaucracies have become part of what actually matters to people "on the ground." (Herzfeld 2001: 663, 665)

The Mediterranean, from this theoretical standpoint, can also be considered as the locus of différance (to take Derrida's notion as a jumping-off point): "If it is true, Paul Valéry maintained, that the Mediterranean can be conceived as a "machine à faire de la civilization," this region is also in many ways a "machine" producing differences and conflicts along ever-changing borders. Thus, the Mediterranean can be seen as a field of "différance," as a texture of differences continuously reshaped" (Albera and Blok 2001: 24). It is because of this very instability, which is both continuous and desired, that the Mediterranean seems to constitute a paradigm for discussion in contemporary anthropology (Bromberger and Durand 2001: 747), to the point of being the field that expresses and reflects the discipline's epistemological quandaries (Albera and Blok 2001: 26–27): and thus, as Michael Herzfeld emphasizes, the instabilities of anthropology's ontologies correspond to the instability of what anthropology studies (2001: 665).

More Voices

I find myself, actually, very attached to this Mediterranean patrimony of creativity. In my opinion, it offers a real space for conviviality and understanding and weaves the threads of a solid intimacy. . . . Our neighboring Mediterranean "West" is not a monolithic block, enveloped in technology and arrogance, bent on casting glances of superior disdain at its neighbors across the way to the south. The West is an aggregation of groups and regions, criss-crossed by a dialectic of the disclosed and the hidden, one that impels it to realize its deepest essence. The Mediterranean is an expression of this dialectic and operates in the deepest sense as a multiple identity. . . . For this reason, I feel the necessity of a Mediterranean Sea that defines itself as an identity, as a project that incorporates pluralism, difference and vibrant cross-fertilization. At that point, the risks of a war between cultures will disappear and the Mediterranean outlook will become a viable way to suppress, on northern shores, the burdensome racist superiorities of hack politicians and, on southern ones, the despotism and indifference of governments. (Barrada 2002: 22–25)

Mediterranean: the power of a word from whose center rises a song of childhood. . . . Mediterranean. From the first, a surface made for the launching of a dream, you slide along a path it has invented and then it decides to follow another. . . . But the Mediterranean, as its name suggests, is a liquid story. . . . This is why my memory becomes a seascape. It bestows on me a melded blue, where identities recombine and grow and nourish one another, without my ever needing to revisit a single fragment of my Mediterranean past to separate and isolate it from the rest. (Belhaj Yahia 2003: 17–18)

O who knows Ionian Gulf O Sea of Duclea / O sea cursed by jingling panderers / O upper sea O at long last Bay of Venice / a just name for every colored eye / that fixes upon it. (Maniacco 1998: 10)

Is the Mediterranean a circle? And if it is, how shall we ever relate without a French or German axis of rotation? In other words, how can we ever relate directly, at least in the cultural field, without going through the great capitals?. . . . Are we perhaps about to witness the birth of a new literature, marked by hybridity and freed through linguistic theft, capable of becoming a bridge of communication that puts an end to the literature of orientalism and of orientalism in reverse? [The] new Mediterranean horizon, a horizon that fascinates us today because it opens a window in this blind wall between North and South, lays the foundations of a new collaborative relationship. (Khuri 2002: 38)

All this confirms, without a doubt, what all Mediterranean people know, that the Mediterranean doesn't exist. . . . This is why I have the clear sensation that the Mediterranean, rather than existing for itself, is a necessary condition for the existence of its inhabitants. (Theodoropoulos 2002: 39–40)

There is no one Mediterranean culture: there are many, in the bosom of only one Mediterranean. (Matvejevic 1998: 31)

Harmonic Circularity

In 2003, Dounia, jointly with Tunisian poet Moncef Ghachem, issued a book entitled, *Dalle sponde del mare bianco* (From the Shores of the White Sea) that featured a selection Ghachem's poems accompanied by a CD made during a live concert in Acireale (Catania, Sicily), at which Moncef Ghachem (and others) recited his poetry.

Born in 1946, in Mahdia (the "sister city" of Mazara del Vallo in Sicily), Ghachem is, by his own admission, a fisherman poet: "in the heart of my fisherman family I encountered poetry. And since I was on the sea by night and day, it lavished on me some of its memory, its mystery and fragments of its song" (Ferrini 2003: 5). According to Costanza Ferrini, "The continuous see-saw of his verses, from the mobility of the sea to the solidity of the shore, forms the rhythm of Ghachem's universe, in which one element continues into the other without a break, in harmonic circularity, with all the lacerations inherent in both. The conversation between land and sea, past and present is articulated in prolonged silent gestures that generate a lonely landscape, throbbing like a body. It is hard to establish where the horizon of this unity of absence and presence, evocation and the senses ends" (6).

Ghachem's Mediterranean is at once a familiar place, an environment of solitary and communal labor, a region that at once connects and divides, a mobile element of inspiration and a symbolic space through which a multiplicity of relationships can be expressed. This polyphony of significations is now enriched through Ghachem and Dounia's collaboration. For example, in the song *Lambuca*, two voices recite the same text in Arabic and Sicilian—which is a mosaic of fishermen's conversations from Mahdia and Mazara del Vallo and also a reflection on these kinds of dialogues:

Mukhhtaf lifluca fi esciuca / Ukhai mraueh blàmbuca / Gaiedtha giarida murmiya / Ala assimiya / Il hut ia ualad il mahdiya / Ua dukhul il laila bmuzica / Uakhi bibuscira arica / Uimid il hèt il baladiya / Bfundiya / Ualhut arus il mahdiya / Hiia.

L'ancora da varca furriau / fratuzzu! Torna cca lampuca / ca chiama intr'a nassa / ittata a tramuntana / o pisci! Figghiu ri Mahdia / o spirò c'è fistin'i nozz'e musica / fratuzzu! cecchi scerra / vai a ghittari na ciappedda / supra u muru ru cumuni / o pisci! Maritu ri Mahdia / heeeeeee.

The boat's anchor is turning / little brother! Come back with the *lampuga*[5] / that calls from the bow-net / thrown to the north / O fish! Son of Mahdia / tonight there will be a wedding feast with music / little brother! you are looking for trouble / go and throw a pebble / over the town wall / O fish! Husband of Mahdia / heeeeeee.

The workplace environment (fishing) is communal, as is the means of expression. Ghachem seems to suggest that across the sea and on the sea, the personal and collective identities of the Tunisians of Mahdia and the Sicilians of Mazara del Vallo define themselves with reference to each other; the long story of collaboration and opposition (which is linguistic as well) between the two communities momentarily reassembles itself in his verses. Dounia's music in *Lampuca*, is, once again, "minimalist" (Ghachem and Dounia 2003: 84), a rhythmic-harmonic pattern repeated over and over with variations—performed on double bass, acoustic guitar and darabuka—delineates an imaginary Mediterranean without explicitly quoting either Tunisian or Sicilian musical forms, but rather suggests an open, Mediterranean space, a soundscape on which Ghachem's poetry is reflected. Poetry and music are here two Mediterranean lingua francas that mirror and lead back to each other.

Conclusion

In the song *Cutieddu e mola* by Cecilia Pitino and Dounia, the Mediterranean is at once a metaphor and an epistemologic project. It seems to me that this song and more in general, Dounia's compositions, represent in music a theoretical outlook that has been defined as "Mediterranean thinking":

> The Mediterranean is much a network of reflections, connections and intersubjectivities as it is a geopolitical site. In a word, it is a process as well as a place, suggesting an epistemology that may be called "Mediterranean thinking." Water, both as a mirror and as liquid substance, plays a defining role in Mediterranean thinking. A form of aquacentric inquiry, Mediterranean thinking distinguishes between the materiality of earth and sea, juxtaposing the fixed and the fluid, as well as the near and the far in time and space. (Cooke 2000: 294)

According to Miriam Cooke (2000: 298), placing oneself in the perspective of "Mediterranean thinking" (as theoretically elaborated by Franco Cassano in his *Il pensiero meridiano*, 1996), opens the possibility of reconceptualizing the Mediterranean as both a physical and virtual place. The concepts of center and margin are undermined in a manner analogous to the supposed indivisibility of identity, language and culture—and also musical forms.

The music of Dounia and of Cecilia Pitino is the music of a Mediterranean without a center, in which identities are changeable, it is the

music of the "seacoast border" that "disrupts the dominion of 'identity,'
and obliges us to accommodate differences" (Cassano 1996: 24).[6] It
belongs to that Mediterranean experienced as fluid, "an interregional
arena that is in constant flux, with individual moving, meeting and
changing habits of heart and mind" (Cooke 2000: 298–99). Through
their music (and in their music) Dounia admits the positive hybridity of
every Mediterranean identity, without obscuring hybridity's painful
aspect, as remarked by Slavoj Zizek, since they don't downplay the
trauma of having to cross frontiers without being able to settle in any
one place. They don't merely glorify the mixed nature of the migratory
postmodern subject, but they also confront the reality of suffering
(2003: 72–73). Dounia achieves in music that process of authentic
communication born of the consciousness of "solidarity in a communal
struggle," that emerges, according to Zizek, when it is clear that "the
blind alley with no way out is common to me and to the 'other'" (71)
and which permits them to establish a real alternative to the Orientalist
perspective (Said 1991: 27).

On another level, it is not really possible to evaluate Dounia's music in the light of the practices of discourse that are usually applied to
"world music." The cultural imperialistic perspective does not really
apply to their compositions; and, in my view, neither do the antitheses
of West/rest, self/other, hegemony/counter-hegemony have much heu-
ristic value (Brusila 2003: 11–88, 221–31). In Dounia and Cecilia Pitino's music, a dialogue seems to take place between "different others,"
who represent different possibilities, never defined once and for all, of
a changing Mediterranean self. In other words, I don't think that these
musical experiences that express "the fluidity of the Mediterranean as
an epistemological project" (Cooke 2000: 299) can be understood by
means of fixed analytical frames. I believe that an ethnomusicological
perspective of these Mediterranean musics can be attained by accepting
the suggestions along the lines, for example, of Ingrid Monson (1999):
reclaiming for ethnomusicology the ability to say something about
these new musical experiences through a greater theoretical openness
(see also Plastino 2003a: 9–10). It is probably opportune to stand outside the debate between those who identify forms of local resistance in
the global popular music market and those for whom the global musical
market destroys and obliterates local music in all its forms. I think it is
time to reestablish an ethnomusicology that distinguishes between the
fact of hybridity and the ends for which it is employed, that "can speak
to the full range of interlocking cultural levels" (Monson 1999: 60). If
the Mediterranean serves as a paradigm of contemporary anthropological discourse, then perhaps there are Mediterranean musics (as I have

tried to show here) that can be paradigmatic of new theoretical directions in ethnomusicology.

Notes

1. In Arabic *dounia* means "life," "world" and "universe" and is also a woman's name.

2. From the liner notes of *New World*.

3. Again, from the liner notes of *New World*.

4. Lortat-Jacob (2001: 539) recalls Costantin Brăiloiu's affirmation of the Mediterranean as a "*maniére d'etat d'âme.*"

5. A fish (coryphaena hippura).

6. Dounia's compositions and collaborative undertakings can also be seen in the context of the history of "Mediterranean" music in Italy (the band is considered an offspring of Kunsertu, another Sicilian world music group; see Catalano 1999: 89–94). The emergence in Italy of performance-styles defined as "Mediterranean" occurred in the '70s and '80s, when there was a perceived necessity to engage the Mediterranean as a cultural area. "Mediterranean" was considered an element of Italian subjectivity—not as a negative pole or exotic vacation locale—and its music, as Franco Cassano writes (2000: 49–61), encouraged and accompanied this engagement. This is not the place to list the participants or to comprehensively describe this complex phenomenon, which occurred in the sometimes quite divergent fields of pop, folk revival (and "post-folk"), progressive rock, jazz and jazz-rock (see Fabbri 2001; Ferrari 2003 and Plastino 2003b: 270–72). But some tendencies can be mentioned. In Italy, the definition "Mediterranean music" was used to express:

(i) forms of collaboration (musicians and singers from other Mediterranean countries performing with Italian colleagues);

(ii) forms of hybridization (musics and musical instruments of other Mediterranean countries performed and played within and with Italian folk and popular music and musical instruments);

(iii) forms di imitation (Italian musicians and singers imitating the musics of other Mediterranean countries in an Orientalist way).

Moreover, the Mediterranean redefined and imagined by Italians through their music was predominantly Arabic and playing "Mediterranean music" in Italy was and still is, often considered (by instrumentalists, singers and audiences) a political statement. In some respects, Dounia is a part of this Italian musical scene and represent its latest development.

Bibliography

Albera, Dionigi and Anton Blok. "The Mediterranean as a Field of Ethnological Study: A Retrospective," 15–37 in *L'anthropologie de la Méditerranée* (Anthropology of the Mediterranean), edited by Dionigi Albera, Anton Blok and Christian Bromberger. Paris: Maisonneuve et Larose, 2001.

Barrada, Muhammad. 2002. "Progetto per un sogno," 15–27 in *Rappresentare il Mediterraneo . Lo sguardo marocchino*, edited by Muhammad Barrada and 'Abd al-Magid Qadduri. Messina: Mesogea, 2002.

Belhaj Yahia, Emma. "Costruire sul paesaggio marino," 15–27 in *Rappresentare il Mediterraneo . Lo sguardo tunisino*, edited by Emma Belhaj Yahia and Sadok Boubaker. Messina: Mesogea, 2003.

Bromberger, Christian and Jean-Yves Durand. "Faut-il jeter la Méditerranée avec l'eau du bain?" 733–56 in *L'anthropologie de la Méditerranée* (Anthropology of the Mediterranean), edited by Dionigi Albera, Anton Blok and Christian Bromberger. Paris: Maisonneuve et Larose, 2001.

Brusila, Johannes. "Local Music, not from Here." *The Discourse of World Music Examined through Three Zimbabwean Case Studies: The Bhundu Boys, Virginia Mukwesha and Sunduza.* Helsinki: Finnish Society for Ethnomusicology, 2003.

Cassano, Franco. *Il pensiero meridiano.* Roma and Bari: Laterza, 1996.

———. "Contro tutti i fondamentalismi: il nuovo Mediterraneo," 37–69 in. *Rappresentare il Mediterraneo. Lo sguardo italiano*, edited by Consolo Vincenzo and Franco Cassano. Messina: Mesogea, 2000.

Catalano, Roberto. "Mediterranean World-Music: Experiencing Sicilian-Arab Sounds." Ph.D. dissertation, UCLA, 1999.

Cooke, Miriam. "Mediterranean Thinking: from Netizen to Medizen" *The Geographical Review* 82, no. 2 (2000): 290–300.

Dounia. *New World.* Altrosud—Il Manifesto—Officina CD 070, 2001 (compact disc).

Fabbri, Franco. "Nowhere Land: The Construction of a 'Mediterranean' Identity in Italian Popular Music." in *Music and Anthropology* 6 (2001) http://www.muspe.unibo.it/period/ma/index/number6/fabbri/fab_0.htm.

Ferrari, Luca. *Folk geneticamente modificato. Musiche e musicisti della moderna tradizione dell'Italia dei McDonald's.* Viterbo: Nuovi Equilibri, 2003.

Ferrini, Costanza. "Il canto di Moncef Ghachem," 5–8 in *Dalle sponde del mare bianco*, edited by Moncef Ghachem and Dounia. Messina: Mesogea, 2003.

Ghachem, Moncef, and Dounia. *Dalle sponde del mare bianco.* Messina: Mesogea (book and compact disc), 2003.

Herzfeld, Michael. "Ethnographic and Epistemological Refractions of Mediterranean Identity." 663–83 in *L'anthropologie de la Méditerranée* (Anthropology of the Mediterranean), edited by Dionigi Albera, Anton Blok and Christian Bromberger. Paris: Maisonneuve et Larose, 2001.

Khuri, Elias. "Beirut e il Mediterraneo. Doppia lingua e lingua plurale," 15–40 in *Raccontare il Mediterraneo Lo sguardo libanese*, edited by Elias Khuri and Ahmad Beydoun Messina: Mesogea, 2002.

Léothaud, Gilles, and Bernard Lortat-Jacob. "La voix méditerranéenne; une identité problématique." 9–14 in *La vocalité dans les pays d'Europe méridionale et dans le bassin méditerranéen.* La Falourdière: Modal, 2002.

Lomax, Alan. *Cantometrics. An Approach to the Anthropology of Music.* Berkeley: The University of California Extension Media Center, 1976.

Lortat-Jacob, Bernard. "S'entendre pour chanter: Une approche anthropologique du chant en Sardaigne." 539–54 in *L'anthropologie de la Méditerranée* (Anthropology of the Mediterranean), edited by Dionigi Albera, Anton Blok and Christian Bromberger. Paris: Maisonneuve et Larose, 2001.

Magrini, Tullia. "Where Does Mediterranean Music Begin?", *Narodna Umjetnost* 36, no. 1 (1999): 173–82.

———. "Introduction: Studying Gender in Mediterranean Musical Cultures." 1–32 in *Music and Gender. Perspectives from the Mediterranean*, edited by Tullia Magrini. Chicago: University of Chicago Press, 2003.

Maniacco, Tito. *Mediterraneo.* Sequals: Grafiche Tielle ("Quaderni del Menocchio"), 1998.

Matvejevic, Predrag. *Il Mediterraneo e l'Europa: Lezioni al Collège de*

France. Milano: Garzanti, 1998.

Monson, Ingrid. "Riffs, Repetition and Theories of Globalization." *Ethnomusicology* 43, no. 1 (1999): 31–65.

Pitino, Cecilia. *Far lunari.* World Music WM 030, 2003 (compact disc).

Plastino, Goffredo. "Introduction: Sailing the Mediterranean Musics." 1–36 in *Mediterranean Mosaic: Popular Music and Global Sound,* edited by Goffredo Plastino. New York: Routledge, 2003a.

———. "Inventing Ethnic Music: Fabrizio De André's *Creuza de mä* and the Creation of *Musica mediterranea* in Italy." 267–286 in *Mediterranean Mosaic: Popular Music and Global Sound,* edited by Goffredo Plastino. New York: Routledge, 2003b.

Said, Edward W. *Orientalismo.* Torino: Bollati Boringhieri, 1991.

Theodoropoulos, Takis. "Alcune storie sul Mediterraneo, mare senza misteri," 17–43 in, *Takis and Rania Polycandroti, Raccontare il Mediterraneo: Lo sguardo greco,* edited by Takis Theodoropoulos. Messina: Mesogea, 2002.

Zizek, Slavoj. *Difesa dell'intolleranza.* Troina: Città Aperta, 2003.

Part 5
The Traveling Mediterranean

Chapter Ten

Algerian Raï into Beur Raï: The Music of Return

Gabriele Marranci

Introduction

In this chapter, I discuss how the popular-traditional Algerian musical meta-genre known as raï blossomed during the 1990s while acknowledging its longer history. It developed a role as an important marker of Algerian immigrant identity while becoming part of the "world music" scene and later attracted the attention of international pop stars such as Sting (for example, in the song *Desert Rose*). Several forms of raï coexist today, which have achieved particular meanings for their respective audiences. On the two sides of the Mediterranean, in Algeria and in France, raï has elicited different emotional responses in its listeners. In order to try to understand these responses I conducted fieldwork in 1998 and 1999 among Algerian immigrants in France.

Raï grew out of the relationship between the urban culture of Oran in Algeria and the rural culture of the surrounding countryside villages. At the end of the nineteenth century, during the period of French colonization, Algeria saw an increase in rural migration to the coastal towns. Not only did this internal migration facilitate economic and demographic changes, but also cultural and, consequently, musical innovations. As a consequence of these changes, the bedui[1] singing style began to fuse with the urbanized zendani style, the resultant mix characterized by popular themes and provocative texts, in which love and sex were the main ingredients (Rouanet 1905). The male singers of this new style were called cheikhs and the females, cheikhats (masters) and they sang in the Arab cafés. During the French colonization there were two types of cafés: the French cafés, attended mainly by the French population and the Arab cafés, attended mainly by Arabs. The latter were located around the port areas and in local bordellos. This naturally affected the way in which Algerians in general viewed this music.

In traditional Algerian society, it was normal to engage a professional maddahat religious singing group to provide the necessary music for a successful wedding party.[2] Nevertheless, families from a rural background could rarely afford one of the maddahat groups and rather than holding wedding parties without music, they preferred to engage the controversial cheikhs and cheikhats. These singers improvised the lyrics of their songs and filled the gaps between verses with words like Aïe! Aïe! or ya lalla, the expression ya-raï becoming the most popular.[3] Gradually, this new musical element in their performances became more popular than the traditional religious songs they could perform. (It should be noted that before World War II, maddahats would refuse to sing nonreligious songs). Hence, despite their status, increasingly the cheikhats (rarely the cheikhs) were invited to sing their ya-raï (or simply raï as it soon became known) at weddings.

During World War II, with the presence of foreign troops and in particular French and North American soldiers, radios were increasingly to be found in the bars and cafés of Algerian cities, increasing the possibility of intercultural contacts. Algerians could now more easily hear American popular music (Daoudi and Miliani 1996). The cheikhs and cheikhats working in these coffee shops, bars and cabarets began to adapt their repertoire by including elements of the blues, big band, early bebop and boogie-woogie, along with rhythms such as the foxtrot. At the same time, the presence of the troops influenced some Algerian singers to question strict Islamic social rules. Indeed, Remiti, one of the most famous cheikhats, even scandalously alluded to sexual liberation for Algerian women (Virolle 1995), challenging two fundamental tenets of the Islamic faith, the modesty and virginity of women. In 1954 one of the most famous raï singers, Houari Blaoui, systematically started to mix Algerian traditional music with American musical styles, achieving success with a young Algerian audience, which started to consider the cheikhats, such as Remitti, as old fashioned.

As we have seen, by the end of the 1940s, raï became a recognized Algerian repertoire, especially among the younger generation, despite the fact that many Algerians still considered the texts of raï inappropriate because of the love stories they narrated. Indeed, there was a generational gap in the musical preferences of the older and the younger Algerians, the latter, in the 1950s, seeing raï as more appropriate to their lifestyles and identities. Thus, during wedding parties the demand for raï increased to such a level that even the maddahats, whose repertoire was mainly religious, had to perform the less "scandalous" raï songs. Given the strict Algerian gender segregation norms respected during the weddings, new young singers, who often came from poor families (such as Khaled) had the opportunity to sing raï for the male guests, opening the door to performance as an important source of income.

Raï, under the influence of this new generation, was continuing to assimilate musical ideas from other cultures, indeed the bedui style became eclipsed. Yet the new version was developing side-by-side with the cheikhs' and cheikhats' original raï. In 1974, to avoid possible confusion, Messaoud Bellemou, an influential raï musician, coined the successful term pop-raï to emphasize the stylistic differences between the young singers' style and that of the cheikhs. During the 1980s, the young raï singers, now called *cheb* (meaning "young" in Arabic), introduced electronic keyboards into their performances.

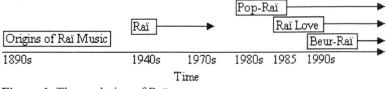
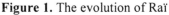

Figure 1. The evolution of Raï

Yet this was not the only "revolution." The chebs and *chebats* (the female pop-raï singers), started to record their songs on audiocassettes, which were then sold at a cheap price in a growing number of "music kiosks." The incredible success of their raï, however, not only produced a lucrative black market in the cassettes but also resulted in the exploitation of raï singers whose copyright was not protected. The recordings of the most famous pop-raï singers (and in particular, Cheb Khaled, nicknamed the "king of Raï," and Cheb Hasni, whose style became known as raï-love[4]) found their way from Algeria, across the Mediterranean, to Algerian immigrants in France (Marranci 2001).

Algerian Music in Paris

From this point we begin to consider raï as a phenomenon plugged into a global cultural economy. Two useful theoretical concepts, the environmental variable and the global disjunctive variable, feature in the work of Arjun Appadurai. For Appadurai, the environmental variable is a set of physical and metaphysical spaces facilitating contact with "cultural otherness." In this dimension, raï singers may elaborate and reconstruct elements of different cultures as a new hyphenated musical product. Here, the in-between is not incertitude but a permeable border between different cultural experiences. Appadurai (1996: 32) considers the global disjunctive variable as the "new global cultural economy, a complex, overlapping, disjunctive order that cannot any longer be understood in terms of existing center-periphery models." To explain this point Appadurai has developed his well-known theory of "scapes": mediascape, technoscape, financescape, ideoscape and ethnoscape.[5]

Raï has been subject to different phases of musical globalization. Although even before the 1980s some Algerian raï singers had traveled to France and sometimes performed in the cabaret in French neighborhoods with a majority Maghrebi population, it was only with the so-called Bobigny Concert, in 1986, that raï started to attract Algerians living in France and, in particular, Paris. The Immigrants' Association of Paris and the Parisian municipality organized the concert in Bobigny, a suburb of Paris, from 23–26 January 1986, inviting the most famous Algerian raï singers, including Zahouania, Hamid, Fadela, Kahled and Hasni, whose raï-love style was becoming increasingly popular.[6]

This was an important event for the history of pop-raï in France for three principal reasons:

(i)   Many Algerian immigrants had known raï only through the audio cassettes sold in the Arab neighborhoods such as Berbés (the most famous Maghrebi neighborhood in Paris). So, for many young Algerians, the concert in Bobigny was the first occasion to see and hear live the voices of their favorite singers.

(ii)   Perhaps more importantly, the concert allowed the Algerian raï singers to make contracts with French record companies, such as EMI.

(iii) The French mass media amplified the success of the concert with some enthusiastic newspaper reviews (for instance, *Le Monde* and *Le Nouvel Observateur*).

Raï enjoyed a growing international success, reaching other important European capitals such as New York and London, with the voices of Chebs Khaled, Hasni and Mami. A new musical style emerged which was called French-raï and was global in reach.[7]

However, at the beginning of the 1990s, if raï was welcomed in the West, the same could not be said for its reception in Algeria, where tensions between Islamic fundamentalists and the government resulted in civil war. Cheb Hasni was murdered in 1994, allegedly by an Islamic commando, who had accused his music of being anti-Islamic because of its lyrics, which allude to divorce and extramarital relations. According to some journalists and commentators (for instance, Loari and Senouci 1999), raï singers responded to the assassination by emigrating to Western countries.

The economic advantages of this action were clear. French record companies could guarantee copyright protection to raï singers, who were often exploited by Algerian producers. Although many of the most important and famous raï singers had left Algeria, a new generation replaced them. Yet this new generation of Algerian singers living in Algeria (like Cheb Bilal) maintained a traditional approach to raï.

The Development of Beur-Raï

French scholars such as Tribalat (1995), Lepoutre (1997) and Manço (1999) have seen the Beurs of Paris as trapped within a "double couture," in-between the Algerian heritage of their parents and their life in France. Towards the end of the 1990s, another raï style developed in France, the so-called Beur-raï, which may be seen as a response to this predicament. At the time of this writing, Faudel is the leading exponent of this style (Marranci 2003) which is musically heterogeneous (drawing on aspects of Western popular music such as rap, techno and reggae, as well as disco) and textually traditional (even going back to the tradition of the maddahats). Other young Beurs continue to try to emulate Faudel's success as record companies look for new Beur-raï voices.

Studies of Algerian immigrants, such as those by Miliani (1995), Derderian (1996) and Gross, McMurray and Swedenburg (1992), reveal a certain attitude towards raï. Gross, McMurray and Swedenburg see raï as "a kind of protective shield for immigrants who are experiencing the disruptions, dislocations and insecurities of migration, who feel vulnerable to racist discrimination and economic marginality and who wish to maintain an originary [sic], imaginary communal identification" (1992: 148).

The preferred repertoire of Algerian immigrants to France has always been the music from Kabylia, a mountainous area in northeastern Algeria lying on the coastline between Algiers and Bejaïa and the popular music of Algiers, called cha'abi.[8] For instance, Idir, a renowned Kabyli singer, who came to Paris during 1976, emphasized that the music from his region was for many Algerian immigrants in France a unique comfort during their "exile" (Derderian 1996). The texts of these songs expressed immigrant workers' everyday difficulties and loneliness, but they also dealt with the political problems of their homeland. From the texts of these songs, it can be understood that immigrants did not foresee a permanent life in France. They wanted to maintain their Kabylian or Algerian identity in the hope that they might return home.

By the late 1970s, Algerian immigrants had effectively become "permanent immigrants": for many, the return to their homeland or, in the case of the second generations, their fathers' or even grandfathers' homeland, Algeria, became only wishful thinking, perhaps even a myth. Hence, the music from Kabylia or other regional repertoires such as cha'abi no longer seemed to adequately represent Algerian immigrant identity. It has already been noted how the concert held in Bobigny in 1986 was an important starting point for the diffusion of raï, succeeding in de-ghettoizing pop-raï from cafés in Barbès and music shops in the Arab neighborhoods of Paris. Cheb Hasni had a particular and important role in this. His songs became a sort of musical bridge across the Mediterranean between Algerians in Algeria and Algerians in France (Virolle 1995; Daoudi and Miliani 1996 and Shade-Poulsen 1997).

Sounding the Music of Return: The Beurs Adopt Raï

Tullia Magrini has observed that "Sound groups are formed by people who choose a certain music mainly because they may identify themselves with the values they connect to that." She also emphasized that:

> Different sound group[s] may coexist in a single place. . . . Sound groups may tend to coincide sometimes with ethnic groups, generational groups, or social classes in a layered society. But differently from ethnic or generational groups, sound groups are open. Thus, the choice to belong to a particular sound group may become a powerful means for self-representation within a society and may conform to or contrast with the habits of a particular place, class, gender, etc. (Magrini 2000: 329)

Using this concept, different sound groups interpret raï in different ways. For example, for an Algerian living in Algeria the tormented love story of a Hasni song may represent the pain of unrequited love. However, the same song has the potential to affect an Algerian immigrant in Paris rather differently; it may, for instance, serve as a metaphor of love phor of love for the homeland. In order to understand this metaphoric process it is important to emphasize that love and courtship have a particular set of meanings for Algerians. In Algeria, because of the strict Islamic moral code pervading society, young people cannot meet freely, but in many cases, must use stratagems to do so. Furthermore, traditional families prefer arranged marriages, which often leave no freedom of choice to the future spouses. The "clandestine" love stories narrated by the texts of raï, the allusive music and pop's association with Western society, become symbols not only of personal, but also social, freedom. However, these clandestine love stories have little possibility of success, as family honor and reputation are still strong social forces in Algeria (Virolle 1995), such that the majority prefer to forego their freedom rather than risking social and familial ostracism.

Algerian immigrants may use the metaphor of love and the cathartic potential of raï in different ways. During fieldwork in Paris (in 1999) one of my informants emphasized, when speaking of love in raï, "Algeria is like a beautiful woman that you had to leave but you still love." One can see then, that French raï can become the *music of return* for Algerian immigrants. Indeed raï music is less regionally and politically, marked than the other Algerian repertoires such as Kabyle music.

As we have seen, not only have the Beurs responded by forming another raï "sound group," but also adapted raï to their cultural needs. Today, there are many Beur singers and groups, such as Cheb Faudel and less well-known figures as Cheb Rani, Raï Kum and Seba Malik (Daoudi 2000: 69–76). Beur raï has affirmed the success of a new generation that claims a new France, a France in which ethnic diversity is celebrated. They express through raï their identities which refuse both assimilation and racial, religious and ethnic stereotyping. Refusing the concept of "in-betweens" (Bhabha 1994) and "halfies" (Abu-Lughod 1991), the second- and third-generation Algerians want to emphasize their originality and be accepted for what they are: Beur.

Conclusions

In its move from Algeria to France, raï has provided for the needs of various generations of immigrants. They have each been able to locate themselves in particular sound groups furnished by both Algerian traditional music and Western styles. This throws up questions about the processes of globalization as posited by Appadurai and the experience of postcolonial cultures by Bhabha. We have seen in the way that raï has been reconfigured in a global diasporic context in which music plays an important role in shaping identity and social status. Raï music has been a fundamental factor in the revaluation of the so-called Beur culture and the role it might have in a multicultural France. In singing, Beurs discover what it is to be "Beur" in new and positive dimensions that facilitate the difficult process of developing mutual understanding between them and French society.

Notes

1. Traditional Algerian country singing style characterized by a syncopated rhythm, often played on traditional percussion instruments such as the darabuka.

2. Groups of women singers that "liven up" marriage parties with religious songs.

3. Word for word: "oh my thought."

4. Raï love was particularly important because, by avoiding the controversial texts of some raï songs, became socially acceptable even within the Algerian families. Also, the new generations found in Hasni's raï love the metaphor of their difficult lives in Algeria and the complex gender relationships.

5. Ethnoscape deals with the personal sphere, mediascape is the account of reality based on images, technoscape refers to the sphere through which various technologies move, financescape is the area through which money and financial transactions flow and ideoscape is the locus of ideologies of states and the counter-ideologies of movements aimed at opposing those states. Examining how these "scapes" interact, Appadurai has observed that: "cultural processes today are products of the infinitely varied mutual contest of sameness and difference on a stage characterized by radical disjunctures between different sorts of global flows and the uncertain landscapes created in and through these disjunctures" (1996: 43).

6. For aspects concerning raï and gender, see Virolle (1995: 80–128).

7. For a biography of the singers and more details on the development of this genre, see Marranci (2003).

8. Cha'abi is an Algerian repertoire predominant in the Algerian capital, Algiers. Musically influenced by other Northern African styles, the texts often refer to recent events in the history of the country as well as personal experiences of the singers. Today the cha'abi, which in

Arabic means "urban," is undergoing a process of modernization similar to that of raï music, although less globalized.

Bibliography

Abu-Lughod, Lila. "Writing against Culture" 137–62 in *Recapturing Anthropology: Working in the Present*, edited by R. G. Fox. Santa Fe: School of American Research Press, 1999.

Appadurai, Arjun. *Modernity at Large: Cultural Dimensions of Globalization*. Minneapolis: University of Minnesota Press, 1996.

Bhabha, Homi. *The Location of Culture*. London: Routledge, 1994.

Daoudi, Bouziane. *Le Raï*. Paris: Librio Musique, 2000.

Daoudi, Bouziane, and Hadj Miliani. *L'aventure du raï*. Paris: Edition du Seuil, 1996.

Derderian, Richard L. "Popular Music from the North African Immigrant Community: Multiculturalism in Contemporary France 1945–94." *Contemporary France Civilisation* 20, no. 1 (1996): 203–16.

Gross, Joan, David McMurray and Ted Swedenburg. "Arab Noise and Ramadan Nights." *Middle East Report* 22, no. 5 (1992): 120–55.

Lepoutre, David. *Cœur de banlieue*. Paris: Editions Odile Jacob, 1997.

Loari, Marcello, and Chawky Senouci. *La battaglia del raï*. Milano: Zelig, 1999.

Magrini, Tullia. "From Music Makers to Virtual Singers: New Musics and Puzzled Scholars." 320–30 in *Musicology and Sister Disciplines: Past, Present, Future*, edited by D. Greer. London: Oxford University Press, 2000.

Manço, Altay. *Intégration et identités*. Paris: De Boeck Université, 1999.

Marranci, Gabriele. "Le Raï aujourd'hui: entre métisage musical et world music moderene." *Cahiers de Musiques Traditionnelles* 13 (2000).

———. "A Complex Identity and its Musical Representation: Beur and Raï Music in Paris." *Music and Anthropology* 5 (2001)

———. "Pop-Raï: from Local Tradition to Globalization" 102–21 in *Mediterranean Mosaic: Popular Music and Global Sounds*, edited by Goffredo Plastino. New York: Routledge, 2003.

Miliani, Hadj. "Banlieues entre rap et raï." *Hommes and Migrations* 1191 (1995): 24–30.

Rouanet, J. "La Chanson Populaire Arabe en Algie." *La Revue Musi-*

cale V (1905): 166–67.

Shade-Poulsen, Marc. "Which World: on the Diffusion of Algerian Raï to West." 59–85 in *Siting Culture*, edited by Karen Fog Olwig and Kirsten Hastrup, London: Routledge, 1997.

Tribalat, Michèle. *Faire France* Paris: La Découverte-Essais, 1995.

Virolle, Marie. *La chanson raï*. Paris: Karthala, 1995.

Chapter Eleven

On Imagining the Mediterranean

David Cooper

Introduction

In a discussion of the lullaby *Seo Hú Leó* in his anthology *The Petrie Collection of the Ancient Music of Ireland* ([1855] 2002: 106), the antiquarian George Petrie drew attention to the similarity between the melody of this Irish traditional song and tunes from North India and Iran (then known as Hindustan and Persia respectively).[1] Later in the same work, writing about another Gaelic-language lullaby, *Do Chuirfinnse Féin mo Leanbh a Chodladh* (I Would Put My Own Child to Sleep), Petrie readdressed the theme, noting that:

> Such affinity with Eastern melody is not confined to the nurse-tunes of Ireland, but that it will be no less found in the ancient funeral caoines, as well as in the ploughman's tunes and other airs of occupation—airs simple indeed in construction, but always touching in expression; and I cannot but consider it as an evidence of the early antiquity of such melodies in Ireland and as an ethnological fact of much historic interest, not hitherto sufficiently attended to. (169)

This judgment may seem to exemplify the "random comparisons, made for capricious reasons" which as Nettl (1983: 53) remarks, "make even the most devoted comparative musicologists cringe." However, Petrie was not the first and certainly would not be the last writer to imagine connections between the traditional culture of Ireland and what was regarded as the "East." For example, sixty years later, on 12 May 1918, Philip Heseltine (better known as Peter Warlock) delivered an illustrated lecture entitled "What Music Is" at the Abbey Theatre, Dublin, during which he attempted to demonstrate parallels between the musics of Ireland and India with the help of an Indian musician and an Irish sean-nós singer.[2]

In more recent times, the Irish composer and academic Seán Ó Riada, who proved highly influential in the development of a pioneering mode of traditional performance with the formation of the ensemble

Ceoltóirí Cualann (the forerunner of The Chieftains) in the early 1960s, was drawn to the music of North Africa, the Middle East and India.[3] According to his friend Garech a Brún, "Seán had sensed the connection between *true* Irish music and the music of the Arab and Indian worlds, as also that of the Far East" (Harris and Freyer 1981: 185).[4] In a talk broadcast on RTE radio in 1962, Ó Riada observed that Irish traditional music was not European at all, but was "closer to some forms of Oriental music" (Ó Riada 1982: 20).[5] It was not, he suggested, founded upon the extensional, goal-directed formal principles of Western art music, but on repeating cycles in which ornamentation, rather than the development and integration of contrasting material, was the fundamental creative element:

> The basic pattern of the song remains in each verse, but the events, the ornaments vary. This does not necessarily mean that the musician who does not use variation is a bad one; he is a passive holder of tradition. The musician who makes good variations is, on the other hand, a creative contributor [to] the tradition. He makes it grow and develop. (22)[6]

While Ó Riada's account of the structural principles of Gaelic song may seem coherent on musicological grounds, perhaps a political motivation for distinguishing the genre from European art music may also be inferred. In his analysis, the culturally "pure" Gaelic music predated the influence of invading Vikings, Normans and Anglo-Saxons, the innate conservatism of the people keeping "Irish music alive for us, its basic characteristics unchanged, with very little outside influence" (20). In the terms of postcolonial theory, sean-nós, as a signifier of precolonial Ireland, offered Ó Riada a means of abrogating the musical language of Britain, the former colonial center and privileging that of the marginalized Gaeltacht by means of an "authentic" Irish music that offered a pure, "uncontaminated" musical identity.[7] Through its melismatic and highly ornamented melody (which may also be found in some "Eastern" musics) and its rhythmic freedom, sean-nós seemed to express the difference and otherness of Ireland,[8] especially when contrasted with the clichéd view of the English vernacular as foursquare, plain and stodgy—"cowpat music" as the art music molded upon it has sometimes been uncharitably characterized.[9]

Charles Acton (1914–99), the long-time music critic of *The Irish Times*, touched upon mythological migratory connections between North Africa, Spain and Ireland in his brief monograph *Irish Music and Musicians*. Claims of such links made their first appearance in the twelfth-century manuscript *Lebor Gabála Érren* (Book of the Taking of Ireland), which traced the legendary inhabitants of Ireland back to the time of Noah. Of the invaders alluded to in *Lebor Gabála Érren*, perhaps the most significant in terms of contemporary Irish national consciousness are the sons of Míl Espáine, the Milesians or Gaedels (Gaels), who purportedly came from Spain. Acton, looking slightly farther south across the Mediterranean and seeing perhaps that there may have been a grain of truth in some of these myths of invasion, remarked that:

> The rules of warfare and politics in pastoral, mediaeval Ireland were extraordinarily similar to those of the Bedouin up to 1940. And the decoration of "old-style" (sean nós) Irish singing of the great slow airs is very like desert Arab music. Those songs, unlike other European musics, have their own rhythm, without the normal foundation of any regular pulse.
>
> Northern migrations have left us with a fabulous wealth of artifacts. Their musical heritage is still a matter of guesswork. The south-Mediterranean route has left us with a directly recognizable heritage of the rhythm and decoration of the slow air and possibly of the bagpipe gracing. (Acton 1978: 8)

Ó Riada's and Acton's assessments of sean-nós were acknowledged by the Irish filmmaker and writer, Bob Quinn, in his 1983 trilogy of television films and 1986 book, *Atlantean*.[10] Quinn (who made no claims to be a scholarly writer) drew on data from a wide range of academic disciplines to develop the argument that Ireland, through the influence of traders and adventurers, had come into close cultural contact with the Mediterranean region. For Quinn, the exotic characteristics of sean-nós singing (especially that found in Connemara, the area he made his home) and above all in the employment of melisma,[11] bore the imprint of these contacts. A major focus of his attention was the North African region of the Maghreb and in particular Morocco, whose Arab-Berber inhabitants, he suggested, shared many characteristics, musical and otherwise, with those of Ireland. Quinn's aims in pointing out these similarities seem to have been to deconstruct the dominant myth of Ireland as a land peopled by Celts and to reveal "the diverse richness that lies beneath" (1986: 27). An ability to replace an exclusive and homogeneous concept of racial purity found in romantic nationalism with one that was both inclusive and heterogeneous was for Quinn a sign of a people's maturity and self-confidence. For Martin McLoone (2000: 133), "Quinn scrutinizes the whole of Celtic mythology in Ireland in an ironic and absurdist manner"; furthermore, "his films exist in an ironic relationship with both tradition and modernity, on the one hand castigating cultural nationalism's use, or abuse, of Gaelic Ireland while at the same time, being deeply suspicious of the modernity represented by Dublin (and Hollywood)."

Brian McIlroy (1989: 69) has suggested that the publication of Quinn's work in book form might encourage scholars to "take up more thoroughly his observations on the similarities, among others, of sean-nós singing, language and the sheela na gig figures in Ireland with their counterparts in North Africa and the Middle East." Before accepting this challenge and exploring some of the musical implications of Quinn's thesis, we would do well to review the main musical features of western-Irish sean-nós singing:

(i) **Accompaniment**. Although many contemporary singers often perform with instrumental accompaniment, sean-nós is fundamentally an unaccompanied, monophonic genre.

(ii) **Modality**. As is the case with much Western-European traditional music, song tunes are usually either pentatonic, or use modes that may conveniently be defined as Ionian, Dorian, Mixolydian or Aeolian.

(iii) **Ornamentation**. A prime feature of southwestern Irish sean-nós is the elaborate embellishment of song skeletons. Figure 1 illustrates various strategies for decorating melodic intervals found in some areas of Ireland,[12] these ornaments paralleling the short trills, turns, nota cambiata figures and auxiliary and passing notes widely found in Western art music. Movement is frequently by step, whether diatonic or pentatonic and the use of portamento is common, particularly at phrase endings.

(iv) **Rhythm and tempo**. A fluid approach to rhythm tends to be adopted by singers (and instrumentalists performing slow airs), usually in a leisurely tempo and as a result of this listeners (see, for example, Acton's remarks cited above) sometimes report difficulty in locating an underlying pulse.

(v) **Intonation**. Early in the twentieth century, with the aid of Erich von Hornbostel's laboratory at the University of Berlin, Richard Henebry conducted elementary acoustical research which broadly suggested that Irish traditional musicians did not conform to either equal temperament, or for that matter any fixed intonation system, while singing.[13] Henebry, an uncompromising Irish nationalist, contrasted the "dead" modern scale, with its fixed and unmovable intervals, with the "living" natural singing of the traditional performer and noted that:

In the latter we find a myriad intervals, each used in obedience to some mysterious and subtle laws, that are, no doubt, the fundamental motives of human expression. For the place of a given note will change, for instance, with the meaning above all, with the stress which has a constant or multiple relation to the meaning and again, a place will make varying reactions to upward and downward progressions. (1928: 40–41)

Some of Henebry's data relating to the interval of a major second is analyzed in table 1 and this reveals significant flexibility of intonation in the airs he examined.[14] Henebry's basic conclusions have been confirmed by more recent scientific work, including that of this author. As is the case with much traditional music, transcriptions using Western staff notation can be misleading in that they fail to fully convey the subtle pitch relationships inherent in live performance.

Melodic interval	Mean frequency in cents	Standard deviation
A–B	210.2	56.2
G–A	187.5	40.4
A–G	184.2	51.9
E–F#	206.4	45.4
F#–E	219.8	42.0

Table 1. Average frequencies in cents and standard deviations of melodic major 2nds in data from Henebry's *Handbook of Irish Music*. An equal-tempered second is exactly 200 cents.

(vi) **Form**. Traditional Irish songs are generally strophic, usually in four or eight lines and although other forms are found, simple AABA and ABBA structures predominate. Songs may have tens or even dozens of verses and each of these, when sung by musicians steeped in the tradition, can be ornamented in subtly differing ways, such that a kind of variation form is produced. Two specific principles of metrical organization are found in song in the Gaelic language (which is influenced by the bardic tradition): syllabic or quantitative meter, in which a regular pattern of syllables is present, and accentual or qualitative meter in which the number of syllables varies, but the number of accents remains constant. The use of internal rhyme and assonance is widespread in Irish-language verse.

(vii) **Timbre**. There are very many different approaches to voice
production in Irish traditional singing, from the full-throated
and hard-edged tone found in some eastern European traditional styles, through the rather nasalized sounds of singers
such as Joe Heaney and Pat Phádraic Tom Ó Conghaile, to the
smoother timbre of some recent performers (for example, the
Donegal singer, Mairéad Ní Mhaonaigh).

Figure 1. Samples of sean-nós ornamentation. The opening pair of
notes on each line presents the unornamented interval.

A transcription of the first two lines of the melody of the song *Bean a'*
Leanna (Woman of the Alehouse), sung by Pat Phádraic Tom Ó Conghaile from Spiddal near Galway appears in figure 2. This song illustrates some of the tendencies noted above and in particular, rhythmic
elasticity and filigree ornament. One must be wary, however, when
making assumptions about the antiquity of such "old style" techniques
simply from the degree of embellishment that the songs display.
Shields remarks that "modern learners of traditional Irish singing often
rely chiefly on decoration of the melody to give their singing idiomatic
character," and that even traditional singers themselves "may also mul-
tiply ornaments after exposure to modern kinds of celebrity" (1993:
126). He demonstrates that the mid-Ulsterman Geordie Hanna had in-

creased the degree of decoration by some 20 percent in a 1978 recording of the song *Lisburn Town* relative to one made in 1969 (126–
27). From this point of view, it is illuminating to examine Liam de Noraidh's 1940s transcriptions of Munster songs in his collection *Ceol ón
Mumhain* (Music from Munster, 1965), which range from the heavily
decorated (for example, Domhnall Ó hArachtáin's *Bruach na Carraige
Báine* [26–27] or Seán Ó Cíobháin's *Caoineadh na Luasach* [31]) to
the simple and unadorned (Séamus Ó Cionnfhaolaigh's *An Ceannaí
Bán* [47]).

Figure 2. Transcription of the first two lines of the melody *Bean a'
Leanna*, sung by Pat Phádraic Tom Ó Conghaile.[15]

If southwestern Irish sean-nós can be related to the musical practices of
the Maghreb, as Acton and Quinn argue, which genres of music from
that region are they envisaging? Quinn draws on a nineteenth-century
anecdote in his discussion:

> When a Lebanese visitor to the Royal Irish Academy in the 1850s
> was asked to read from an ancient copy of the Qur'an which the
> academy possessed, he proceeded to chant it in the style of a muez-
> zin.[16] Coming up the stairs at the same time was Eugene O'Curry, a
> well-known antiquarian and native Gaelic speaker. As soon as the
> visitor stopped, O'Curry took up the refrain—but he continued in the
> strain of a Keener, or sean-nós singer of the West of Ireland. The
> people present said they could not distinguish between the two forms
> of chant or the words used. They came to the conclusion that the two
> forms were related. (1986: 29)[17]

While a number of cultural and linguistic connections between Morocco (which is, of course, culturally very different from Lebanon) and
Ireland are explored in *Atlantean*, Quinn by no means fully investigates
the musical ones. Morocco possesses an incredibly rich and diverse
musical tradition. The variety of the music found within the nation-

state of Morocco underlines its ethnic mixture as reflected in musical practice,[18] with the genre of Arabo-Andalusian music or al-âla and its close relative al-gharnâti (which is also found in Algeria), forming the most influential category of Arab-Moroccan art music.[19] The Arabo-Andalusian tradition was brought from Baghdad to Spain (Córdoba and Granada) in the ninth century and arrived in North Africa around the thirteenth century with the Arab expulsion from Spain.[20] Its characteristic musical form is the nûba, a suite in five extended movements for voices and orchestra (a combination of oud, rabâb, violins and percussion), based on a single ṭab' (an Arab mode or maqâm).[21] Each of the five movements (mizân) lasts between fifteen and seventy minutes, has an associated meter,[22] and is composed of an instrumental prelude and a series of çan'a or vocal sections. Arabo-Andalusian music (like most Arab music) is based on the systematic division of the octave into twenty-four nonequal-tempered quartertones rather than the twelve semitones of the Western system.

A common interval in the Arab maqâm is the three-quarter tone, often used to subdivide pitches lying a minor third apart (for example, between D and F in the râst tetrachord) into two almost equal-sized intervals, rather than the tone plus semitone division (or vice versa) of the Western system and it is probably this feature, as much as any, which engenders its unfamiliar or exotic color for the Western listener. It was noted above that Irish sean-nós performances (particularly those from earlier generations) demonstrate a largely unregulated approach to intonation (whereas maqâm is very regulated, systematized, sophisticated and highly theorized in terms of art music); and in my own study of the style of the Ulster fiddler and singer Joe Holmes, I have noted the pronounced tendency to perform the leading note in an intermediate position between the minor and major species, such that the interval of the minor third between the submediant and upper tonic is fairly evenly split into two three-quarter tones.[23] For Irish musicians this is certainly *not* a theorized practice and it seems unlikely that it came about as a response to external influences such as those of the southern Mediterranean; in fact it is probably symptomatic of the flexible approach to modality found in many European traditional musics.[24]

If Arabo-Andalusian music is representative of urban Arab-Moroccan art music, then that of the rwais, itinerant professional performers (at once composers, comedians, poets, singers, dancers, instrumentalists and storytellers) from the High Atlas and Sus regions of the southwest of the country, is characteristic of one strand of indigenous Berber culture. Unlike the ṭab'-based modality of Arabo-Andalusian music, with its distinctive quarter or three-quarter tone intervals (common to most Arab, Turkish and south-central Asian music), the music of the rwais is essentially pentatonic.[25] Much of it, like the jigs and hornpipes of Ireland, is in compound duple or quadruple time, a feature that has encouraged bands such as Mugar (see below) to attempt a musical synthesis of Irish and Berber styles.[26]

However, neither of these two important representatives of Moroccan music-making can really be seen to relate to Irish sean-nós in style or in approach; neither for that matter does the music of the Gnawas, or the genre called ahwash, the popular amateur dance music found in Berber villages. Nevertheless, the journalist Luke Verling, like the unidentified source in Quinn's story of O'Curry cited above, observes a correspondence between Arab-Berber Islamic chant and sean-nós. In an article published in *The Limerick Leader* in January 2002, which describes a visit to Morocco, Verling notes that:

> The Koran was sung in the streets, in a style sounding very like Irish sean nós singing. Their similarity has been well noted and discussed by people such as Bob Quinn—for whose film, The [sic] *Atlantean*, Dr de Courcy Ireland brought recordings of Arabic music back to Ireland from a previous research trip—Seán Ó Riada and many others. Nevertheless, when you hear that singing, live, there, the arguments connecting North Africa with Ireland seem more a certainty than a theory. The same applies to meeting red-haired, blue-eyed Berbers in Tetouan.[27]

The chanting of the Qur'an by scholars called tôlba is, as Schuyler notes, a "foreign" tradition borrowed from Arab music by the Berbers, (1979: 65) though the rwais do perform chants as part of their pitch for money in marketplace performances (1984: 101). Of course, to regard the Qur'anic chant as singing is to apply a Western gloss to a form of religious recitation that is simply not regarded as music by the "performer." However, the chant found in Morocco, particularly the Arabo-Andalusian style found in northern Morocco, is heavily influenced by maqâm-based principles of construction.

Touma identifies the essential features of such Arab Qur'anic recitation:

> Not infrequently, the reading actually involves a complete maqâm presentation. . . . In every melodic passage, just as during a secular performance, the performer realizes a tone level centered on one tone of the maqâm row. The presentation of the mandatory phrases at the beginning and end of the Koran reading is always restricted to the first tone of the maqâm row. Other characteristics are the relatively

slow tempo of the singing, the many long sustained tones, the melismas on consonants as well as on vowels, the register changes at the interval of an octave and the long pauses of up to ten seconds between melodic passages. During these pauses, the faithful burst into spontaneous applause, especially when an excellent Koran reader, by modulating to neighboring maqâm rows or by abruptly finishing a melodic passage on a high tone, manages to heighten the inner tension of the listeners until they have no choice but to release it with exclamations praising God. (1996: 155)

Figure 3 presents a transcription of the melody of the first four lines of a Qur'anic chant in the Arabo-Andalusian style intoned by Abu Bakr Siddiq, an Imam from Ksar Kebir, near Laroche, which illustrates some of the phenomena identified by Touma. Although there are some superficial stylistic similarities with Irish sean-nós (and for that matter, Scottish-Gaelic song), such as the relatively slow tempo and the use of related forms of ornamentation, the underlying approach to both modality and musical structure is very different. As has already been noted, sean-nós involves the decoration of songs which have pre-formed melodic frameworks, their semi-improvisational decorative elements supporting the interpretation of the text but not functioning as a means of elaborating a larger-scale goal-directed structure. One might be tempted to argue a closer relationship between Arabo-Andalusian Qur'anic chant and the Gaelic psalm-singing tradition of Presbyterians from the Isle of Lewis, though it seems less plausible to assume trading or other relations between this region and North Africa as causative factors.[28]

Hugh Shields is surely correct when he remarks in *Narrative Singing in Ireland* (1993: 124) that if the Western and Southwestern styles of sean-nós have international links, they are more likely to be found "in Europe than in Africa or the Middle-East (as is sometimes suggested)." Acton compared sean-nós to Spanish cante jondo or the "deep song" of the Spanish-Andalusian flamenco tradition,[29] whose "oriental" character Felipe Pedrell viewed as emerging as much from the influence of Byzantine chant as from Arab music.[30] If we look further north in Spain, to the province of Cácares in the Extremadura region, where Alan Lomax collected a large number of field recordings, we find a similarly highly ornamented style.[31] In these recordings and in Manuel García-Matos's transcriptions of Extremaduran music in *Cancionero Popular de la Provincia de Cáceres* (1982), there are highly decorated song genres, with regular strophic forms that are more closely comparable to those of Irish sean-nós than Moroccan Qur'anic chant.

Figure 3. The opening section of a Qur'anic chant transcribed by the author from a recording of Abu Bakr Siddiq from Ksar Kebir.[32]

Further north still, at the northwest tip of Spain, lies Galicia, where a type of song called alalá (a term curiously similar to al-âla, the Arab-Moroccan word for the Arabo-Andalusian music discussed above) is one of the major regional musical forms. Writing in the 1930s, Walter Starkie, professor of Spanish at the University of Dublin who took on the role of an itinerant minstrel during his vacations, describes performances of both alalá and instrumental music, relating them to his experiences of Irish music:

> An *alalá* is sung to four-line *coplas* and the Galician singer gives free reins to his improvisation, introducing grace-notes and trills *ad libitum*. Every kind of emotion enters into the *alalá*. There are cradle-songs, ploughing songs, muleteer songs, but in all of them there is a sense of melancholy, or *morriña* as a Gallego would call it, such as we get in the Irish songs. After a few glasses of wine the old man started to play a *muiñera*, or "dance of the miller's wife," which made me feel as though I had been transported back to a harvest *Ceilidhe* in Ireland. (1934: 188)

Starkie's musical companion on this occasion, Tió Anselmo, a Galician living in Bilbao, regarded him as a fellow Celt, an epithet which the Catholic Starkie found hard to accept as an appropriate ethnic descriptor for himself, remarking that the Irish only became Celts once they emigrated from Ireland. While Galicia is now popularly regarded as a

"Celtic" region (see Chapman 1994), there is no doubt that there have been important links between Catholic Spain and Ireland for many centuries, the latter offering a route by which the interests of England could be damaged. In the 1530s, for instance, Spanish agents encouraged Munster chieftains to ally themselves to King Charles V and in 1601 an abortive uprising led by Hugh Roe O'Donnell had the support of around 4000 Spanish troops who landed at Kinsale but were besieged by the English army and forced to retreat. O'Donnell's failure led to his own retirement to Spain, just one of the many Irishmen and women who would seek refuge or settle there. Equally, the Iberian Peninsula was a powerful trading partner of Ireland's from Tudor times and devout Irish Catholics regularly went on pilgrimages to Spain.

In light of these exchanges, a connection between the traditional musics of the two countries may not seem entirely implausible. The musicologist Julián Ribera traced the Galician melody *La Molinera* through the British Isles and northern Europe and noted that, "En Irlanda, donde también se cree que está una de las más antiguas músicas de Europa, se nota claramente que hay muchas melodies populares procedentes de España y de la familia de «La Molinera»" (1925: 24).[33]

Starkie conjectured that, as Irish pilgrims traveled through Galicia to Santiago de Compostela, they would have been very likely to come into contact with juglares (minstrels) and exchanged melodies, such as *La Molinera*, with them (1934: 193–94). On their return to Ireland, the pilgrims would have performed the melodies they picked up, albeit adapted to local taste and thus transmitted them to the local community.[34] One of the tunes of apparently Galician provenance taught to Starkie by Tió Anselmo was a muiñera (a dance like a double jig) entitled *Tantarán que los Higos son Verdos* (Tarantán for the Figs They Are Green). Starkie remarks that "whenever I have played it in Ireland, Scotland or Wales the Gaelic lads and lasses danced to it as if it had sprung out of the soul of the Celt," but cautions us against inferring that this correspondence inevitably indicates a shared Celtic musical culture (192–93). Drawing on Ribera's paper, he notes that:

> I have always thought that it was the most Galician mill-danced [*sic*] tune of all until I read Ribera's study on Galician music. He states that it must have been very popular in other regions of Spain before it was considered the exclusive property of Galicia. The theme is well known in Catalonia and in the sixteenth century it was sung in Castile. Even the rhythm, which seems so characteristically Galician, was very common among the Spanish Moors in the days of Salinas, the great musician of the sixteenth century. (1934: 193)

Of course, as well as embracing melodies from other regions, Irish musicians have enthusiastically adopted new instrumental resources, sometimes adapting them to their requirements. The violin, flute and piano were readily absorbed from art music, while the accordion, concertina, banjo and guitar were borrowed from other vernacular musics. Although musicians have undoubtedly played together when given the opportunity, it is arguable that the performance of traditional music (whatever the instrument), prior to the twentieth century, was largely the domain of the individual, rather than the ensemble, before the early twentieth-century creation of the so-called Céilí band. It was noted earlier that Seán Ó Riada had developed a new mode of instrumental performance in the later 1950s by devising his Irish orchestra Ceoltóirí Cualann as a replacement for the Céilí band, the mainstay of popular dances in both towns and villages. According to Ó Riada (1982: 73), the Céilí band was conceived in 1926 by the first director of Irish Broadcasting, Seamus Clandillon, though in fact it seems that the term was used at least as early as 1918 for an ensemble which performed at the St. Patrick's Day Céilí in Notting Hill, London (see Quinn 1999). Ó Riada poured scorn on the Céilí band as it had developed by the 1960s, feeling that it had been sullied by the influence of jazz and swing bands. Originally the bands had been composed of fiddles, flutes and accordions, but the later additions of piano, drum kit, bass and ultimately (in Ó Riada's words, "the final insult") saxophones, guitars and banjos had corrupted them. Their performances, he remarked, resulted in "a rhythmic but meaningless noise with as much relation to music as the buzzing of a bluebottle in an upturned jam jar" (Ó Riada 1982: 73–74).

To reform the Céilí band, Ó Riada turned to the basic principles of the Arab orchestra, proposing a grouping whose wind section involved the uillean pipes, flute and tin whistle and a string section formed of fiddles, with accordions to provide weight in tutti sections. It is arguable that his most original and brilliant addition was a frame drum called the bodhrán, an instrument played with a double-ended beater that was hardly known at the time and was used principally in the mummers' (the "Wren Boys") activities in Kerry, Limerick and Clare held on St. Stephen's Day. The bodhrán, whose primary function (other than when occasionally used as a percussion instrument) seems to have been as a household storage container or farming utensil until Ó Riada's adoption of it (see Schiller 2001: 94–96), is related both to the Arab bendîr or târ and to the Spanish tambourine. Interestingly, pre-revival performers were known to add metal jingles to the bodhrán,

presumably in emulation of the tambourine.[35] Ó Riada's other controversial addition to his ensemble was the harpsichord, whose tone he felt
made a much better substitute for the metal-strung Irish harp than the
instruments available at the time.[36] The performance principle of the
orchestra was that of variation: after the outlining a tune's "skeleton,"
soloists or small subgroups would ornament it, "the more variation the
better, so long as it has its roots in the tradition and serves to extend
that tradition rather than destroy it by running counter to it" (Ó Riada
1982: 74).

The selection of tone-color for Ceoltóirí Cualann (and its immediate successors, such as the Chieftains) was premised on a hierarchical
concept of musical authenticity in which, by and large, the instruments
that had been associated with Irish traditional music for the longest
time held precedence. Thus banjos or guitars were held in some contempt as modern interlopers, foreign to the tradition. Ó Riada's acceptance of the harpsichord as a surrogate for the harp, however, betrays
his Western art music origins (as does, perhaps, his tendency to perform in "concert dress") and his use of the instrument until his final
years was tied to conventional art music practice. Gráinne Yeats remarks that:

> His arrangements were full, rich and often chromatic, using modula-
> tions impossible on the harp. [. . .] He loved to make ingenious ar-
> rangements in which he interwove phrases from one tune with
> phrases of another to make an unusual whole. He sometimes added a
> little bit of classical music, as in "Ding Dong Dedero," where a few
> bars of an 18th century minuet make a brief appearance. In fact he
> used the harpsichord largely as he would have the piano, with full
> chords and plentiful use of modulations. (Yeats 1981: 85)

Nowadays, instruments of Mediterranean origin—bouzoukis, mando-
lins, mandolas, even darabukas—which Ó Riada would probably have
spurned as inauthentic regularly find a place in the contemporary Irish
"traditional" music ensemble.[37] The onset of this specific Mediterranean influence and especially the introduction of the bouzouki, can be
fairly accurately pinpointed to the mid 1960s and to the band
Sweeney's Men. A friend of Johnny Moynihan, one of the original
members of the group, had brought a bouzouki back from a Greek holi-
day and presented him with it.[38] Apparently Moynihan found the instrument easier to handle than the mandolin and introduced fellow band
member Andy Irvine to it.[39] The contrapuntal interplay between
Moynihan's bouzouki and Irvine's mandolin is heard to particularly

fine effect on the track *Rattlin' Roarin' Willie* from the 1968 album, *Sweeney's Men* and this type of interaction became a feature of the performance style of the band Planxty, which was formed in 1972 by Irvine, Christy Moore, Liam O'Flynn and Dónal Lunny (the inventor of the flat-backed version of the instrument which became known as the Irish bouzouki).[40] The influence of Lunny over the three decades since the formation of Planxty has been substantial, both as solo and backing musician and as producer and it is probably as much due to him as any other performer that the bouzouki is regularly found within Irish traditional bands.

This embracing of Mediterranean instruments by Irish musicians in the 1960s predates the invention of the "world music" marketing category by some twenty years,[41] and it is unlikely that it was motivated by the rather naïve syncretic impulses which gave rise to the "world fusion" of Ancient Future (founded in 1978) or more recent bands such as Afro Celts. It is more reasonable to see it as the outcome of a more inclusive and perhaps more developmental, attitude towards traditional performance, embodying a concern not simply to adhere to the narrower notions of authenticity of an Ó Riada, either in terms of instrumental resources or performance practices, at the expense of the renewal of the tradition.

Conclusion

If there is, perhaps, too little solid evidence to justify notions of ancient links between sean-nós and North African musical practices, it is clear that such relationships, even if imagined, can provide useful inspiration for creative musicians. If we consider the French-Moroccan band Mugar's CD *Kabily-Touseg*, which, under the direct influence of Quinn's vision of a shared Atlantean connection, brings together Berber musicians and 'Celtic' music, we find in its more successful moments music which is both novel and satisfying. The CD liner notes that "traditional repertoire and original compositions, loans and exchanges, blends and confrontations together weave this repertoire which makes of their differences their source for creation." This would seem to me to be a healthy attitude, for it is through cultural contact that traditional music remakes itself. I have noted elsewhere, in respect to Bartók's views as expressed in the essay "Race Purity in Music" that while he:

regards internationalization as detrimental to the development and continuation of peasant music, he believes that the best means of circumventing it is by allowing peasant [*sic*] musics from different cultures to interact, for by doing so the "material of each, however heterogeneous in origin, receives its marked individuality" (Bartók [1942] 1976: no. 5, 30).

The preservation of a culture, by artificially segregating it from alien influences, restricts the potential gene pool, resulting in a poverty-stricken and stagnant music. (Cooper 1999)[42]

If the exchanges and interactions between the Mediterranean region and Ireland result in the enhancement of their respective musics (as was the case with Starkie's muiñera), this would seem to be of benefit to the development of traditional music in an age of transnationalism and globalization. However, if the consequence is simply a mishmash of half-digested clichés, the subtle tokens which act as carriers of intracultural meaning will be erased. In time, of course, new meanings will accrue to these composite tokens and the musical instabilities that arise from the contact of divergent cultural materials may to all appearances be resolved. In either case, the music which results may well stimulate the imaginations of future generations of listeners, to hear in it evidence of affinities with "remote" and "distant" cultures.

Notes

1. George Petrie (b. 1790) was an Irish artist, antiquary, violinist and collector of traditional music. The most likely source for Petrie's knowledge was William Hamilton Bird's *The Oriental Miscellany; being a collection of the most favourite Airs of Hindoostan, compiled and adapted for the Harpsichord* (Calcutta: J. Cooper, 1789), a work which is cited in Edward Bunting's 1840 collection *The Ancient Music of Ireland*.

2. Malcolm Gillies, *Bartók in Britain* (Oxford: Clarendon Press, 1989), 22. See Smith (1994: 136–37) and Grey (1934: 159–60). The term *sean-nós* (Gaelic for "old style") indicates the generally highly ornamented style of the western and southwestern regions of Ireland. It is not clear when this term was first used—my assumption is that it is of recent origin. It is unclear which part of India Heseltine was referring to.

3. Seán Ó Riada (1931–71) was born as John Reidy but adopted the Gaelicized version of his name by 1960. In the 1950s he studied in

Paris and was influenced by both Florent Schmidt and Olivier Messiaen. He was attracted to serial technique and adopted it in a fairly crude way as part of his compositional language in his early concert works, such as *Nomos No. 1: Hercules Dux Ferrariae* for strings (1957). See Harris and Freyer (1981).

4. My emphasis.

5. Seán Ó Riada, *Our Musical Heritage*, edited by Thomas Kinsella and Tomás Ó Canainn (Mountrath: The Dolment Press, 1982), 20.

6. This would, of course, be equally true for British and Scottish traditional music and for most, if not all, traditions worldwide.

7. The word *Gaeltacht* refers to the regions of Ireland where Gaelic is still spoken as a first language.

8. Vic Gammon notes that this is "very much comparable to A. L. Lloyd's view of English song after the effects of enclosure. I criticise this in my essay on Lloyd in *Singer, Song and Scholar*, edited by Russell." Personal communication.

9. The author has observed this response from students exploring Irish traditional music in classes at the University of Leeds. The perception of sean-nós and by implication the culture from which it springs, as a carrier of difference suggests a kind of "internal exoticism."

10. The original *Atlantean* series was directed by Quinn in 1983 as a trilogy of television programs. A book based on the series, with the same title, was published in 1986 by Quartet books. Subsequently Quinn has made two more films on related subjects: *Allah and Alcuin* of 1997 and *Navigatio: Atlantean II* of 1998.

11. Interestingly, Quinn maintains the Gaelic spelling "Conamara" (great sea) rather than the standard "Connemara," throughout *Atlantean*.

12. These are derived from transcriptions in Cowdery (1990) and O'Rourke (1990). It should be noted that the approach to melodic ornamentation does vary considerably from region to region and that, for example, the styles found in Ulster (including Donegal) tend to be less highly decorated than those of the southwest.

13. See Richard Henebry, *A Handbook of Irish Music* (Cork: Cork University Press, 1928), 282–316. Henebry's phonograph field recordings were of fourteen songs taken from traditional singers in County Waterford. Hornbostel used a device called the Appun tonometer, which apparently had a resolution of 1 hertz, for the analysis. One must acknowledge the fact that in more recent times singers and performers increasingly demonstrate the tendency to pitch in equal temperament.

14. Henebry lists intervals and relevant sizes in cents in a table. For reference, an equal-tempered major second is 200 cents and there are two major seconds in a just intoned diatonic system (9/8 and 10/9 which equate to 203.9 cents and 182.4 cents respectively).

15. Track 4 of the cassette *Tógfaidh mé mo Sheolta*, Cló Iar-Chonnachta, CIC 088, 1993. Transcribed by the author.

16. The Muezzin is the person who calls Moslems to prayer at the mosque, traditionally calling out the adhat or call to prayer from a minaret.

17. *Keening* (from the Irish *caoine*) is a women's funereal chant for which there is considerable evidence at least as far back as the seventeenth century. Some of the earliest transcriptions of caoines appear in volume 4 of the *Transactions* of the Royal Irish Academy (1782).

18. Although its population is officially described as 99 percent Arab-Berber, the autochthonous ethnic group is the Imazighen or Berbers, many of whom intermarried with Arab invaders, settlers or refugees (following their expulsion from southern Spain). While the majority of inhabitants may be classified as being of Berber descent, as with Ireland, it is very difficult to identify a "pure" strain. In recent times a movement has been established to promote Berber culture against alleged discrimination resulting from government-inspired "Arabization," and to advance the cause of the Berber language (Tamazight). This Arabization can be compared to the process of Magyarisation found in Hungary in the second half of the nineteenth century in which "only Hungarian citizens 'of a separate mother tongue' were formally recognised and nominally accorded equal civic rights, the unrestricted use of their native language in the lower levels of the administration, the judicial system and elementary and secondary schools" (Hoensch [1984: 28–9]). See also El-biad (1990: 24–44); Grandguillaume (1991: 45–54); Seckinger (1998: 68–89) and Sirles (1999: 115–29).

It should also be noted that there also are minority groups of Black Moroccans of sub-Saharan descent (the Gnawa), many of whom are professionally involved in music-making (often for therapeutic functions) (see Langlois [1998: 135–56]), and of Berber Jews, who, as Schuyler notes "were probably local converts, rather than immigrants from the East, or refugees from the Spanish reconquista" (1979: 80).

19. See Aydoun (2001: 24–25) for a discussion of the problem of denomination of "Andalusian music."

20. Habib Hassan Touma, *The Music of the Arabs*, translated by Laurie Schwartz (Portland: Amadeus Press, 1996), 68.

21. See Touma (1996: 71–83) for a detailed analysis of the first section of a performance of a nûba mâya.

22. These are called al baçit, al qaîm wa nisf, btayhi, darj and quddâm and are in 6, 8, 8 (3+3+2), 4 and 3 times respectively.

23. This characteristic is also built into the scale of the Scottish highland bagpipe, in which the fourth (C#) is considerably flatter than the equal-tempered version.

24. For example, it is also found in Norwegian Hardanger fiddle music.

25. As is a substantial proportion of Irish music . . . and of course, much Scottish, African, Chinese and U.S. music (among many others).

26. Mugar, *Kabily-touseg*, Tempo Maker Productions, 34502–2.

27. Luke Verling, "The Road to Morocco," *Limerick Leader* (online edition), Saturday, 19 January 2002, http://www.limerickleader.ie/issues/20020119/morocco.html [18 May, 2002]. Dr. John de Courcy Ireland is a veteran maritime historian and broadcaster.

28. The CD *Gaelic Psalms from Lewis*, CDTRAX9006, includes recordings of six psalms drawn from the archive of the School of Scottish Studies, University of Edinburgh.

29. Quoted in Quinn (1986: 19). Quinn's source is given as "Seannós and the Arab style," *Irish Times*, 4 November, 1974.

30. See de Falla's discussion (1979: 101–5). He cites Pedrell's *Cancionero Musical Español*.

31. Issued as *The Spanish Recordings: Extremadura*, The Alan Lomax Collection, Rounder 82161–1763–2.

32. From the CD *A Dip in the Ocean*, QASIDA QCD002.

33. This roughly translates as "In Ireland, which is thought to have one of the oldest musics of Europe, clearly there are many popular melodies coming from Spain and of 'the Miller's wife' family" (author's translation).

34. This kind of interchange of musical characteristics between countries was a phenomenon (in a different context) that the composer Béla Bartók ([1942] 1976) saw as a particularly powerful means of perpetually rejuvenating and enriching music and avoiding stagnation.

35. Vic Gammon notes that "there were some pretty large tambourines used in England, twelve inches and more across." Personal communication. The bendîr and târ are frame drums similar in structure to the bodhrán.

36. Towards the end of his life he managed to locate an authentic instrument and rewire it with copper strings. The CD *Ó Riada's Farewell* (Ceirníní Cladaigh, CC12CD), recorded in August 1971, two months before his death, illustrates his use of the harpsichord as a surrogate harp.

37. The Irish bouzouki is a flat-back version of the traditional Greek fretted instrument. The darbuka is a single-headed drum with an hourglass or goblet shape.

38. http://www.irishmusicweb.ie/texts/moynihan.html [10 April 2002].

39. The mandolin was a mainstay of bluegrass, a form of American country music whose development owed something to the influence of Americans of "Scotch-Irish" descent (that is Ulster Protestants).

40. Transatlantic TRA170. In a personal communication, Vic Gammon noted that:

> Planxty comes out of the English folk revival (which in turn took its inspiration from the USA) before they made it big in Ireland and the world. (I remember booking Christy Moore in about 1968/9 for £5! He lived in Manchester at the time; one of his great inspirations was and remained Ewan MacColl). Andy Irvin lived in this wonderful (read down-at-heel) house in the Archway in London that was packed full of famous and not so famous folkies.
>
> If O'Riada felt he needed to justify the harpsichord as a substitute harp, no such problems arose in the folk revival context. The basic instrumentation of the English/British revival was American, the guitar dominated, the banjo was used, the mandolin sometimes, the fiddle occasionally. (Note: Luke Kelly of the Dubliners originally played with the Ian Campbell Folk Group which consisted of Scots, Irish and English people based in Birmingham—the group itself was based on the Weavers, Pete Seeger's 1940s/50s group.) Irvine's early inspiration was Woody Guthrie.

41. The term *world music* was established as a marketing category at a meeting of recording companies and other interested parties on Monday 29 June 1987. See the minutes of the meeting of an "International Pop Label Meeting" held at the Empress of Russia on St. John Street, Islington. http://www.frootsmag.com/content/features/world_mu sic_history/minutes/page03.html [2 June 2002]. However, as Kevin Dawe notes (personal communication) "there was a course on World Music and Dance at QUB from 1976 and I believe courses at Wesleyan and UCLA had such names in the late 1960s."

42. A distinction is made between the artificial isolation of a culture and the "natural" state of such regions as the Arab areas of North Africa, which, Bartók (wrongly) hypothesizes, have seen few migrations or intermarriages with other races (Bartók [1942] 1976: no. 5, 31).

Bibliography

Acton, Charles. *Irish Music and Musicians*. Dublin: Eason and Son Ltd., 1978.

Aydoun, Ahmed. *Musiques du Maroc*. 2nd ed. Casablanca, Marseille: Editions Eddif et Éditions Autres Temps, 2001.

Bartók, Béla. "Race Purity in Music." 29–32 in *Béla Bartók Essays*, edited by Benjamin Suchoff. Lincoln: University of Nebraska Press, 1976.

Brún, Garech a. "My Friend Seán Ó Riada." 182–89 in *Integrating Tradition: The Achievement of Seán Ó Riada*, edited by Bernard Harris and Grattan Freyer. Terrybaun: Irish Humanities Centre and Keohanes, 1981.

Chapman, Malcolm. "Thoughts on Celtic Music." 29–44 in *Ethnicity, Identity and Music: The Musical Construction of Place*, edited by Martin Stokes. Oxford: Berg, 1994.

Cooper, David. "Béla Bartók and the Question of Race Purity in Music." 16–32 in *Musical Constructions of Nationalism: Essays on the History and Ideology of European Musical Culture 1800–1945*, edited by Michael Murphy and Harry White. Cork: Cork University Press, 1999.

Cowdery, James R. *The Melodic Tradition of Ireland*. Kent, Ohio: The Kent State University Press, 1990.

De Falla, Manuel. "El Canto Jondo." 99–117 in *On Music and Musicians*, translated by David Urman and J.M. Thomson. London: Marion Boyars Ltd., 1979.

De Noraidh, Liam. *Ceol ón Mumhan*. Baile Átha Cliath: An Clóchomhar Tta, 1965.

El-biad, M. "The Role of Some Population Sectors in the Progress of Arabization in Morocco." *International Journal of the Sociology of Language* 87 (1990): 24–44.

García-Matos, Manuel. *Cancionero Popular de la Provincia de Cáceres*. Vol. 2, Lírica Popular de la Alta Extremadura. Barcelona: C.S.I.M., I.E.M., J.R.E., 1982.

Gillies, Malcolm. *Bartók in Britain*. Oxford: Clarendon Press, 1989.

Grandguillaume, Gilbert. "Arabisation et languages maternelles dans la contexte national au Maghreb." *International Journal of the Sociology of Language* 87 (1991): 45–54.

Grey, Cecil. *Peter Warlock: A Memoir of Philip Heseltine*. London: Jonathan Cape Ltd., 1934.

Harris, Bernard, and Grattan Freyer, eds. *Integrating Tradition: The*

Achievement of Seán Ó Riada. Terrybaun: Irish Humanities Centre and Keohanes, 1981.

Henebry, Richard. *A Handbook of Irish Music*. Cork: Cork University Press, 1928.

Hoensch, J. K. *A History of Modern Hungary*. Harlow: Longman, 1984.

Langlois, Tony. "The Gnawa of Oujda: Music at the Margins in Morocco." *The World of Music* 40, no. 1 (1998): 135–56.

Stewart Macalister, R. A., ed. and trans. *Lebor Gabála Érenn* (The book of the taking of Ireland). Dublin: Educational Co. of Ireland for Irish Texts Society, 1938–1956 (Ponsonby and Gibbs, 1938–41, republished by Dublin University Press, 1956).

McIlroy, Brian. *World Cinema 4: Ireland*. Trowbridge: Flicks Books, 1989.

McLoone, Martin. *Irish Film: The Emergence of a Contemporary Cinema*. London: The British Film Institute, 2000.

Nettl, Bruno. *The Study of Ethnomusicology: Twenty-Nine Issues and Concepts*. Urbana: The University of Illinois Press, 1983.

Ó Riada, Seán. *Our Musical Heritage*, edited by Thomas Kinsella and Tomás Ó Canainn. Mountrath: The Dolment Press, 1982.

O'Rourke, Brian. *Pale Rainbow: An Dubh ina Bhán*. Blackrock: Irish Academic Press, 1990.

Petrie, George. *The Petrie Collection of the Ancient Music of Ireland*, 1st edition, edited by David Cooper. Cork: Cork University Press, 2002.

Quinn, Bob. *Atlantean*. London: Quartet Books, 1986.

Quinn, Seán. "Céilí Band" 60–64 in *The Companion to Irish Traditional Music*, edited by Fintan Vallely. Cork: Cork University Press, 1999.

Ribera, Julián. "De Música y Métrica Gallegas." 7–35 in *Homenaje Ofrecido a Menéndez Pidal*, Vol. 3, edited by Tomo Tercero. Madrid: Librería y Casa Editorial Hernando (S.A.), 1925.

Schiller, Rina. *The Lambeg and the Bodhrán: Drums of Ireland*. Belfast: The Institute of Irish Studies, 2001.

Schuyler, Philip D. "Rwais and Ahwash: Opposing Tendencies in Moroccan Berber Music and Society." *The World of Music* 21, no. 1 (1979): 65, 80.

———. "Berber Professional Musicians in Performance." 91–148 in *Performance Practice: Ethnomusicological Perspectives*, edited by Gerard Behague. Westport: Greenwood Press, 1984.

Seckinger, B. "Implementing Morocco's Arabization Policy: Two Problems of Classification." 68–89 in *With Forked Tongues: What are National Languages Good For?* edited by F. Coulmas, Ann Arbor: Karoma, 1998.

Shields, Hugh. *Narrative Singing in Ireland.* Dublin: Irish Academic Press, 1993.

Sirles, Craig A. "Politics and Arabization: The Evolution of Post-independence North Africa." *International Journal of the Sociology of Language* 137 (1999): 115–29.

Smith, B. *Peter Warlock: The Life of Philip Heseltine.* Oxford: Oxford University Press, 1994.

Starkie, Walter. *Spanish Raggle-Taggle: Adventures with a Fiddle in North Spain.* London: John Murray, 1934.

Touma, Habib Hassan. *The Music of the Arabs.* Translated by Laurie Schwartz. Portland: Amadeus Press, 1996.

Yeats, Gráinne. "The Rediscovery of Carolan." 78–94 in *Integrating Tradition: The Achievement of Seán Ó Riada*, edited by Bernard Harris and Grattan Freyer. Terrybaun: Irish Humanities Centre and Keohanes, 1981.

Index

About the Contributors

Caroline Bithell is lecturer in ethnomusicology at the University of Wales, Bangor. She has published on a number of different aspects of traditional and contemporary music in Corsica, which has been the main focus of her research since 1993. She is currently preparing a book, to appear in the Scarecrow Press's Europea series. Particular interests include polyphonic singing traditions, music and politics, music and gender and world music.

Loren Chuse is an ethnomusicologist with a doctorate in ethnomusicology from the University of California, Los Angeles, whose work centers on the music of Spain, the Mediterranean and Latin America. Her research interests focus on the construction and negotiation of social identity in musical performance, with special emphases on issues of gender and the participation of women in expressive culture. She is currently collaborating with the department of anthropology at the University of Sevilla, where she is participating with a Spanish research team on the project *Women in Flamenco: Ethnicity, Education and Power. Confronting New Professional Challenges.*

David Cooper is professor of music and technology and head of the School of Music at the University of Leeds. His research interests include Irish traditional music, film music, Bartók and the applications of science and technology to music. He is the author of the Cambridge Music Handbook on Bartók's *Concerto for Orchestra* (1996), *Bernard Herrmann's* Vertigo: *A Film Score Handbook* (Greenwood Press 2001) and a new edition of George Petrie's *The Petrie Collection* (Cork 2002). He is currently completing a study of Bernard Herrmann's score to *The Ghost and Mrs. Muir* (Scarecrow Press).

Ruth Davis is senior lecturer in ethnomusicology at Cambridge University and fellow and director of studies in music at Corpus Christi College, Cambridge. She has published and broadcast extensively in North African and Middle-Eastern music, especially on her original field research in Tunisia. Her current research focuses on the recordings and writings of Robert Lachmann in British Mandate Palestine in the late 1930s. Her book *Ma'luf: Reflections on the Arab Andalusian Music of Tunisia* was published by Scarecrow Press in 2004.

Kevin Dawe is lecturer in ethnomusicology in the School of Music at the University of Leeds where he is also a member of the Centre for Mediterranean Studies and the Centre for African Studies. He has worked as a professional musician and ethnomusicologist in a variety of cultural contexts including field research in Greece, Spain and Papua New Guinea. He has published articles in journals such as *The British Journal of Ethnomusicology*, *World of Music*, *Popular Music*, *Popular Music and Society* and the *Galpin Society Journal* and has written several book chapters. He is the editor of *Island Musics* (2004, Berg) and coeditor of *Guitar Cultures* (2001, Berg). He is currently writing up a monograph on his field research in Crete. Kevin is a member of the editorial board and currently reviews editor for *Ethnomusicology Forum* (Routledge).

Eno Koço is senior teaching fellow in performance classes and permanent conductor of the University of Leeds Philharmonia at the University of Leeds, School of Music. He is the author of *Treatise on Orchestration* (Tirana 1977), *Albanian Musical Life in the 1930s* (Tirana 2000), *Albanian Urban Lyric Song in the 1930s* (Tirana 2002) and *Korçare Distinctive Song* (Tirana 2003), as well as several articles in Albanian and English published in *Kultura Popullore* and *Studia Albanica*. He has made numerous recordings of Albanian music.

Tony Langlois teaches at the School of Media and Performing Arts at the University of Ulster. His Ph.D. study of North African popular culture was gained at Queen's University, Belfast in 1997. His published articles consider musical relations to gender, race and politics in Algeria and Morocco and "rave" music in the UK. In addition to academic pursuits, Tony has also worked in the areas of community and race relations in Northern Ireland.

Gabriele Marranci is a lecturer in the anthropology of Islam at the School of Divinity and Religious Studies, University of Aberdeen. His main area of interest relates to cultural and identity aspects of the Muslim diaspora in Europe. He has recently conducted fieldwork in Northern Ireland about the local Islamic community. He has published several book chapters and articles in journals such as *Ethnologies*, *Building Environment* and *Culture and Religion* and participates at international meetings and conferences. Currently, he is writing a book concerning the concepts of jihad among ordinary Muslims for Berg Books.

John Morgan O'Connell is a senior lecturer in ethnomusicology at the University of Limerick (Ireland). He is a graduate of Oxford University, the Guildhall School of Music and the University of California (Los Angeles), where he completed his Ph.D. in ethnomusicology on Turkish classical music. He has taught ethnomusicology at Mimar Sınan Üniversitesi (Turkey) and Otago University (New Zealand). He has recently been awarded a Senior Fulbright Scholarship to continue his research into central Asian expressive culture at Brown University in association with the Aga Khan Foundation. In 2004, John Morgan O'Connell hosted the 15th ICTM Colloquium in Ireland.

Goffredo Plastino is a lecturer at the International Centre for Music Studies of the University of Newcastle, England. He is also the editor of *Italian Treasury*, a series of CDs in the *Alan Lomax Collection* (Rounder Records), from the 1954–1955 Italian recordings by Alan Lomax and Diego Carpitella. His publications include *Mediterranean Mosaic: Popular Music and Global Sounds* (as editor: Routledge 2003), *Tambores del Bajo Aragón* (PRAMES 2001) and *Mappa delle voci: rap, raggamuffin e tradizione in Italia* (Meltemi 1996). He is currently working on a book on music, violence and crime in Calabria (Southern Italy).

Dafni Tragaki studied ethnomusicology at Goldsmiths University of London and has recently received her Ph.D., titled "Urban Ethnomusicology in the City of Thessaloniki (Northern Greece): The Case of Rebetiko Song Revival Today." She is currently teaching Ethnomusicology at the University of Thessaly (Greece), Department of History, Archaeology and Social Anthropology and at the University of Macedonia (Thessaloniki), Department of Music Science and Art.